AN ETHOS
OF BLACKNESS

BLACK LIVES IN THE DIASPORA:
PAST / PRESENT / FUTURE

BLACK LIVES IN THE DIASPORA: PAST / PRESENT / FUTURE

EDITORIAL BOARD

Howard University

Clarence Lusane, Rubin Patterson, Nikki Taylor, Amy Yeboah Quarkume

Columbia University

Kevin Fellezs, Farah Jasmine Griffin, Frank Guridy, Josef Sorett

Black Lives in the Diaspora: Past / Present / Future is a book series that focuses on Black lives in a global diasporic context. Published in partnership with Howard University's College of Arts and Sciences and Columbia University's African American and African Diaspora Studies Department, it builds on Columbia University Press's publishing programs in history, sociology, religion, philosophy, and literature as well as African American and African Diaspora studies. The series showcases scholarship and writing that enriches our understanding of Black experiences in the past, present, and future with the goal of reaching beyond the academy to intervene in urgent national and international conversations about the experiences of people of African descent. The series anchors an exchange across two global educational institutions, both located in historical capitals of Black life and culture.

Imani D. Owens, *Turn the World Upside Down: Empire and Unruly Forms of Black Folk Culture in the U.S. and Caribbean*

Gladys L. Mitchell-Walthour, *The Politics of Survival: Black Women Social Welfare Beneficiaries in Brazil and the United States*

James V. Koch and Omari S. Swinton, *Vital and Valuable: The relevance of HBCUs to American Life and Education*

For a complete list of books in the series, please see the Columbia University Press website.

AN ETHOS OF BLACKNESS

RASTAFARI COSMOLOGY, CULTURE, AND CONSCIOUSNESS

VIVALDI JEAN-MARIE

Columbia University Press *New York*

Columbia University Press
Publishers Since 1893
New York   Chichester, West Sussex
cup.columbia.edu

Copyright © 2023 Columbia University Press
All rights reserved

Cataloging-in-Publication Data is available from the Library of Congress.

ISBN 9780231209762 (hardback)
ISBN 9780231209779 (trade paperback)
ISBN 9780231558105 (ebook)

LCCN 2023004254

Cover design: Chang Jae Lee
Cover image: © Universal History Archive/UIG/Bridgeman Images

CONTENTS

Preface vii

1 Resistance to British Colonialism and the Rise of Two Forms of Subjectivity in "Yamaye" 1

2 The Genealogy of Rastafari Cosmology and Its Distinctive Ethos of Blackness 29

3 Rastafari Cosmology, Natural Artifacts, and the Ethos of Blackness 65

4 Rastafari's Theology of Blackness: A Eurocentric God Cannot Love Africans and People of African Descent 101

5 Rastafari I-Talk and Black Consciousness 127

6 The Limit of Rastafari Cosmology: Gender Inequality and the Failure to Liberate Rasta Women 157

Notes 189
Bibliography 201
Index 219

PREFACE

An Ethos of Blackness: Rastafari Cosmology, Culture, and Consciousness provides a detailed elaboration of the norms, culture, religious practices, and epistemological boundaries of Rastafari in order to argue that they are advancing Rastafari's distinctive postcolonial ideals of Blackness for people of African descent. Rastafari's norms, culture, and religious practices constitute Rastafari cosmology. The six chapters of this book demonstrate that Rastafari cosmology is remedial in promoting an alternative system of norms, culture, and religious practices to those established by colonial and postcolonial institutions to define Blackness for people of African descent. The account of the book is unique in drawing out the implications of the religious, cultural, and aesthetic conventions of Rastafari. It shows that, by means of their religious, cultural, and aesthetic conventions, Rastas seek to define a normative guideline for people of African descent to conceptualize themselves according to an Afrocentric ethos. Rigorous and sensitive philosophical reflections on the normative implications of Rastafari's religious, cultural, and aesthetic conventions reveal that Rastas sought to elaborate an alternative conception of Blackness around Afrocentricity and in resistance to the Eurocentric and colonial conception of Blackness. The uniqueness of Rastafari is that Rastas grasped that people of African descent may only transcend Eurocentric postcolonial oppression by espousing a normative guideline that is consistent with their original Afrocentricity.

The aim of the first chapter, "Resistance to British Colonialism and the Rise of Two Forms of Subjectivity in 'Yamaye,'" is to argue that centuries of overt, covert, normative, and spiritual resistance practices of slaves to British colonialism in Jamaica have informed the cosmology of Rastafari. The argument is built on the elaboration of two forms of subjectivity that were espoused by people of African descent in response to the institution of slavery on the Jamaican plantations. These forms of subjectivity are the Anglo-Jamaican and the Afro-Jamaican. It concludes that the spiritual and normative ethos inherent in the Afro-Jamaican form of subjectivity has framed the Afrocentric norms, beliefs, rituals, and conventions that constitute Rastafari cosmology.

The second chapter, "The Genealogy of Rastafari Cosmology and Its Distinctive Ethos of Blackness," sets out to show how the Rastafari movement emerged at the intersection of Jamaican Revivalism and Garveyism. The tenet of Revivalism informed the Afrocentric religious beliefs and practices of the Rastafari movement. Garveyism supplied the socioethical and cultural guidelines of Rasta communities. The complex system of norms, religious beliefs, cultural practices, and social attitudes that result from Garveyism and Revivalism constitute Rastafari cosmology. Then, I build on this argument to show that the complex set of norms, religious beliefs, cultural practices, and social attitudes inherent in Rastafari cosmology define a distinctive ethos of Blackness that is intrinsically tied to the Rastafari movement. The goal is to show that this distinctive account of Black identity—which emerged during the second half of the nineteenth century, on the basis of the Black Native Baptist tenet—shaped the endeavors of the Rastafari movement in the twentieth century, and more specifically Rastas' notion of Black identity and their emphasis on the end of oppression. The chapter emphasizes the role of religious events and the unity of the slave communities that carried out the Morant Bay Rebellion of 1865 as key to elucidating the link between slavery, religion, and communal unity as preambles to the Rastafari movement.

The chapter "Rastafari Cosmology, Natural Artifacts, and the Ethos of Blackness" elaborates the thesis that, in Rastafari cosmology, resistance to postcolonial institutions and the technological oppression of natural artifacts are an intrinsic dimension of Rastas' ethos of Blackness. Technological oppression of natural artifacts means the exploitation of natural artifacts through technological means for profit and overconsumption. I begin by showing that resistance to the technological oppression of natural artifacts is the logical implication of Rasta communities' striving to align their lifestyle with the guiding notion of *Ital livity*, which stands for "a commitment to using things in their natural or organic states."[1] In Rastas' mindset, Ital livity consists of a lifestyle whose practices provide a cosmic energy commonly known in their communities as "earthforce." Ital livity and earthforce are achievable through a naturalist inclination according to which Rastas structure their lifestyle around the imperative to create an egalitarian relationship with natural artifacts, which must be freed from technological oppression. Egalitarian relationship with natural artifacts stands for an egalitarian and balanced relationship between humans and natural artifacts. On the premise of this thesis, I then draw the conclusion that Rastas' ethos of Blackness, which includes the creation of nonoppressive communities for people of African descent, encompasses the freedom of natural artifacts from technological oppression as well. Put differently, in Rastafari cosmology's ethos of Blackness, freedom from oppression for people of African descent is isomorphic with the freedom of natural artifacts from technological oppression.

In the fourth chapter, "Rastafari's Theology of Blackness: A Eurocentric God Cannot Love Africans and People of African Descent," the argument is that Rastafari cosmology is in tune with the alienating component of orthodox Christianity toward Africans and people of African descent—namely, the theological conundrum that a Eurocentric God is unfit to love and guide Africans and people of African descent. And further, that Rastafari cosmology recognizes this theological conundrum and elaborates a Black theology as a solution. Then, on the premise of the discussion of Rastafari Black theology and hermeneutic, the chapter delineates how a messianic model is inherent in Rastas' reception and interpretation of biblical scriptures as it draws continuity between religiosity and the social amelioration of people of African descent's circumstances. Finally, it shows that Rastafari Black theology, on the basis of its advancement of the messianic model, frames Rastas' attitudes toward both their present and future by conditioning them to view the present and future as temporal media for the redemption of the Black Messiah.

"Rastafari I-Talk and Black Consciousness" takes up the Rasta vernacular, *I-talk*, which is a pivotal dimension of Rastafari cosmology. The chapter begins by elaborating the intricacies and details of Rasta I-talk to contextualize it vis-à-vis the context of Jamaican institutions. The elaboration of the intricacies of Rasta I-talk sets up the platform for the argument of this chapter—namely, that Rasta I-talk articulates Rasta Black consciousness. The account of Rasta Black consciousness complements the elaboration of Rastas' ethos of Blackness by showing that I-talk is the cultural mechanism that Rastas use to attune the constituents of their ethos of Blackness with their objective and inner realities. Given that consciousness is polysemous, in the context of Rasta Black consciousness, it means the coordination of Rastas' realities with their Afrocentricity. The goal is to show that Rasta Black consciousness, via I-talk, stands as the cognitive and spiritual synthesis of Rastas' realities with their Afrocentricity.

The last chapter, "The Limit of Rastafari Cosmology: Gender Inequality and the Failure to Liberate Rasta Women," focuses on Rastas' failure to redress the sexist attitudes and practices toward women that were prominent during colonialism and postcolonialism, and the fact that this failure impedes the fulfillment of Rastafari cosmology's ambition to liberate all people of African descent from oppression. It shows that male Rastas' sexism toward women is further reinforced by Jamaican religious institutions—namely, the depiction of women in biblical scriptures and the economic subordination of women in both the colonial and postcolonial periods. In this chapter, I conclude that the persistence of gender inequality impairs Rastafari cosmology's advancement of freedom from oppression for all people of African descent because Rasta women remain oppressed in Rasta communities.

An Ethos of Blackness is written for all interested readers and scholars of religious studies, Caribbean religious traditions, and African Diaspora studies. This account is pertinent to current debates about the lack of and need to create discursive space for Black topics in academia by drawing attention to Rastafari's understated take on Blackness for people of African descent. My hope is that it will be embraced by readers and researchers who are promoting the inclusion of Black topics in academia. The distinctiveness of this book consists in the elaboration of Rastafari's discourse on Blackness, which is an aspect that is overlooked in the existing literature. These chapters present the rigorous framework to tease out this discourse on Blackness in a cohesive fashion.

Moreover, this book informs readers about the distinctive strategies that Rasta communities created to refigure the social, cultural, and religious experiences of people of African descent according to an Afrocentric regime. Readers will learn about a coherent approach to Black identity that strives to transcend the colonialist and postcolonialist accounts of Blackness. Finally, it fills a gap in the literature about Black lives in the Diaspora since there is no existing publication that teases out Rastafari' advancement of a distinctive ethos of Blackness.

AN ETHOS
OF BLACKNESS

1

RESISTANCE TO BRITISH COLONIALISM AND THE RISE OF TWO FORMS OF SUBJECTIVITY IN "YAMAYE"

But my hand was made strong
By the hand of the Almighty
We forward in this generation
Triumphantly
　　　　　　　—Bob Marley, "Redemption Song" (1980)

The colonist and the colonized are old acquaintances. And consequently, the colonist is right when he says he "knows" them. It is the colonist who fabricated *and* continues to fabricate *the colonized subject. The colonist derives his validity, i.e., his wealth, from the colonial system.*
　　　　　　　—Frantz Fanon, *The Wretched of the Earth* (1961)

The aim of this chapter is to argue that centuries of overt, covert, normative, and spiritual resistance practices of African slaves to British colonialism in Jamaica have informed the cosmology of Rastafari. The argument of the chapter is built on the elaboration of two forms of subjectivity that were espoused by people of African descent in response to the institution of slavery on the Jamaican plantations. These forms of subjectivity are the Anglo-Jamaican and Afro-Jamaican. It concludes that the spiritual and normative ethos inherent in the Afro-Jamaican form of subjectivity has framed the Afrocentric norms, beliefs, rituals, and conventions that are intrinsic to Rastafari cosmology.

The prevalence of slaves' resistance practices on the plantations established their resistance as an inherent component of British colonialism in Jamaica. Resistance practices emerged concurrently with the institution of British colonialism in Jamaica. It is by virtue of the simultaneity of resistance and slavery that it is reasonable to think of resistance practices as an inherent component of the history of British colonialism in Jamaica. They stand as proof that for centuries the African slaves on Jamaican plantations relied on resistance practices as the technology to seek their freedom and more importantly to elaborate an alternative conceptualization of themselves. The invention of Afro-Jamaican subjectivity heralded the rise of Rastafari's cosmology, which is informed by the normative ethos that arose out of the slaves' resistance. In contrast, Anglo-Jamaican subjectivity encapsulates the slaves' internalization and performance of British colonials' social, cultural, religious, and judicial norms.

As the embodiment of the British colonials' institutions by people of African descent in Jamaica, the Anglo-Jamaican form of subjectivity stands as the opposite of the Afrocentric conceptualization of themselves that the African slaves sought to forge. Anglo-Jamaican and Afro-Jamaican subjectivities had different existential aims. The notion of an Afrocentric conceptualization means that the slaves, from various African countries, strove to shape themselves and to behave as bearers of African social practices, cultural mores, and religious beliefs they inherited from their previous contexts in Africa.

The argument of the chapter is elaborated on the fact that the system of British colonial institutions in Jamaica had two key aims. First, it set out primarily to enrich the British metropolis by using slave labor to exploit natural resources in Jamaica. Second, it set out methodically to invent the Anglo-Jamaican subjects by imposing the rule of British sociocultural and judicial norms in Jamaica. The invention of Anglo-Jamaican subjects is the fulfilment of the first aim of British colonialism because the subdued and compliant Anglo-Jamaican subjects were conditioned via slavery to further British colonials' material interests. Also, they were primed through systematic conditioning to regard themselves as British Jamaicans and loyalists of the metropolis.

Accordingly, the rise of resistance in Jamaica evolved with the rule of British colonialism in having two aims. Slaves' resistance in Jamaica was geared toward the end of physical slavery. Also, it aimed to resist the British colonials' strategies to promote the creed of Anglo-Jamaican subjectivity. The African slaves envisioned the Afrocentric conceptualization as the suitable alternative to the creed of Anglo-Jamaican subjectivity. For the African slaves, this conceptualization was the psychological requisite for their physical freedom and the dominant incentive of their resistance.

Hence, since its inception as a colony, Jamaica may be framed as a battleground between these two regimes of social practices, cultural norms, and religious beliefs and mores. The British colonial and the Afrocentric conceptualization regimes have always been the psychological premises of the open conflicts and resistances in the colonial context of Jamaica. The ultimate goal has always been to promote the dominance of either Anglo-Jamaican subjectivity or the Afrocentric conceptualization. The communities that elude this dichotomy are the Maroons. By virtue of their treaty in 1739 with the English settlers, Maroons secured their freedom legally and became runaway slave catchers and mercenaries for the colonial regime in Jamaica. They eluded the dichotomy because their interests were mainly financial and the preservation of their freedom as Maroon communities in the mountains. The Maroons did not have any loyalty to either the European settlers or the slaves in Jamaica. It will be shown that they were the first communities of people of African descent to pursue their financial interest and freedom without allegiance to either the African slaves or the white masters.

Thus, it is in the context of framing resistance and forms of subjectivity around the competition for normative dominance over Jamaica as a colony that the term cosmology is more suitable to capture the immaterial outcome of the material processes involved in slavery. Rastafari cosmology, in the balance of the book, is used to articulate the attitudes, self-consciousness, conventions, and the overall ethos that were born out of the Rastafari movement in the twentieth century to further the advancement of the Afrocentric conceptualization that their African forebears initiated at the inception of British colonialism in Jamaica.

THE NEW WORLD AS THE JUXTAPOSITION OF CULTURES, RELIGIONS, AND SOCIAL TRADITIONS

For the sake of this project, an adequate grasp of the concept of the New World, as an overhaul of the Eurocentric conception of the New World, requires acknowledgment of the diverse historical and social heritage of the Indigenous peoples who populated the Americas prior to the arrival of the European settlers.

Also important to recognize is the fact that the historical and social traditions of the Indigenous populations became more complex and hybrid as the European settlers started to bring African slaves to the Americas. The synthesis of the social, cultural, and religious traditions of the Indigenous populations with those of the European settlers and the social, cultural, and religious traditions of the millions of African slaves brought to the Americas are thus the grounds for viewing the New World, more specifically the Caribbean, as the seat of the juxtaposition of cultures, religions, and social traditions. The evolution of Jamaica from the arrival of Christopher Columbus in 1494 to the modern day is one illustration of this juxtaposition. In the following observation, Philip Sherlock and Hazel Bennett advance a characterization of Jamaica that endorses this view of Jamaica:

> Africa is present everywhere in Jamaica. She has been here for five centuries. She walks the dark valleys and sun-baked savannas, the coastal plains and sculptured mountain slopes. She reveals herself in the physical appearance of nine out of every ten Jamaicans, in their body language, everyday talk, in their way with words, their crafts, customs, cults, in their attitudes and modes of self-expression. She is the homeland of a vigorous creative people who, out of a past of fire, exploitation and suffering preserved a passion for freedom and justice and built these values into the Jamaican way of life. Britain is also present. She was dominant in Jamaica for three centuries. She is present in churches and schools, in the institutions and forms of law and government. Her presence lingers in old great houses, around broken fortifications and in eighteenth-century sugar ports. Today she lives in her powerful, supple language, an open sesame to one of mankind's great treasuries of literature and to communication with countless millions of people throughout

the world. The Taino is slowly becoming a reality. Recent studies have shown that the Tainos survived longer than was thought. Few though they were, they resisted forced labour and the last survivors established a base in the Dry Harbour Mountains of St Ann and another in the Blue Mountains, probably at Nanny Town. Three important Taino carvings have been found and authenticated. The story of the Tainos is woven in the story of the African-Jamaicans, the 'old indigenous' melding with those who became the 'new indigenous.'[1]

In the above observation, it is evident that the heterogeneous constitution of Jamaica must be the fundamental premise to understand the heterogeneous nature of the Jamaican people. As the authors emphasize, Afro-Jamaicans became the new Indigenous people. The new Indigenous people are nonetheless continuous with the old Indigenous people by virtue of inheriting and working the land that the old Indigenous population had labored on previously. Both people of African descent and Indigenous communities appropriated Jamaica's physical environment through their labor. This transformation occurred through the ruthless decimation of the Indigenous communities by Europeans. A parallel system of ideological, material, and aesthetic depopulation and repopulation was enacted through the sweeping genocides that exterminated vast populations of Indigenous Caribbeans who were replaced through systematic repopulation by Europeans and enslaved Africans.[2]

The appropriation of the land through slavery and systematic repopulation occurred over many centuries of labor as African slaves developed the material means to define their social, cultural, and religious traditions in continuous rapport with Europeans. The process of appropriating Jamaica's physical environment was concurrent with the African slaves' conceptualizing themselves as African Jamaicans. This occurred as they brokered their social, cultural, and religious traditions with those of the European settlers. Trevor Burnard makes the following observation about the slaves' mediating their social, cultural, and linguistic heritage on the Jamaican plantations:

> West African societies had sufficient commonalities, especially linguistic commonalities, to enable slaves to communicate intelligibly with one another and share a common cosmological understanding. Moreover, the nature of the slave trade and the structure of the slave community on large plantations ensured that West Indian slaves lived among sufficiently large concentrations of their fellow countrymen to allow many African traditions to be transplanted to the New World, including language. Bilingualism and multilingualism were common in Africa. Jamaica was probably multilingual from its colonization, and linguists argue that a Gold Coast language, Twi-Asante, very quickly became a lingua franca among slaves, in addition to Creole English.[3]

The slaves' Afrocentric conceptualization of themselves arose as they labored on the plantations and adapted to the British colonial institutions. Also, the Tainos' cultural traditions syncretized with the diverse African traditions of the slaves as they internalized the norms of the British colonialist institutions. It is a known fact that the Maroon communities included Indigenous people as well as people of African descent. Hence, the slaves' Afrocentric conceptualization is inherently heterogeneous because it includes norms and conventions of Africans, Tainos, and the British colonial institutions. This process of coming to think of themselves as pluralities is normatively complex and defines the slaves' subjectivity as a sociocultural mélange as they strive to resist the dominant colonial ethos.

A broader outlook on Jamaica should regard it as a context defined by the synthesis and juxtaposition of Tainos, British, and

African social, cultural, and religious traditions. Also, this take elucidates the competition that ensued for cultural, social, and religious dominance in Jamaica. The logical extension of Jamaica as a synthetic juxtaposition of Tainos, British, and Africans is the rise of conflicts aimed to promote the dominance of one regime of social, cultural, and religious norms and practices over the other. British settlers set out to systematically establish the Anglo-Jamaican form of subjectivity as the internalization of their regime by the African slaves. In the minds of the British settlers, the Anglo-Jamaican subject was an existential medium to preserve and further their institutional control and wealth in Jamaica. The systematic conditioning and the psychological attitude of the Anglo-Jamaican subject were guarantees for maintaining the colonial regime and the enrichment of Great Britain. Edward Long was an English settler in Jamaica who was committed to advancing Anglo-Jamaican subjectivity in Jamaica to profit Britain. He made a firm distinction between newly arrived Africans, whom he thought of as savages almost without merit, and established or Creole slaves, whom he believed could be made very useful members of society when treated—as he thought they invariably were already—by a kind master. One way to increase the number of Creole slaves and to remind people to treat slaves well was to place an onerous tax on slaves acquired in the slave trade for four or five years, "except for re-exportation."[4] It is noteworthy that, in Long's vision for Jamaica as a prosperous and beneficial island for Britain, the Africans' disposition constitutes the nascent resistance attitude which led to the various revolts. Long's remark is proof that the agents of the British colonial institutions were cognizant of the fact that two forms of subjectivity were emerging. During British colonialism, Creole slaves and African slaves were the two embodiments of the Anglo-Jamaican and the Afrocentric subjects. Both forms of subjectivity are creations of the British colonial regime in Jamaica. The set of attitudes, beliefs, norms, and conventions inherent in both forms of subjectivity are still prominent in contemporary Jamaican society. This fact led Rex Nettleford to observe that the Anglo-Jamaican form of subjectivity or the attitudes of the Creole slaves still prevail in contemporary Jamaica: "Jamaica bought into a hybrid, creolization model that valorized assimilation away from a historical antecedent of slavery and Africa, and mimicry of European cultural values and aesthetics."[5]

It is in reaction to the British ideal of Anglo-Jamaican subjectivity that the African slaves devised their mechanism of resistance and created communal ties to safeguard their Afrocentric mores. It is also noteworthy that there is another form of heterogeneity that emerged among the Africans on the plantations because as inheritors of various African social, cultural, and religious traditions the African slaves had to broker and synthesize their rich traditions into a coherent system of norms to distinguish them as an Afrocentric people. This endeavor, which unfolded over many centuries, heralded the birth of various religious communities throughout Jamaica including Revivalism and Rastafari during the early phase of the twentieth century.

SUGAR PLANTATIONS AND THE INVENTION OF BLACK AND WHITE IN JAMAICA

The British colonial system invented a society that aimed exclusively at generating and maximizing wealth around the cultivation of sugar on Jamaican plantations. It is important to bear in mind that the land, Yamaye (Tainos' name for the land), morphed into Jamaica as the result of the vast transactions of the British colonial institutions around sugar production. It is also key to keep in mind that, at its inception, the British settlers and the Africans were both foreigners in Yamaye. For both groups, which came from two different continents with different natural environments, Yamaye stood as being merely an immense foreign arable land. The British settlers left Great Britain for Yamaye with the aim of enrichment. And the Africans were captured and brought to Yamaye as tools of labor on the sugar plantations. The extensive colonial transactions that were put in place to exploit the sugar plantations and the arable land's resources led to the invention of a judicial, cultural, social, and religious system. This complex system conceived Jamaica as a New World entity.

Settlers and slaves were the two social groups that created and enacted this new system. The point is to be cognizant of the fact that the original Yamaye provided the material and natural basis for the sociocultural norms around which the British settlers and Africans, via the exploitation of sugar plantations, slowly managed to invent Jamaica as their home away from their original home. Slave labor on sugar plantations is the kernel of Jamaica's contribution to British wealth. Most of Jamaica's hundreds of thousands of slaves, male and mainly female, were engaged in backbreaking field labor that was done by hand. Largely exposed in the acres of cane, they were a highly visible presence on every sugar plantation. After planting, the cane took about eleven or twelve months to mature. They worked under armed drivers and overseers from sunup to sundown six days a week and, during harvest time, five to six months a year, were also compelled to work at night in rotating gangs to "feed" the mills that would turn the cane into molasses, rum, and sugar.[6]

Though Jamaica emerged as a substitute for their original home, it elevated the profile of the settlers as wealthy Europeans and cast the conception of Africans as mere tools for sugar production. Jamaica's wealth accrued almost entirely to its white population. On the eve of the American Revolution, white Jamaicans were among the wealthiest subjects in the British Empire. In 1774 per capita white wealth was £2,201, with white men having an average wealth amounting to £4,403. The average white in Jamaica was 36.6 times as wealthy as the average white in the thirteen colonies, 52.3 times as wealthy as the average white in England and Wales, and 57.6 times as wealthy as the average white in New England.[7] The characterization of British settlers as White Jamaicans is, thus, an invention of British colonialism in Jamaica. It is equally noteworthy that, by virtue of the wealth acquired, the status of White Jamaicans surpassed the status of their countrymen in England. British colonialism defined Whiteness as a category that was financially superior to slaves, British citizens in Britain, and whites in the other British colonies. Jamaican society was created for sugar; Jamaican customs and culture were fashioned by sugar; sugar, for two hundred years, was the only reason behind Jamaica's existence as a center of human cohabitation. The society created by sugar was rigid, base, and greedy. It consumed life, energy, and thought and fertilized the Industrial Revolution of England with the profits from its labor.[8] Jamaica, by virtue of the exploitation of the sugar plantations, emerged as a melting pot for exiled groups of Europeans and Africans.

The rise of Jamaica as the byproduct of the complex system of cultural, social, judicial, and religious conventions around sugar plantations put in place the two distinct subjects of European colonialism in the Americas. By means of physical distinctions, Black and White emerged as the crudest means of demarcation in the colonial Americas and the Caribbean. In Jamaica, British settlers, initially foreigners in Yamaye, espoused the label "White." The distinctive citizenship of the millions of Africans, from various African countries, was eclipsed by the label "Black." Slavery not only made Britons brutal; it made them self-indulgent, indolent, and full of overbearing pride. In a society where being a worker meant being Black and where Blackness was a sign of ineradicable inferiority, working was a mark of servile status. Whites were expected to be lazy, listless, and self-indulgent in part because these were qualities to which no Black person could aspire.[9]

Thus, it is important to grasp that, in the British colonial context of Jamaica, White and Black were imposed as group characterization in the dynamic of slavery for the exploitation of sugar plantations. The average productivity of enslaved people working in sugar cultivation, as measured by the pounds of sugar produced per worker, doubled between 1750 and 1810, with productivity increases especially apparent between the end of the Seven Years' War and the start of the American Revolution.[10] Each characterization is then imbued with a specific set of rules and regulations to legitimize inequality and the exploitation of slaves. Whiteness was, thus, associated with wealth; in contrast, Blackness was associated with slaves and sugar workers. Furthermore, the English settlers, by means of the system of Negro Jurisprudence, took up the task of assigning the social standing of the slaves in their colonies. This system delineated the legal conduct, treatment, and regulation of slaves.

> The island was administered by the governor and a council of 12 men; a house of assembly with 30 or more elected representatives; and a local council of justices and vestry in each parish. All representatives were selected from among local white freeholders and paid officials. The council of 12 was nominated by the Colonial Office in England on the recommendation of the governor. It was

both an advisory and an executive body, dealing with matters such as the jurisdiction of civil courts, law and order and the framing of acts and ordinances in keeping with English law. In time it became the Upper House of the legislature.[11]

The system of Negro Jurisprudence was the English equivalent of the Black Codes that regulated the conduct, treatment, and regulation of slaves in the United States colonies, and the French Code Noir in the French colonies. By means of the Black Codes, Negro Jurisprudence, and the Code Noir, the European settlers invented a social context that was ruled by violence, cruelty, and methodical dehumanization with White and Black as polar opposites. The slave, as the Black entity, was the victim of violence, cruelty, and systemic dehumanization because, unlike the European settlers who were able to claim and return to their respective homes in Europe, the Black entity remained permanently exiled and lost their respective African identity. The characterization "Black" and its colonial heritage remain as a permanent memento of the massive homelessness and dehumanization of people of African descent in the European colonies. Furthermore, the deployment of the European codes of regulations in their various colonies forced their indoctrination by both the slaves and settlers in the colonies. In the context of Jamaica, this process of conditioning the slaves to abide by the norms of the Negro Jurisprudence led to their internalization. Hence, the Anglo-Jamaican subjects are the embodiment of this process; they are incarnations of the system of religious, social, cultural, and legal norms that were invented to manage the slaves as tools for sugar production.

It is against the backdrop of the invention of the Anglo-Jamaicans that slaves' resistance and conflicts throughout the Caribbean must be grasped as deliberate media to resist the edicts of the Black Codes, the system of Negro Jurisprudence, and the Code Noir. Salvaging their humanity and advancing their Afrocentric conceptualization was always the unifying motif of the slave revolts, which are usually depicted as mere chaos. The logical extension of the slaves' revolts and technology of resistance imposed a form of subjectivity in the European colonies that eluded the purview of the European codes of regulations. From the angle of the European codes of regulation in the colonies, the outcome was predicted to be a mere duality: the European settler as White and the African slave as Black. Slave revolts and the various overt and covert techniques of resistance in Jamaica promoted the Afrocentric subject as an unprecedented form of subjectivity.

STRATEGIES OF SLAVES' RESISTANCE IN JAMAICA

As stated above, a broad grasp of the dynamics of slavery in Jamaica must account for both the oppressive practices with the aim of exploiting slaves for production and the various strategies that slaves deployed to resist these oppressive practices. Strategies of resistance have been an inherent component of the relationship between slaves and masters on the plantations. The spirit of resistance and an attempt to postulate alternative social realities in freedom have always been concurrent with slavery and the inclination to resistance has informed the ethos of Rastafari, which flourished during the twentieth century in Jamaica.

The brutality of slavery and its harsh exploitation practices did not quell the resistance disposition of the African slaves in Jamaica. The slaves managed to invent overt and covert strategies to resist slavery. These strategies conveyed the message to the masters that, despite physical subjugation, the slaves remained confident in their human dignity. The assertion of human dignity in the face of physical subjugation was grounded in the African cultural and social inheritance of the slaves on the Jamaican plantations. The slaves' bent to resist assumed two media of expression. One medium was covert and passive; the other was overt violence. In some instances, violent resistance was undertaken by a single individual or carried out by a group of individuals in an organized fashion. Both media of violence share in common the slaves' understanding that refusal to produce and destruction of the masters' properties are efficient means for undermining the slave regime. In their minds, sabotaging the master's goods and properties and unwillingness to produce were the most effective means to deal blows to the slave regime.

Evasion was one of the passive strategies of resistance that gave rise to the Maroon communities in Jamaica. Feigning sickness and deliberate suicide were also prevalent means of resistance. Resistance had been a mainstay of Jamaican slavery even before the British conquest in 1655. Under the Spanish, Maroon communities that included peoples of African and Arawak descent had been established in Jamaica's mountainous terrain. Left behind by the Spanish, the ranks of these defiant self-liberated people only grew under British colonization, as successive groups of slaves fled their mainly British owners.[12] The fact that slaves were treated as commercial entities that slave owners bought and sold led the slaves to infer that their suicide would amount to destruction of their master's property. The prominence of suicide among slaves reveals that the slaves internalized their treatment as commercial goods and tools of labor for their masters' acquisition of wealth. The most popular form of passive resistance, however, was evasion of work under various pretenses, the most common of which was illness. Several writers have observed that many slaves went to the extreme lengths of injuring themselves either by reopening old sores or allowing the "chigga worms in their feet to remain there, thus making them limp. . . . The belief in return to Guinea after death induced many to commit suicide. Mass suicides were not uncommon, particularly among slaves from Ghana. A large number of the slaves involved in the unsuccessful slave rebellion of 1760 committed mass suicide in the woods, sometimes in bodies as large as twenty-five of them."[13] The slaves' rationale was that since slavery prevented them from conceiving distinctive plans for their existence as social agents and their destiny was strictly bound to generate wealth for another person, then ending their life stands as the only existential choice that they may fulfill freely while simultaneously undermining the master's scheme to acquire wealth. As a means of resistance, individual or communal suicide provided the only medium for slaves' existential freedom under British colonialism.

Individual violence was sophisticated and often subtle. To carry out individual violence, the slaves had to feign complete submission to the master. Also, the slaves had to be fully acquainted with the master's habits and routines because one of the most prevailing forms of individual violence was poisoning the master. The legal penalty for a slave imagining the death of a white person or threatening to injure him in any way, except in the defense of his master's property, was death. Despite the severity of this law and the barbarous manner in which it was executed (usually the culprit was burned to death), the incidences of masters dying at the hands of their slaves were not uncommon. The slaves were expert at exacting vengeance on the master, especially through the African obeah-man from whom most of the poison originally came.[14] The slaves had to be aware of the master's habits and diet to determine the propitious time. Also, poisoning required extensive knowledge of the virtues of the herbs that were available. Thus, the African slaves relied on poisoning more than their Creole counterparts because of their extensive knowledge of herbs' potencies they had acquired in their original homeland.

The eruption of collective violence was frequent throughout Jamaica. The frequency of the violent revolts is proof that it was an undeniable component of the dynamics between masters and slaves on the island. It instilled in the rebels the consciousness that they held power only collectively. Bonding in groups assured both survival in runaway communities and the conviction among slaves that they were not completely powerless as the masters wanted them to believe. This subtle assumption was prominent among both slaves and masters, which is why masters forbade slaves to gather outside of working hours on the plantations and religious worship was closely monitored and sometimes forbidden. Collective violence unfolded as spontaneous revolts, planned revolts, and independent revolts.

Spontaneous revolts arose out of a slave seeking revenge or the availability of a propitious context to harm the master and members of his household. This type of revolt was driven by deep-seated hate and usually brought catharsis to the individual slave who ultimately wanted to escape without having any elaborate plan. Planned revolts were carried out by large groups of slaves throughout the island or all the slaves on a specific plantation. The African slaves learned to cooperate in elaborating plans of attack that required knowledge of the island or the involved plantation's geography, at times when the white masters were most vulnerable and the goal was to resume life as free communities after the revolt. The success of these planned revolts contributed to the slaves' self-conceptualization as being fit to self-manage as free social agents independently of the masters' rules and exploitation.

The contexts and frameworks of the relationship between slaves and masters were the premises of frequent revolts in Jamaica. The frequency of the revolts makes colonial Jamaica unique by the fact that it is second only to Brazil in having the highest number of slave revolts. This fact also suggests the distinctive antislavery attitude that was prominent among the African slaves. Moreover, the regularity of the revolts highlights that the slaves on the Jamaican plantations grasped that constant revolts would eventually end the regime of British slavery. They learned that rebellion is more effective when it is organized and carried out collectively. One significant component of the rebellious undertakings that made them so common is that the bulk of the slaves in Jamaica were African adults. The distinction between African and Creole slaves is central to appreciating the fact that the African slaves had lived freely in their respective cultural and social institutions in Jamaica and were captured and enslaved during their adulthood. Orlando Patterson makes the following observation regarding the impact of this fact:

> The second general cause accounting for the frequency of Jamaican slave revolts is to be found in the ratio between Creole and African slaves. Naturally, a slave population which had a higher proportion of slaves who were born freemen and were enslaved only as adults would exhibit a greater tendency to revolt than one in which there was a higher proportion of Creoles who were born into the system and socialized in it. It is significant that almost every one of the revolts of the seventeenth and eighteenth centuries was instigated and carried out by African slaves (and their children born in the rebel camps). Another factor explaining the revolts of the island was its geography. The mountainous interior

of the country with its intricate, innumerable ravines, naturally concealed mountain passes, precipices and forests, was ideal for guerilla warfare. In this respect the African slaves, used to jungle warfare of their own country, had an insurmountable advantage over their British masters.[15]

The fact that the African slaves on the Jamaican plantations had previously been acculturated in their respective cultural context and that some of them had extensive experience with carrying out warfare played a central role in their ability to mobilize and organize rebellions in Jamaica. It is equally noteworthy that the African slaves were experienced in managing themselves as free social agents independently of the European slave masters' rule. As such, they were agents and preservers of diverse African cultural and social practices. These systems of African cultural, religious, and social norms crossed the Atlantic unscathed through the African slaves' psyche. As acculturated African adults, they were naturally impervious to indoctrination by British and European cultural norms prevailing in colonial Jamaica. In addition, the dichotomy between African slaves and Creole slaves and its mediation with the slave regime plays a key role in shaping the two forms of subjectivity—namely, the Anglo-Jamaican subjectivity and the Afrocentric subjectivity. The African slaves preserved and managed to transmit their sociocultural wealth of values, beliefs, and norms to their descendants. In contrast, it is important to acknowledge that the Creole slaves, who were born and socialized in the slaves' regime, were more susceptible to espousing the Anglo-Jamaican form of subjectivity. And the African slaves were naturally inclined to perpetuate the Afrocentric form of subjectivity by virtue of its continuity with their original acculturation in African social, religious, and political institutions. Thus, the strand of

Afrocentric cultural, social, and religious practices has always prevailed in Jamaica since the inception of slavery. The Afrocentric form of subjectivity initially secured its grounding in colonial Jamaica by means of covert and overt resistance. It evolved, then, through the socialization of children by advocates of an Afrocentric worldview and religious groups. The Afrocentric form of subjectivity has been preserved and disseminated via both religious and secular media in Jamaica. As I will show in the next section, the African slaves practiced Obeah and Myalism in colonial Jamaica. The latter is the precursor of Revivalism during the first half of the twentieth century in Jamaica, which in turn shaped the cosmology of Rastafari. The following chapters show how this African strand is the stalwart Afrocentric root of Jamaican Rastafari cosmology.

It is undeniable that the revolts of African slaves and submissiveness of Creole slaves were the formative frameworks of the Anglo-Jamaican and the Afrocentric forms of subjectivity in colonial Jamaica. But there is another colonial group that had an impact on the social attitudes of Creole and African slaves.

The Afrocentric and Anglo-Jamaican forms of subjectivity evolved in a mediating relationship with the white masters' institutions and another prominent social group—namely, the Maroons. The Maroons defined their standing in the colonies as free communities with distinctive financial interests, which they pursued by availing themselves for hire as catchers of runaway slaves and as mercenaries. The Maroons were a distinctive group because they did not have communal ties with either the African slaves who spearheaded the revolts or the submissive Creole slaves despite being of African descent. They stood as various autonomous communities in Jamaica and the other European colonies. In the account below, Trevor Burnard provides the genealogy of the Maroons' ascension to being communities that enjoy freedom, legal recognition, and financial comfort in colonial Jamaica.

> The colonial Jamaican state was the major beneficiary of the settlement of the First Maroon War, even more than Maroons themselves, though Maroon success in not being defeated in the 1730s allowed them a remarkable amount of autonomy within the British empire. The signing of the treaty between Britain and the Maroons in 1739 signaled the beginnings of the transformation of state power in Jamaica through the same kind of fiscal-military tactics that were revolutionizing state formation in Britain and Ireland. Maroons fell comfortably into a new imperial role as policemen and auxiliaries in wartime. [Edward] Trelawny's 'mild government' of the Maroons transformed white Jamaicans' greatest internal foe into a considerable supporter of the plantation regime. Among their many services, Maroons opened the highways and prevented or suppressed all insurrections of the Negro and other slaves. In addition, they never failed to bring back all runaway slaves to the service of their respective masters and kept the peace and found ease and prosperity under the protection of the laws.[16]

It is reasonable to infer from Burnard's rendition that the Maroons' roles were complex in Jamaica. Their roles were to serve as police and act as mercenaries for the British while enjoying financial benefits. That is why the Maroons were perceived by the revolting slaves as an extension of the white masters' interest in maintaining the slave regime and as individuals to fear and distrust. On the other hand, the white masters perceived them as media of brutish force for hire to regulate their slaves. Given their status as free communities and their detachment from plantation slavery, the Maroons were thus positioned to grasp that slavery was primarily a system aimed at creating wealth. The Maroons were the communities of people of African descent in the colonies who understood that the slave regime operated under the dichotomy of White and Black people as superficial categories to justify exploitation and the acquisition of wealth. Thus, the standings of the Maroons, the African insurrectionists, and the Creole slaves are proof that resistance in Jamaica was multifaceted in its purpose. The Maroons' resistance culminated in their positioning to benefit financially and socially from the slave regime. And given that the regime was conducive to their financial and social ease, they viewed the end of the regime as the end of their sociofinancial privilege. In contrast, the African slaves strove to end the slave regime because it was the only alternative for them to achieve self-realization as free social agents with human dignity. The submissive Creole slaves merely viewed themselves as social and cultural extensions of their white masters. Their birth and socialization in the colonial regime prevented them from forging any consciousness of themselves as distinct from their masters' mores and rules.

THE AFRICAN SLAVES' SPIRITUAL AND NORMATIVE RESISTANCE

Resistance assumed many forms in the confrontations between slaves and masters on the Jamaican plantations. It has been shown above that resistance may assume overt violent manifestations and may be passive and covert, as well. Another form of resistance that assumed a prominent role in the antagonism between masters and slaves in Jamaica was the African slaves' preservation and dissemination of their system of spiritual beliefs and religious ceremonies, and their use of natural artifacts in healing practices and magical incantations. Spiritual and normative resistance is worthy of consideration because it encompasses the original norms, spiritual beliefs, and relationships between the African slaves and natural artifacts. Given the immaterial nature of the norms, spiritual beliefs and knowledge of the healing and magical power of herbs, they remained unscathed from the physical and material oppression of slavery. Spiritual and normative resistance unfolded on the ground of ancestral knowledge and spirituality; they remained in the slaves' collective consciousness given that they were originally acquired in the respective African context of the slaves. Although they underwent some mediation in the non-African social and material environment of the colonies, they mostly remain as sociospiritual institutions that survived in the slaves' original consciousness and were transmitted to posterity. Also, reflection on and scrutiny of these beliefs and practices shows that they are still prominent in contemporary Jamaica specifically among Rastas' commitment to the curative power of herbs.

The African slaves' spiritual beliefs, norms, and knowledge of herbs were immense, given the numerous regions and tribes in Africa that the slaves were taken from. The African slaves' spiritual and knowledge capital of herbs went through syncretism to produce a shared and collective spiritual outcome. This outcome encapsulated the spirituality and knowledge of herbs from the various African countries of the slaves. The syncretistic mediation of these spiritual beliefs, norms, and knowledge of herbs among the different backgrounds slaves who populated the Jamaican plantations yielded two dominant systems of spiritual beliefs, practices, and herbs in Jamaica. This mediation process happened through slaves instructing and learning from other slaves about their spiritual beliefs, norms, and knowledge of African herbs. The collective knowledge that this process of mutual learning created constitutes their mediation and syncretistic outcome. The rise of Myalism and Obeah during slavery is the outcome of the syncretism and mediation that the spiritual beliefs, practices, and herbs underwent on the plantations in Jamaica. Myalism and Obeah also encapsulated the spiritual and normative resistance of the African slaves to the British religious institution and provided the slaves with a set of spiritual beliefs that helped them cope with the psychological oppression of the institution of slavery in Jamaica. Also, the fact that Myalism and Obeah were established spiritual beliefs and practices during the slave regime in Jamaica is proof that they coexisted with the institution of British slavery and provided the means for adherents to preserve their spiritual identity. The preservation of their spiritual identity, via Myalism and Obeah, supplied the slaves a psychological shield against the religious indoctrination of the slave regime. They were syncretistic and flexible by nature and provided a forum for the slaves to feel that their respective inherited spirituality was validated by their peers. Orlando Patterson provides a detailed and critical account of the continuity between the various religious rituals of the slaves in Jamaica and their endemic contexts in Africa. Paterson begins by emphasizing that Myalism and Obeah were syncretistic:

> To begin with it must be noted that the clearly defined categories of supernatural practices which one finds in Africa were not to be found in Jamaica, where elements of ancestor worship, of the various divinities and of the cult of the dead, were all incoherently combined in the supernatural beliefs of the slaves.... Obeah was essentially a type of sorcery which largely involved harming others at the request of clients, by the use of charms, poisons, and shadow catching. It was an individual practice,

performed by a professional who was paid by his clients. [Obeah] undoubtedly had its origins largely in West African practices.... Myalism, on the other hand, was obviously a form of anti-witchcraft and anti-sorcery. The proponents of myalism were just as aware of the techniques and 'wons' of the obeah men but used then for good rather than evil.... The most important difference from obeah, however, was the fact that it was not an individual practice between practitioner and client, but was organized more as a kind of cult with a unique dance ritual. To a certain extent myalism may be said to approximate closely to standard West African medicine. There are certain elements in it, however, which seem to be of religious origin. The dance ritual of 'death' and 'resurrection,' for instance, bears some resemblance to the 'Resurrection' rite of the Mawu-Lisa ceremonies performed on initiates as the first test of entry into the sky cult of Dahomey. Throughout West Africa, and particularly among the Ga, there were certain good-medicine-men who specialized in immunizing people from witchcraft and in curing people who had been made witches. Almost the same practice is found among Jamaican obeah-men; and the opposite art of releasing these tied up shadows, among the myal-men.[17]

Orlando Patterson's insightful and detailed account of the continuity between Myalism and Obeah captures the spiritual anchorage they supplied to the slave practitioners. We can infer from the dynamics of their rituals that Myalism and Obeah performed as an institution of justice among the slaves. The obeah-men handled complaints and inflicted punishments for their clients and the myal-men were hired to reverse punishments and evil curses. The roles and expectations of the slaves as clients of the obeah-men and myal-men cast them as administrators of spiritual justice. Obeah and Myalism supplied the slaves with an alternative juridical system for seeking justice. The purpose of Obeah and Myalism, thus, was dual; they were spiritual and juridical inventions. They provided an alternative for slave communities that were excluded from the British institutions of justice and religion. Myalism and Obeah are Afrocentric spiritual institutions that have prevailed in Jamaica since British colonialism.

In addition, the rituals and performance of Obeah and Myalism were paradoxical, in colonial Jamaica, in illustrating "open secrecy." To the gaze of the white masters, these performances amounted to theatrical displays in which slaves danced, sang, and used natural artifacts as part of the performances. But they were secretive because the white masters were not in tune with the shared spirituality of the slaves, which rendered the performances meaningful to them. It is by virtue of this spiritual institutional function that Myalism and Obeah were resistance mechanisms, which are still embraced and cherished by Jamaican adherents in the twenty-first century. Rasta scholars are cognizant of the central role that Myalism, via Revivalism, played in shaping the cosmology of the Rastafari movement and Rastas' belief in a triune constitution of the self. The renowned Rasta scholar Barry Chevannes delineates the spiritual and normative continuity between Myalism, Revivalism, and Rastafari in the following observation:

> In this tendency toward decentralized engagement with the society, the Rastafari movement very closely resembles the movement from which it could be said to have emerged, Revivalism. The Revival movement took shape as an 1860 development of Myalism, a Pan-African religion that had emerged a hundred years before to forge a united multiethnic front against slavery. Rastafari grew out of Revival in the sense that it had nothing on

which to peg the new vision, other than the ritual processes of Revival including baptism.... To better appreciate the profundity of the changes underway in Rastafari theology of death, it is useful to summarize the Revival-based folk beliefs about it. The human being is a composite of spirit, body, shadow, and soul. The soul is the life principle, and the shadow the personality, which is subject to the malign influence of obeah.[18]

In this discerning account, Chevannes skillfully articulates the spiritual and normative influence of Myalism, via Revivalism, on Rastafari creed. It is also remarkable that Rastafari cosmology retains the Myal and Obeah belief in the self having a "shadow" component, which is susceptible to the evil of Obeah's witchcraft. The antagonistic relationship between the evil curses of Obeah and the curative virtues of Myalism are preserved in Rastafari cosmology as well.

In conclusion, the centuries of overt, covert, normative, and spiritual resistance practices of African slaves toward British colonialism in Jamaica have informed the cosmology of Rastafari through Myalism and Obeah's creed. Knowledge of the curative virtues of herbs in Myalism remains a core Rastafari practice. In Rastafari cosmology, it preserves its resistance to the colonial institution by the fact that Rastas often seek natural and herbal cures as alternatives to the scientific medical cures, which they perceive as unnatural and an ineffective means by Babylon to subjugate human beings. Also, Rastas' skepticism toward Babylon or mainstream Jamaican normative and spiritual institutions, which they consider anti-Afrocentric, parallels the skepticism of the communities of African slaves who created Myalism and Obeah during British colonialism. In Rastafari cosmology, British slavery and its sociospiritual institutions still prevail in Jamaica as Babylon. And the ultimate goal of Rastafari cosmology is to provide the Afrocentric media of resistance to these institutions. Moreover, Rastafari cosmology encapsulates the original dichotomy between the Anglo-Jamaican and Afrocentric forms of subjectivity that emerged during British colonialism. Rastafari cosmology still provides the sociospiritual form that Jamaicans may choose to espouse Afrocentric subjectivity. Accordingly, the aim of the following chapters is to detail the various norms, conventions, spiritual beliefs, and aesthetics that Rastafari cosmology elaborates to perpetuate the Afrocentric form of subjectivity and to show that they constitute an ethos of Blackness.

2

THE GENEALOGY OF RASTAFARI COSMOLOGY AND ITS DISTINCTIVE ETHOS OF BLACKNESS

This chapter begins by elaborating how the Rastafari movement emerged at the intersection of Jamaican Revivalism and Garveyism. On the one hand, the tenets of Revivalism informed the Afrocentric religious beliefs and practices of the Rastafari movement. On the other, Garveyism supplied the socioethical and cultural guidelines of Rasta communities. As a result, the complex system of norms, religious beliefs, cultural practices, and social attitudes that emerged from Garveyism and Revivalism constitute Rastafari cosmology. Then, on the premise of this elaboration, I argue that the norms, religious beliefs, cultural practices, and social attitudes inherent in Rastafari cosmology define a distinctive ethos of Blackness that is intrinsically tied to the Rastafari movement. I proceed by delineating how the set of events in the Morant Bay Rebellion of 1865 in southeastern Jamaica provided the platform for the elaboration of a distinctive account of Black identity and collective unity as the suitable means to achieve freedom from oppression. To do so, I draw out the centrality of the Native Baptist Church's tenets to show that they were the medium which united the scattered freedmen into insurrectionists. Ultimately, this chapter shows that the distinctive account of Black identity, which emerged during the second half of the nineteenth century on the basis of the Black Native Baptist Church's tenets, shaped the endeavors of the Rastafari movement in the twentieth century, more specifically Rastas' notion of Black identity and their emphasis on the end of oppression. It is imperative to grasp the continuity of the Rastafari movement in the larger context of Jamaican historical evolution and the set of social, cultural, and religious events that influenced its formation. Finally, the conclusion is that the role of religious events and the unity of the slave communities that carried out the Morant Bay Rebellion of 1865 are key for elucidating the link between slavery, religion, and communal unity as the preambles to the Rastafari movement.

The Morant Bay Rebellion was spearheaded by Paul Bogle, a Native Baptist Church preacher. It is noteworthy that the Native Baptist Church arose out of the exclusion of people of African descent from the traditional English Baptist Church in the colony. The English Baptist Church denied people of African descent the privilege of becoming pastors. This denial led to the organization of the Native Baptist Communion circa 1860–1861 through the cooperation of its two leaders George William Gordon and Paul Bogle, mainly in Eastern Jamaica with distinctive tenets to guide people of African descent in the colony. The English settlers' exclusion of people of African descent from the English Baptist Church turned religious oppression into a normative practice. Before the rise of the Native Baptist Church, people of African descent were bereft of a well-defined religious community and religious tenets. George William Gordon and Paul Bogle thus set out to fill this religious void and to mend the religious oppression of people of African descent by establishing the Native Baptist Church. The concomitant collective unity among people of African descent, which made the Morant Bay Rebellion feasible, is concurrent with their attempt to end religious oppression. It is thus consistent with this mission and its byproduct that Paul Bogle spearheaded the rebellion.

On October 11, 1865, Paul Bogle led an animated crowd of hundreds of men and women into the town of Morant Bay, which is located in southeastern Jamaica in the parish of St. Thomas. Some of the main causes of the rebellion were fear of the loss of provisional grounds, burdensome taxes by the planters to counterbalance diminution of their profit, and the worry of being reenslaved. The insurrectionists regarded the landowners and elites, which were predominantly white, as a menace to their livelihood, their privilege to use land, and their ability to obtain just hearings in the courts. The symbolic configuration of the rebellion is equally noteworthy. The rebels were driven by social, economic, and lack of justice issues. Moreover, the racial dimension of the Morant Bay Rebellion was expressed in the rebels' plan: "We will kill every white and Mullato in the Bay. . . . [It] is your colour [Black], don't kill him. You are not to kill your colour."[1] Collective unity to end these social and economic issues, the insurrectionists' religious beliefs, and the leadership of Paul Bogle were the prominent factors that defined people of African descent's racial identity around unity and the demand for social justice. These motifs captured the late nineteenth-century notion of Blackness among people of African descent in Jamaica. Hence, it is reasonable to think that the insurrectionists' confidence in uprising as the means to improve their socioeconomic conditions was reinforced by the tenets and the sense of community that they derived from the Native Baptist Church. It is also remarkable that the two most important rebellions in Jamaica—namely, Paul Bogle's Morant Bay Rebellion of 1865 and Samuel Sharpe's Baptist War slave rebellion of 1832—were led by religious figures. This fact highlights the historical continuity between the formation of religious communities and struggles for social improvement by people of African descent in Jamaica.

Even though the Morant Bay Rebellion caused the British to resume control of the island, it provided the platform for the nascent notion of Black identity on the basis of solidarity among hundreds of insurrectionists toward a common goal. The recognition of a shared destiny and demands for socioeconomic amelioration instilled the notion of Black identity among people of African descent. The anthropologist Charles Price drew the following conclusion from the events of Morant Bay: "The rebellion epitomized the capacity of race and a moral economy of Blackness to mobilize people who otherwise might not have challenged an oppressive social order, an order that they might have considered hopeless and preordained."[2] In this observation, Price is sensitive to the anti-oppression incentive of the rebellion. Black solidarity and anti-oppression remain central motifs of the later Rastafari movement, which is historically influenced by the insurrectionist endeavors of the free people and slave communities. It may be added to Price's standpoint that the Native Baptist Church's tenets, in contrast to traditional Christianity's, were nonfatalistic. This means that the power of the Native Baptist Church's tenets, which made them fit to inspire rebellions, assisted its adherents in conceiving the betterment of their social and economic calamities through uprisings. Unlike traditional Christianity, which portrayed social reality as fatalistic, the Native Baptist Church's tenets proposed the possibility of social and economic uplift and an end to the oppression of its faithful.

The Native Baptist Church stemmed from the syncretism of an endemic version of Christianity on Jamaican plantations with African-inspired folk religious practices, such as Obeah,

Myalism, and Kumina. The common threads of these African-inspired folk religions are their worship of spirits and their belief that spirits in combination with herbs and natural artifacts have healing power. From the outset, the syncretism of these African religious practices and Christianity defined a primordial cosmology—a coherent system of beliefs of the slaves and freedmen with a religious pantheon whose form is essentially Christian and its content comprises complex relations of African spirits with natural artifacts. Throughout its elaboration, the tenets of the Native Baptist Church granted slaves and freedmen a cohesive set of religious practices that reconciled the Christianity of the colonizers with their own African beliefs in the connection between spirits and natural artifacts. Moreover, Native Baptist rituals and beliefs tamed the hostility of slavery in Jamaica by providing slaves and freedmen with a medium of solace and solidarity and, eventually, the platform to elaborate a distinctive account of their Black identity.

It is fair to think that this intrinsic prowess of the Native Baptist Church's tenets in Jamaica informed later Rastas' rejection of the White European God and their adoption of Haile Selassie I as Black divinity. The claim is that the system of beliefs, rituals, solidarity, and the distinctive tenets of the Native Baptist Church constitute the forerunners of the later Rastafari movement. The Native Baptist Church helped define the larger historical and religious context of the Rastafari movement. In Jamaica, during the late nineteenth century, the notion of Blackness was shaped by the tenets of the Native Baptist Church and struggles to end social and economic oppression. The Native Baptist preachers' efforts in Jamaica during the second half of the nineteenth century pioneered the tradition of Afrocentric religious tenets that later shaped Rastafari cosmology—the system of beliefs, norms, and cultural practices and their belief in "earthforce"—the notion that harmony with natural artifacts leads to cosmic unity. Sixty-five years after the Morant Bay Rebellion, Leonard Howell, a founding evangelist of the Rastafari, would preach his message of the expected arrival of the Black Messiah and impending Black redemption to threadbare peasants in the St. Thomas districts of Golden Grove, Trinityville, Leith Hall, and Pear Tree Grove.[3] Howell's gospel intertwined Black identity, religious practices, and social justice. These motifs became more pertinent to the poor and disenfranchised groups of Jamaican society during the first half of the twentieth century. Furthermore, it sheds light on why, during the early phase of the movement, the groups who embraced Rastafari came from the poor and marginalized groups of Jamaican society. Key religious leaders such as Samuel Sharpe, George Gordon and Paul Bogle, and Leonard Howell and the founders of the Rastafari movement initiated a conceptual rebellion in Jamaican society. It consisted in casting an account of Blackness for people of African descent that was free of the colonizers' stigmas and a system of religious beliefs which was sensitive to the African background of Jamaicans.

The message of Leonard Howell, Joseph Hibbert, Archibald Dunkley, and Robert Hinds about the coming of the Black Messiah and a call for Black redemption emphasized the Afrocentric religious aspect of this conceptual rebellion. They drew this emphasis in making the recognition of the dignity of people of African descent and acceptance of their African heritage an imperative for Jamaican society and the colonial institutions. In fact, Leonard Howell's homilies went further than his Native Baptist predecessors in the fact that they displaced the White Christian God and provided Haile Selassie I as a substitute. Howell started to build a following and by 1933 was attracting police attention because of the size and fervency of his open-air meetings; shortly afterward, the first of his several arrests occurred.⁴ Known as the first Rasta, Howell's homilies were not merely prophesying the coming of the Black Messiah; they asserted who the Messiah was in the incarnation of the Ethiopian emperor Haile Selassie I. In contrast to Samuel Sharpe's and Paul Bogle's rebellions, which were undertaken under the guidance of traditional Christianity, Howell's conceptual rebellion unfolded upon the assertion of Haile Selassie I as God, who embodies freedom from oppression, the dignity of people of African descent, and the socioeconomic improvement of poor and marginalized segments of Jamaican society.

Leonard Howell summarized the central aspects of his gospel in a pamphlet entitled *The Promised Key*. *The Promised Key* is a fourteen-page essay in which Howell delineates the suitable practices and taboos of the Rastafari movement while simultaneously depicting some of the key biblical figures as Black. In the short pamphlet, Howell's goal is to reinforce the holiness of Haile Selassie I and to elaborate the creed to complement the worship of Haile Selassie I. Howell provides a system of conventions for Rastas to adopt "holy living." There are many rules to follow in order to achieve holy living. The first rules are dietary: no eating of meat, fish, salt, rum; nothing out of tins or bottles; and so forth. The next set of rules deals with monogamy, mainly being regulations for women and their treatment. Further, "combs, scissors and razors" along with congregational admission to alcoholics, "sadamite thie[ves]," and those who practice birth control, among others, are forbidden. Gambling is not allowed, nor is attending "cinimas," "dancehall" or "whore houses."⁵ It is important to appreciate that in formulating these principles, Howell is behaving primarily as a religious ethicist. In Howell's mind, *The Promised Key* is a testament of religious and social attitudes that Rastas should adopt and a system of norms to guide the formation of Rasta communities. Howell's recommendations may be interpreted to be filling the ethical void of postemancipation—namely, the absence of any set of dietary, social, or cultural rules and practices for freedmen. Furthermore, Howell's recommendations are particularly sensitive to the temper of people of African descent. This fact is apparent in the sections entitled "The Healing," "Balmyard," and "Royal Notice" in which Howell reintroduced the healing yard of African traditional religion, where sufferers take up residence until they are cured. Via these prescribed practices, *The Promised Key* defines the distinctive attitudes and social standing of Rastas who have transcended the prominent colonial norms in Jamaica. Howell's *Promised Key* assisted Rastas in positioning themselves as detached observers of the postcolonial institutions in Jamaica. Finally, by using a lively biblical metaphor, Howell depicts Haile Selassie I for Rastas thus:

> His majesty Ras Tafari is the head over all man for he is the supreme God. His body is the fullness of him that filleth all in all. Now my dear people let this be our goal, forward to the King of Kings must be the cry of our social hope. Forward to the King of Kings to purify our social standards and our way of living, and rebuild and inspire our character. Forward to the King of Kings to learn the worth of manhood and womanhood. Forward to the King of Kings to learn His code of Law from the mount demanding absolute Love, Purity, Honesty, Truthfulness. Forward to the King of Kings to learn His Laws and social order, so that virtue will eventually gain the victory over our body and soul and that truth will drive away falsehood and fraud. Members of the King of Kings, arise for God's sake and put your armour on.[6]

In the above account, Howell portrays Haile Selassie I as the remedy for all the social ills that plague people of African descent. In Howell's mind, it is through Haile Selassie I's divinity that people of African descent will transcend the mores that they inherited from slavery and oppression. Ultimately, the redemption to come via Haile Selassie I's divinity is fit to restore the humanity and ideal social setting for people of African descent; it will be free of fraud, delusions, and misguidance. Howell crafts his portrayal of Haile Selassie I as a divine figure, a redeemer, and a social engineer; in asserting "the King of Kings to purify our social standards," Selassie I is broadcast as a divine figure who is involved in the social dealings of his subjects. His divinity is manifested in socially engineering Rastas' realities.

Though, in order to be fulfilled, Howell's conceptual rebellion required a specific system of socioeconomic practices. Howell's *Promised Key* only details the suitable religious lifestyle of Rastas. It does not explicitly state what Rastas ought to do to bring about their desired social outcomes. Put differently, the end of oppression, restoration of the dignity of people of African descent, and the achievement of socioeconomic improvement of poor and marginalized groups are achievable through a system of principled actions. This system was furnished by Marcus Garvey's Universal Negro Improvement Association in Jamaica during the second half of the twentieth century. Marcus Garvey's social amelioration project falls in line with the undertakings to improve the social conditions of people of African descent in Jamaica that started with the 1832 Baptist War slave rebellion led by Samuel Sharpe. The key distinction of Garvey's approach from this tradition is his pragmatist inclination and skepticism toward religion.

GARVEY'S ETHOS, REVIVALISM, AND THE RISE OF RASTAFARI

Now, I will argue that Garvey's ideals for the social improvement of people of African descent encompass an ethos. Garvey's ethos stands for the social, cultural, and economic principles that he formulated through the Universal Negro Improvement Association to guide people of African descent. I will show that Garvey's ethos provides the system of principled actions that was lacking in the gospels of the founders of Rastafari. The founders of the Rastafari movement elaborated the suitable religious lifestyle of Rastas. The Universal Negro Improvement Association (UNIA) mapped out the socioeconomic steps to bridge the religious lifestyle of Rastas with their expected social outcomes. Marcus Garvey's goal, via the UNIA, was to provide a system of principles that, when applied, would improve the social, economic, and cultural circumstances of people of African descent. The pragmatic bent of these principles displayed Garvey's skepticism toward religion as the suitable means to uplift people of African descent. In his mind, social and economic amelioration of people of African descent is achievable through industry, self-reliance, and competition. As an illustration of his skepticism toward religion, Garvey thinks that praying is begging: "When the Negro by his own initiative lifts himself from his low state to the highest human standard he will be in a position to stop begging and praying, and demand a place that no individual, race or nation will be able to deny him."[7]

Garvey dismisses religious beliefs because he holds them responsible for the social plight of people of African descent. From his perspective, religion merely furthers economic and social marginalization. Instead of religion, Garvey leans toward a pragmatic approach for social and economic betterment. This method encompasses a system of social, economic, and cultural strategies to improve the status of people of African descent. As his essays reveal, Garvey is committed to the view that collective improvement is achievable only through personal and social amelioration. For Garvey, each person of African descent owns the necessary requisites for self-improvement. These individual improvements then uplift people of African descent collectively. Accordingly, he promotes the pursuit of pragmatic values such as self-reliance, organization, progress, and self-achievement. Garveyism was a brand of militant nationalism that gave the black person a sense of identification with the whole of Africa while stressing self-reliance.[8] For him, collective improvement begins with an individual's attempts to improve their social situation. Garvey's agenda sought to align the individual with the group's interest independently of religious affiliation. His vision of economic and social improvement is thus collective and pragmatic. However, implementing this vision of social improvement bore some challenges. Chief among them, in Garvey's assessment, is the resistance among people of African descent to embrace a common social destiny. Garvey does not discuss the root of this tendency, which he deems a core characteristic. He elaborates: "Many have tried to congregate us, but have failed, the reason being that our characteristics are such as to keep us more apart than together. The evil of internal division is wrecking our existence as a people, and if we do not seriously and quickly move in the direction of a readjustment it simply means that our doom becomes imminently conclusive."[9]

Garvey perceives the challenges to fulfilling his collective and pragmatic program to be some core characteristics of people of African descent. Accomplishing the Garveyist vision is hindered by these characteristics and their tendency to undermine a common social identity. Indeed, Garvey seems to attribute the penchant for division to the innate constitution of people of African descent. However, he fails to contemplate the roles of slavery and social and economic ostracization as the root cause of this prominent tendency among peoples of African descent.

Garvey does not explore the source of this inclination toward division even though its centrality to the paradigm of the person of African descent he is advancing is apparent. However, despite his belief that people of African descent have anticollective inclinations, he envisions an ideal collective that continuously strives to overcome these proclivities by pursuing organization, industry, economic competition, and a shared destiny. In applying these principles, this ideal person achieves global respect and recognition as the ultimate step in a self-improvement process that is agreeable to the collective interest of the African Diaspora. Self-improvement that is agreeable to the collective interest is synonymous with Garvey and the UNIA's notion of unity.

Garvey provides the central principles of this self-improvement process in the following statement: "Organization is a great power in directing the affairs of a race or nation toward a given goal. . . . No Negro, let him be American, European, West Indian or African, shall be truly respected until the race as a whole has emancipated itself, through self-achievement and progress, from universal prejudice. The Negro will have to build his own government, industry, art, science, literature and culture, before the world will stop to consider him."[10]

The UNIA advanced organization as the lynchpin to assert the latent dignity and distinctiveness of the African Diaspora. Organization, also, guarantees respect and recognition for the African Diaspora. It requires the coordination of social and economic resources toward a shared goal. Garvey is confident that this process is fit to validate the distinctiveness of people of African descent. Progress and self-achievement are thus concomitant to collective organization. "Progress is the attraction that moves humanity, and to whatever people or race this modern virtue attaches itself, there you will find the splendor of pride and self-esteem that never fail to win the respect and admiration of all. . . . It is the industrial and commercial progress of America that causes Europe and the rest of the world to think appreciatively of the Anglo-American race."[11]

Garvey asserts commercial and industrial progress and self-achievement as the means for collective improvement. They are fit to galvanize the socioeconomic prowess of people of African descent according to a specific set of norms. Second, he believes they are required for global recognition of people of African descent. Thus, for Garvey, the achievement of distinctiveness is intertwined with the validation of African culture. This fact makes it plain that Garvey's ideals for the person of African descent are, in essence, Afrocentric. Progress, self-achievement, and pride are individual virtues to forge a distinctive socioeconomic identity while demanding the validation of African culture. Garvey's ideals thus have both individual and collective aims that are fulfilled around the appropriation of African culture and pride.

Furthermore, his account of industrial and commercial progress as being crucial for both the person of African descent and African culture expresses the materialist underpinnings of Garvey's ethos. This commitment to material wealth as the criterion for global recognition and respect can be inferred from the following claim: "The Negro must be up and doing if he will break down the prejudice of the rest of the world. Prayer alone is not going to improve our condition, nor the policy of watchful waiting. We must strike for ourselves in the course of material achievement, and by our own effort and energy present to the world those forces by which the progress of man is judged."[12]

It is obvious, then, that by progress, Garvey intends material progress. Also, he surreptitiously reinforces his denial of religion as a means for social improvement. This is proof of his espousal of material wealth instead of religion as the suitable means to socioeconomic improvement. In Garvey's mind, the person of African descent, in search of recognition, must commit to a materialist conception of progress in order to reclaim their African heritage. This materialist basis of the ideals of Garveyism puts it in stark contrast to religion as the suitable means for collective improvement.

However, it is important to note that this does not imply that religion is completely absent from Garvey's purview. To the contrary, he endorses a nebulous Afrocentric conception of God as the following claim shows: "If the white man has the idea of a white God let him worship his God as he desires. If the yellow man's God is of his race let him worship his God as he sees it. We as Negroes have found a new deal. We Negroes believe in the God of Ethiopia, the everlasting God, God the Father, God the Son and God the Holy Ghost. The one God of all ages. That is the God in whom we believe, but we shall worship him through the spectacles of Ethiopia."[13]

Garvey's notion of God is inseparable from Ethiopia. In his mind, God does not have any distinctive powers or virtues; the God of Ethiopia is mainly a means to bolster racial identity. Despite promoting the God of Ethiopia like the founders of Rastafari, his objectives remain pragmatic. He does not elaborate on any specific religious practices for worshipping the God of Ethiopia. The postulation of the God of Ethiopia seems to be merely strategical; it stands on an Afrocentric relationship with religion. Furthermore, his materialist ideals supplant an abstract conception of God. His allusion to the God of Ethiopia is meant to encourage pride and appropriation of African culture, specifically Ethiopia. He insisted that religion was a universally experienced phenomenon, and that no man ought to criticize another either for holding to religion in general or for believing in a particular conception of the deity. While he was thus content to have his followers remain within any (Black-led) religious organization, whether Protestant or Catholic, Christian or non-Christian, he was not willing for them to retain the religious ideals or conceptualizations of another race."[14]

Scrutiny of the implications of Garvey's approach to religion makes it plain that his assertion of an Ethiopianist conception of God for the African Diaspora is consistent with his pragmatic vision. For him, the role of religion is to serve as a prop for his Afrocentric notion of identity. This fact leads Tony Martin to observe that "Garvey did not indulge in religion for its own sake, however, but used it as he did art—for furthering his program of race pride and self-reliance. . . . Since religion for Garvey was eminently political, the black God of the UNIA differed from many other Christian gods insofar as a he was a God of self-reliance. He [God] endowed all races equally and left them to their own devices to solve the problem of survival."[15]

Martin accurately depicts the pragmatic function of God in Garvey's agenda. Ethiopianism provides only a frame of reference for the African Diaspora; Garvey does not spell out its rituals, beliefs, and norms. Consider, for example, Garvey's attitude toward the Gospel message "No hungry man can be a good Christian"; he states that "no dirty naked man can be a good Christian, for he is bound to have bad wicked thoughts, therefore, it should be the duty of religion to find physical as well as spiritual food for the body of man."[16] In this formulation, material well-being takes priority over religion and spirituality. Garvey's standpoint clearly asserts the priority of material self-realization. Accordingly, in Garvey's mind, the ideal person of African descent is depicted as industrious and progressive, while claiming African identity through an Ethiopianist frame of reference.

Also, a mandate for promoting the redemption of Africa as the ideal social and cultural context for people of African descent is central to Garveyism. Commentators have often misinterpreted this fact in conflating Garvey's view of Africa with the actual continent itself. For Garvey, African culture is the result of the collective achievements of people of African descent. The common mistake is to think that redemption of Africa, then, depended on establishing a distinct system of norms, social regulations, cultural practices, and governments in a specific geographical location. Instead, at its most fundamental level, the purpose of the Universal Negro Improvement Association was to postulate both the method and infrastructure for the realization of Garvey's ideal African culture. The mission of the UNIA was to lay out the technology for the fulfillment of African culture. Indeed, Garvey is emphatic about the necessity of this method. "Organization is a great power in directing the affairs of a race or nation toward a given goal. To properly develop the desires that are uppermost, we must first concentrate through some system or method, and there is none better than organization. Hence, the Universal Negro Improvement Association appeals to each and every Negro to throw in his lot with those of us who, through organization, are working for the universal emancipation of our race and the redemption of our common country, Africa."[17]

This statement suggests that Garvey's view of Africa is tantamount to the unity of all people of African descent around a specific social, cultural, and economic agenda. In Garvey's mind, African is synonymous with African culture.

A close reading of the above passage also shows that the rise of African culture is conditional on two precedent steps. First, there must be the elaboration of a method, the proper form of organization, which Garvey takes to be suitable for people of

African descent to realize their distinctiveness. Second, all individuals of African descent must make their industrial and economic contribution. The fulfillment of African culture and the distinctiveness of people of African descent depend on collective organization as its method, with material and industrial investments as its constituents. Garvey lays out the strategies and concrete steps to achieve cultural distinctiveness: "The Negro will have to build his own government, industry, art, science, literature and culture, before the world stops to consider him. . . . The race needs workers at this time, not plagiarists, copyists and mere imitators; but men and women who are able to create an independent racial contribution to the world and civilization."[18]

Progress is possible only when people of African descent deploy their autonomy via concrete material investments. Garvey's authentic person of African descent arises when the appropriate method, and the industrial and economic contribution of people of African descent toward their self-improvement have been met.

It is important to note, however, that Garvey's conception of organization has a shortcoming. Indeed, while he emphasizes the acquisition of material wealth as the aim of the collective organization of people of African descent, Garvey's account lacks a specific outline for the distribution of material wealth and the implementation of social regulation and cultural practices to guide people of African descent. Also, his Ethiopianist conception of God is wanting; Garvey has not provided the proper rituals, norms, and beliefs to relate to the God of Ethiopia.

Despite this shortcoming, the inherent pragmatism of Garveyism managed to supply the system of principled actions to complement the Rastafari gospels of Howell, Hibbert, Dunkley, and Hinds. The discussion of Garvey's principles for the improvement of people of African descent is meant to show that they made available the social, economic, and cultural principles that the Rastafari movement embraced during the first half of the twentieth century. The tenets of the Native Baptist Church supplied the religious rituals of the movement. Garvey's pragmatic ethos with its Ethiopianist inspiration informed the social relationship of the early Rastas with the Jamaican sociopolitical institutions during the second half of the twentieth century. Accordingly, it is reasonable to infer that the Rastafari movement was configured at the intersection of these two strands—Garvey's ethos and the tenets of the Native Baptist Church.

The Afrocentric ethos of Garveyism serves as the socioethical compass for Rastas to perform their dual function as religious and social agents. The Rastafarian contention that existence in both colonial and postmodern Jamaica are, in reality, "experience in Babylon," is an ideological harangue that best expressed the depth of the helotage and deracinations that occasioned the metamorphosis of Garvey.[19] Garvey's material prescriptions and his goal to uplift people of African descent were congenial to the struggles of alienated youth and oppressed people of Jamaican society during the rise of the Rastafari movement. The UNIA not only had plans for the universal improvement of the Negro but it also had plans for the immediate upliftment of the Negro in Jamaica.[20] Garvey's principles assisted these segments of Jamaican society to conceptualize a cohesive lifestyle in the postcolonial era. Garveyism complemented the prevailing beliefs of Revivalism inherent in the Rastafari movement; it provided a pragmatic praxis to these religious beliefs, which made their performance by Rastas in the social context feasible.

Garvey's ethos and the mission of the Universal Negro Improvement Association thrived in Jamaica during the second half of the twentieth century because they promoted an Afrocentric conception of identity among Jamaican peasants and disenfranchised groups. Garvey's deportation from the United States to Jamaica and the dissemination of his ethos coincided with the span of Jamaican history during which some groups of Jamaican society were attempting to reclaim their African heritage vis-à-vis British colonialism. Rupert Lewis's observations draw out the universal appeal of Garveyism to different segments of Jamaican society:

> Garveyism and Rastafari are the results of distinct social movements that overlap on certain ideas and personalities and differ in other respects. For example, while Garveyites shared a similar perspective on Africa to that of the Rastafarians, they differed over Selassie's divinity. For Garvey, Selassie was a secular figure, not a religious one, and absolutely not God. Garveyism was broader than Rastafari in social appeal and included a strong element of middle-class Blacks of that era, though it also attracted a strong working-class and rural following. By contrast, Rastafari was definitely rooted in the lower socioeconomic classes. It was a movement among the Jamaican poor, unmediated. The infusion of the middle class into Rastafari came with Black Power in the 1960s.[21]

Lewis supports the observation that the God of Ethiopia, for Garvey, was not a religious entity. Haile Selassie I stands as the secular embodiment of the God of Ethiopia. The divinity of Haile Selassie I consists in his ability to perform and be an exemplar of the materialist principles that Garvey and the UNIA advanced. As a cultural nationalist movement, Rastafari therefore is an authentic affirmation of the redemptive power at the wellspring of the traditional African way of life, in which selfhood/self-reliance, ethnocultural identity, and emancipation from Eurocentric modes of consciousness form the primary focus. As such, the Rastafarian assertion of African authenticity naturally came into direct confrontation with colonial and neocolonial governments.[22] Unsurprisingly, then, Garvey's Black Nationalist message was particularly compelling for people at the bottom of the postcolonial structure of Jamaican society. Garvey was a black-skinned Jamaican, and he sometimes referred to what he called his Maroon heritage. He came, in other words, from the lowest socioeconomic layer of Jamaican society, and his entire political program in later years was designed to elevate that section of society.[23] Garveyism bolstered the struggles of marginalized Jamaicans to overcome social alienation by gearing them with the incentive to embrace their African rootedness. The leavening force of Garveyism and Rastafari had long prepared the psychological and spiritual ground for this outburst of Afrocentricity in the 1960s in the Caribbean ghettoes of the Black Diaspora.[24] The Rastafari movement thus benefited from a constellation of congenial historical, cultural, and social occurrences. The postcolonial era in Jamaica, acknowledgment of African rootedness, and the Revivalist preaching of the Bedwardites—a denomination of the Jamaican Baptist Church that was influenced by the Afrocentric preaching of Alexander Bedward—are the events which were most favorable to the rise of Rastafari.

The theology of Bedwardites' homilies and Revivalist rituals promoted an Afrocentric appropriation of the Bible prior to the dissemination of Garveyism in Kingston, Jamaica, in the 1950s. The ideational trajectory of Garveyism was in sharp opposition to the Euro-Christianizing thrust of white sociocultural hegemony in the Anglophone Caribbean.[25] In this way, the practices and beliefs of Jamaican Revivalism syncretized the African inheritance and religious experience of its adherents with the Judeo-Christian tradition. Jamaican Revivalism was born out of slave rebellion and integrated both a theology and a mechanism of resistance to social oppression of the poor and marginalized in Jamaican society.

Revivalism, the term derived from the Great Revival of 1860–1861, is a religious movement in Jamaica that is a syncretism of the Christian faith and African rituals and beliefs. It can be traced to the Myal movement, which first came to European notice during the Tacky Rebellion of 1760. Myal enabled enslaved Africans to unite and protect themselves against what was perceived as European sorcery. With the arrival of the enslaved Baptist preachers George Leile, Moses Baker, and George Lewis in 1776 and their creation of the class-leader system in which their most talented converts were appointed leaders over new converts, Myal reinterpreted and refashioned the symbols and teachings of Christianity. Important among ritual paraphernalia are water, stones, and herbs. The most important religious services of Jamaican Revivalists are: divine worship, baptismal rites, tables, death rites, dedication of a new church building, and installation of new officers. Divine worship services, held weekly, feature drumming, singing, handclapping, praying, Bible reading, preaching, spirit possession, testimonials, and healing. The moral code of Revivalism is based on that found in the Christian Bible. Taboos among the Revivalists include the eating of pork, using profanity, and going to cemeteries at prohibited times. Revivalism as a form of cultural resistance has helped to shape and reinforce the values of the Jamaican peasantry. In the early twentieth century Revival leader Alexander Bedward combined religion with black nationalist sentiments by urging his followers to rise above their oppression and cast down their oppressors, considered at this time to be the white Jamaican ruling class. Revivalism has played a role in the emergence and development of Rastafarianism.[26]

The Afrocentric theology and cultural resistance thrust of Revivalism persist in Rastafari practices. They influenced Rastas' demand for social validation during the postcolonial era.

The religious component of the Rastafari movement stands on the Revivalists' Afrocentric appropriation of the Bible. Moreover, the creed of Revivalism was conducive to the Rastas' positive reception of Marcus Garvey's message and the Ethiopian emperor Haile Selassie I as a divine figure. Rastas believe that Garvey and Haile Selassie I are endowed with divinity and prophecy on the basis of the Revivalists' Afrocentric interpretation of the Bible that they have inherited. For them, Marcus Garvey was the incarnation of Moses and Haile Selassie I was the last member of the Solomonic dynasty in the lineage of the biblical prophets via his kinship with the Falashas, the Judaic Ethiopian community. The peasants and disenfranchised groups of Jamaican society, more specifically in Kingston where Garvey disseminated his ethos, imbibed Garveyism as a prophecy.

It is important to bear in mind that Garveyism flourished in Jamaica for two reasons. First, the dire social and economic circumstances of poor and marginalized communities made them susceptible to Garvey's message. Due to apathy in Jamaica, Garvey could not initiate his movement in the West Indies until it had been established in New York; and even then, examination of his policies at home and abroad revealed a marked duality—Garvey's nationalism in the United States took on a revolutionary character but his Jamaican policies were strictly reformist.[27] Second, the prevalence of Jamaican Revivalism among the Jamaican peasantry and disenfranchised segments of society was conducive to their religious appropriation of Garveyism and a belief in Haile Selassie I as God. It is noteworthy that Rastafarians compare Garvey to Moses because of their common roles as precursors. Ideologically speaking, then, it was

Garveyism that provided the basis for transcending the limitations in the Revivalist concept of nationalism, which the Bedwardites failed to do.[28] It is thus reasonable to observe that the Revivalist tenets provided the Afrocentric religious practices and beliefs around which disenfranchised Jamaicans united to define the Rastafari movement, and Garveyism supplied their socioethical and cultural guidelines. While Garvey emphasized Africa's social and political redemption, Rastas include in that agenda a spiritual dimension, which they often clothe in Judeo-Christian thought and African concepts.[29]

Rastas' appropriation of Marcus Garvey as a divine figure was consistent with the Judeo-Christian worldview that they inherited from the Revivalist and Bedwardite movements that prevailed in Jamaica prior to the spread of Garveyism. Here, we can see a syncretism of Old Testament prophecy, Gnostic mysticism, and Christian theology fused into a revolutionary rhetoric typical of the movement's unique form of expression.[30] After all, Rasta communities were already prone to interpret their socioeconomic plight as a prelude to their redemption. The spiritual appropriation of Garveyism, however, does not exhaust Rastafari; Garveyism and Rastafarian ideology, in the 1930s, shared some ideological features, but they were distinct movements that happened to coincide. Garvey was not radical enough for the Rastas. The Rastas understood that there was a theological and spiritual basis for the poor self-esteem and the loss of racial pride that afflicted Afro-Jamaicans.[31] The historical and social circumstances of the peasantry and disenfranchised people of Jamaica were congenial to the collaboration of the two movements. Theodore Vincent's account of the living conditions of poor and marginalized Jamaican people in Kingston, Jamaica, in the early twentieth century sheds light on the circumstances that made them susceptible to Garveyism and Rastafari beliefs: "Kingston,

Jamaica, though founded in the mid-1600s, typified the sprawling growth of the Third World. Between 1910 and 1920 huge collages of cardboard and flattened water heaters, with names like Trench Town and Denham Town, mushroomed around the outskirts of central Kingston. Unlike the American Migrants, who left the farm willingly, and usually against the wishes of white owners, blacks in the Third World had often been forced to leave their rural setting."[32]

Moreover, urbanization and immigration within Jamaica during the postcolonial era contributed to the wide reception of Garvey's ethos. This historical phase of Jamaican society happened to be favorable to the rise of Garveyism. This led W. E. B. Du Bois to observe that "he [Garvey] has with singular success capitalized and made vocal the great and long suffering grievances and spirit of protest among the West Indian peasantry."[33] So, the rise of Rastafari occurred at a historical juncture in which the theology of the Native Baptist Church's tenets, through Revivalism, and Garveyism complemented each other. Although Garvey did not actively undertake Blacks' return to Africa, his writings and speeches (published in the *Negro World*, the official newspaper of the UNIA) inspired significant numbers of them to return there. Garvey was a persuasive and eloquent orator, and his articulation of these issues and his personal struggles over these questions undoubtedly set the stage for the millenarian theology of the Rastafari.[34]

Furthermore, differing views of the Ethiopian emperor Haile Selassie I help demonstrate some of the key differences between Garveyism and Rastafari. In keeping with his pragmatism and penchant for racial purity, Garvey regarded Haile Selassie I as the pinnacle of African pride and proof of the suitability of people of African descent to adopt his pragmatic ideals. For Garvey, Haile Selassie I was evidence that, through industry and economic competition, people of African descent could galvanize their latent greatness and ascend to the zenith of the world. Rastas, on the other hand, related to Haile Selassie I via the Revivalist beliefs they had inherited. Revivalist theology conditioned believers to view Haile Selassie I as the physical manifestation of the Messiah. They appropriated him as a palpable manifestation of divinity akin to the biblical prophets. Both celebratory, these differing estimations created different expectations from Garveyites and Rastas for his reign in Ethiopia. For Garvey, Selassie was the tangible realization of the ideals of the UNIA and a living symbol of their ideal Africa. For the Rastas, he was the promised Black prophet who would free people of African descent from their colonial and oppressive sociopolitical circumstances in both Africa and the African Diaspora.

FAVORABLE HISTORICAL AND SOCIAL EVENTS FOR THE ESPOUSAL OF HAILE SELASSIE I

The Rastas' spiritual appropriation of Haile Selassie I as a divine figure bears a psychological aspect. The imperial reign of Haile Selassie I was historically favorable to Rastas' attempt to claim their spiritual history in biblical scriptures. The Native Baptist Church's tenets and Revivalism provided Rastas with their Afrocentric interpretation of biblical scripture. This system of beliefs corroborated Rastas' conceptualization of biblical figures and narratives through an Afrocentric lens. The accomplishments of Marcus Garvey and Haile Selassie I were favorable to Rastas' Afrocentric conceptualization in being received as palpable manifestations of Jah—Black divinity and his prophet Moses. Accordingly, their view of Haile Selassie I syncretizes Judeo-Christian and Afrocentric beliefs. This means that, as a prophetic figure, Haile Selassie I's reign strengthened Rastas' spiritual identity and social standing vis-à-vis the oppressive postcolonial Jamaican institutions. As a predominantly disenfranchised segment of Jamaican society, Rastas asserted their human worth in postcolonial Jamaican society by appropriating Haile Selassie I as a divine emperor. Consequently, the worldview of Rastafari can only be identified by the beliefs and practices that the various groups share: the belief in the divinity of Haile Selassie; repatriation; adherence to some sort of livity; and reasoning.[35] So, Haile Selassie I assumes a dual role in Rastafari cosmology. He serves as both a sociopolitical and religious figure for Rastas to overcome marginalization. His believed divine attributes are in essence the media through which Rasta communities validate themselves and their Afrocentric views.

The coronation of Haile Selassie I as emperor of Ethiopia and the return of Marcus Garvey to Jamaica had a tremendous impact for the nascent Rastafari movement. Rastas interpreted both events as prophetic omens for their religious faith. The fact that Haile Selassie I secured the respect and recognition of European leaders as the most powerful African leader of the early twentieth century further contributed to Rastas' perception of him as a divine figure. He was the first African leader to gain this level of international recognition, which, for Rastas, was living proof of Haile Selassie I's divinity on earth. From their perspective, only the promised Black Messiah could have risen to such prominence. Accordingly, the poor and disenfranchised communities of Jamaican society who joined the Rastafari movement viewed this feat as proof of his divine predestination.

The central role of Haile Selassie I in the movement lies in the authority of the scriptures on his divinity and in the fact that he is Black. His Ethiopian birth further strengthens the belief, for the Bible clearly states that their God would be born in that country.³⁶ Moreover, the various Abyssinian emperors' struggles against European colonial rule consolidated Ethiopia as a stronghold of resistance against European domination. From the perspective of Rastas, Ethiopia is the essence of African greatness on the continent. The rule of Haile Selassie I and Ethiopia thus embody the ideal spiritual, social, and religious context for disenfranchised Rastas. They display the pictures of Emperor Haile Selassie I to remember his contribution to Black liberation and to see their God, the Head Creator in these pictures.³⁷ For Rastas, Ethiopia and Haile Selassie I symbolized Africa's greatness and the inherent divinity of people of African descent. Thus, in many ways, historical events were conducive to the birth of the Rastafari movement. Furthermore, Rastas interpreted the Second World War, the coronation of Haile Selassie I, and his return to power after the Italian invasion of Ethiopia as the realization of prophetic omens.

Another key historical occurrence that corroborated the belief in Haile Selassie I's divinity is his speech at the League of Nations meeting in June 1936, after the Italian invasion of Ethiopia. Haile Selassie I concluded his speech by condemning the Italian invasion with this statement: "It is us today and it will be you tomorrow." Rastas interpret this as a prediction of Adolph Hitler's later invasion of the European continent. Haile Selassie I's return to power exactly five years to the day from the time he went into exile in Europe is another historical event that Rastas hold to be the fulfillment of a prophecy. Haile Selassie I's status as a peacemaker among African countries and his exemplary accomplishment in modernizing Addis Ababa as an international attraction reinforced the perception of him as a model leader for postcolonial nations. These historical factors further shaped Rastas' perception of Selassie I as a holy and powerful emperor.

Rastas received Haile Selassie I as the Black God and Marcus Garvey relied heavily on this reception to advance his ethos and the mission of the UNIA. In Jamaica, Garveyism rectified the colonial heritage inherent in Bedwardite and Revivalist beliefs and shaped the sociocultural attitude of Rastas, chiefly by broadcasting the accomplishments of Haile Selassie I. The Bedwardites, while calling for the Black "followers of Christ" to crush the white "Pharisees, Scribes, and Sadducees," retained the view that white was superior to Black—so that the end of white oppression would at the same time be the transformation of Black into the status of white. This conclusion was discredited by Garvey's teaching that Black people's God must be Black "since we are created in his image and likeness."[38]

The accomplishment of Garvey's dissemination of his ethos and the mission of the UNIA in Jamaica was twofold. First, the movement shaped the collective consciousness of the Jamaican poor, thereby challenging the colonial vestiges pervasive at the time. In doing so, Marcus Garvey and the Universal Negro Improvement Association undermined the effects of the self-destructive doctrines of British colonialism on the most vulnerable segments of Jamaican society. Moreover, they encouraged Rasta communities to forge a conception of God via an Ethiopianist figure. For the poor, the workers, the small farmers, and the unemployed, their social consciousness was formed by the reality of the duality of racial discrimination and economic exploitation and thus nurtured searches for identification with the glory of the African past.[39] This fact prepared Rastas to regard Haile Selassie I as the incarnation of a God in whose image they were created. So, the historical role of the coronation of Haile Selassie I as emperor was very propitious for both Garveyism and Rasta communities because it concretized their religious and Afrocentric beliefs. Rastas relied on the imperial rule of Haile Selassie I to legitimate both their sociopolitical and religious experiences in Jamaican society.

Although Garvey distanced himself from the Rastafari movement, it is undeniable that his system of principled actions was congenial to its development. It is plausible that his dissociation from the Rastafari movement was due to his belief that Rastas, as a marginalized group, did not meet his standard of self-reliance and industry, virtues that are crucial for the authenticity of the Black race. Despite Garvey's refusal to identify with Rastas, his message offered them the opportunity to elaborate a spiritual and sociopolitical ethos. This explains why myths about Garvey are part of the ethnic identity of Jamaica's poor, dispossessed Blacks—once the object of enslavement, still the object of oppression in a society that only now is beginning to demonstrate that it values Black as much as it values white.[40]

Rastas' distrust of the colonial institutions in Jamaica intensified as they attempted to validate their experience within the universal context of the biblical tradition. Assertion of Rasta beliefs and resistance to the social institutions was expressed through their belief that they had been deceived in order to be kept in bondage. Rastas thus viewed the colonial political and social institutions as oppressive forces that spread deceit and confusion among the people. As agents of Babylon—their name for this system—they were media of confusion and deceit. This outlook suggests that, in Rastafari cosmology, politicians are agents of Babylon; for Rastas, social institutions are essentially oppressive. Discovering the hidden "truths" of the Bible about Black people—namely, the awakening of the revelation of the true and Black Messiah—gave the early Rastafarians a conviction that compensated for the miniscule size of the movement overall and brought them into confrontation with the establishment almost as soon as their doctrine began to take hold.[41] The basis of Rastas' tension with social and political institutions is both ethical and religious. It is ethical because Rastafari cosmology advances Afrocentricity, which is inherent in their norms, beliefs, and practices. The Rastafari movement contends with the colonial and Judeo-Christian institutions over the normativity of Jamaican identity. Essentially, Rastas promote Afrocentric normativity as the ideal guide in contrast to colonial normativity, which idealizes Eurocentric mores for Jamaicans. Rastas' religious contention consists in asserting the antithetical stance of Haile Selassie I as Jah—Black divinity—against the oppressive and deceiving sociopolitical institutions that constitute Babylon. It is thus accurate to note that in Rastafari cosmology, Rasta communities, via Jah's edicts, are engaged in an incessant resistance to Babylon in order to advance Afrocentric normativity.

Rastafari cosmology is thus in a paradoxical situation in relation to the Judeo-Christian establishment in Jamaica because Rastas are simultaneously skeptical of Judeo-Christianity while trying to appropriate it according to their Afrocentricity. This paradox is illustrated in the rise of the Youth Black Faith. Emerging in the late 1940s, this group of Rastas believed that the Eurocentric and colonial heritage of the Revivalists needed to be jettisoned in favor of a more practical and Afrocentric system of values. "The Youth Black Faith was founded in 1949 by what we may call activists. They were young, and they were on fire with the doctrine. They were for the most part young men who entered adolescence in the late 1930s, left the country for Kingston, and embraced the faith in the following decade. As one of the most influential members of the Youth Black Faith, Wato describes the leadership of the new group was born out of contempt for the waywardness of the older leaders."[42] In this way, the Youth Black Faith unfolded along the process of reforming the Revivalist tenets they had inherited and embracing Garveyist rectifications of Eurocentric ideals. The Youth Black Faith's embrace of Rastafari and its spread throughout the Caribbean led Patrick Manning to observe that "the most distinctive cultural trend to come out of Caribbean cities in the late twentieth century was reggae music and Rastafarian culture from Jamaica. This messianic religion and its migratory connections interacted with a developing youth culture of Kingston."[43]

Upon his forced return to Jamaica, Garvey immediately launched a vigorous island-wide membership drive to bolster and disseminate the principles of the UNIA among disenfranchised groups. He told his Jamaican followers that his deportation from the United States was in fact a blessing in disguise since it had enabled him to return to the homeland to work for race redemption among his own people.[44] It is noteworthy that Garvey's portrayal of his deportation as a "blessing in disguise" contributed to his spiritual reception by Rasta communities. Indeed, the rise of the Youth Black Faith movement is proof of the shift that the Rastafari movement underwent as a result of Garveyism's influence during this period. One expression of this shift is the Youth Black Faith's invention of a distinctive Rasta aesthetic. Beginning in the late 1940s, Rastas adopted dreadlocks and full beards—for which they are known even today—and developed a dialect, diet, and other cultural practices to demarcate their socioreligious inclinations. It is at this juncture that the aesthetic demarcation of Rastas began to assert their physical communities as an anticolonial segment in Jamaican society and a resistant group to Babylon. At the sociopolitical level, the term *Babylon* is used in reference to the ideological and structural components of Jamaica's social system, which institutionalizes inequity and exploitation. In this respect, Babylon is the complex of economic, political, religious, and educational institutions and values that evolved from the colonial experiment.[45]

Unsurprisingly, the movement's creation of distinctive aesthetic, religious, and social practices immediately turned them into antiestablishment communities. Rastas' invention of a demarcating system of aesthetic, religious, social, and cultural practices casts their communities as antagonists to the colonial principles of Jamaican institutions, causing uneasiness in the Jamaican status quo. On the other hand, Rastas view Jamaican sociopolitical institutions and values as vestiges of oppression. Barry Chevannes thinks that the Rasta aesthetic stands as a tangible rejection of Jamaican social institutions or "Babylon":

> The most outstanding characteristic of the Dreadlocks is, of course, his hair, a sacred and inalienable part of his identity. It defines his status. The longer his locks the greater his standing as a professor of the faith. He affectionately called his hair his crown, comparing it to the real crown of his king, Selassie, and sometimes to the mane of the lion, a symbol of male strength. The Dreadlocks reform trend within the Rastafari movement set out to purge the movement of many of the Revivalisms that had been retained in ritual and organizational life, and in doing so to challenge many of the social and religious norms taken for granted. Their matted hair was a symbol of this.[46]

Thus, by virtue of their embrace of the Native Baptist Church's tenets and Garvey's ethos, Rastas are perceived as actively engaged in the refutation of colonialist practices and the implicit Eurocentrism of the sociopolitical institutions via their distinctive aesthetic. They became embodied critiques of Jamaican institutions by promoting an Afrocentric ethos as alternative guidelines for people of African descent. The Rastafarians—living examples of Jamaican social and cultural deprivation—are now the prophets preaching to the elite about the conditions of squalor.[47]

In conclusion, the tradition of continuity between religion and rebellion in the evolution of Jamaica—which started with Samuel Sharpe's 1832 Baptist War slave rebellion and then Paul Bogle's Morant Bay Rebellion of 1865—created the platform for the conceptual rebellion carried out by the gospels of the founders of the Rastafari movement and Garvey's ethos of principled actions. The Rastafari movement transcended the Eurocentric account of God and created an alternative system of guidelines for people of African descent. Another central accomplishment of the Rastafari movement is the promotion of Black divinity in the image of people of African descent on the premise that God's servants should be in God's image. This highlights the view of God shared by oppressed peoples and reinforces the idea that, for them, God must be tangible and must manifest in their daily dealings to alleviate their oppression. Rastas appropriated God and made their appropriation obvious by asserting themselves as concrete images of Black divinity through Haile Selassie I. The Rastafarians went one up on Garvey. They did not argue that God should be Black, they just assumed it.[48] In doing so, the Rastafari movement corrected the inherent flaw in the Native Baptist Church's tenets—namely, their commitment to the White European God despite the congeniality of their beliefs to the betterment of people of African descent. These corrective steps to improve the sociocultural experience and inner realities of people of African descent in accordance with an Afrocentric regime of religious tenets and norms constitute Rastafari cosmology's ethos of Blackness.

Moreover, the formulation of a distinctive ethos of Blackness is inherent in the rise of Rastafari cosmology and the creation of the Rasta movement. The development of the Rastafari movement is concurrent with the elaboration of Rastas' ethos of Blackness for people of African descent. Rastas' ethos of Blackness is multifaceted. Its historical foundation began with Samuel Sharpe's 1832 Baptist War slave rebellion and then Paul Bogle's Morant Bay Rebellion of 1865. This fact makes resistance to the oppression of people of African descent a key feature of Rastas' ethos of Blackness. Rastas' ethos of blackness inherits the Afrocentric spirituality of Revivalism and the Native Baptist Church's tenets. Michael Barnett makes the following observation regarding the centrality of Revivalism and Baptism in Rastafari Cosmology:

Rastafari grew out of Revival in the sense that it had nothing on which to peg the new vision, other than the ritual processes of Revival, including even baptism. Until the revolt of the Youth Black Faith radicals beginning in the late 1940s, the doctrinal innovation was the principal distinguishing mark of the Rastafari. Even as late as the mid-1970s, the Revival influence in Nyahbinghi celebrations was still evident, including its choruses sung to the slower, more somber Nyahbinghi kete drum beat instead of the quick-tempo rattler, and with critical word changes, such as "Zion" for "heaven."[49]

Moreover, Rastas' ethos of Blackness managed to create alternative religious and sociocultural norms for people of African descent. Rastas' Blackness is balanced by Garveyist pragmatist principles while remaining sensitive to the spiritual, cultural, and socioethical needs of people of African descent to function as cohesive communities. It is reasonable to think that the elaboration of a distinctive ethos of Blackness led Rastafari to expand beyond its religious and cultural heritage in Revivalism and

Baptism. The formulation of an ethos of Blackness defines Rastafari's distinction in the Caribbean. Also, Rastas managed to broadcast and position their distinctive ethos of Blackness vis-à-vis Babylon by embodying it in a unique aesthetic and sociocultural practices. Finally, by means of their unique ethos of Blackness along with their aesthetic, religious beliefs, and religious practices that promote African conceptions of people of African descent, Rastafari cosmology complies with the paradigm of Afrocentricity that "positions African ideals at the center of analyses involving African culture and behavior, traditions, and history."[50] Hence, the elaboration of Rastas' ethos of Blackness is proof of the complex intellection about the plight of people of African descent and the suitable technology to correct the ills of colonialism and neocolonialist institutions imposed on people of African descent.

3

RASTAFARI COSMOLOGY, NATURAL ARTIFACTS, AND THE ETHOS OF BLACKNESS

My argument in this chapter is that, in Rastafari cosmology, resistance to both postcolonial institutions and the technological oppression of natural artifacts is an intrinsic dimension of Rastas' ethos of Blackness. Technological oppression of natural artifacts means the exploitation of natural artifacts through technological means for profit and overconsumption. I begin by showing that resistance to the technological oppression of natural artifacts is the logical implication of Rasta communities' endeavor to align their lifestyle with the guiding notion of *Ital livity*, which can be defined as "a commitment to using things in their natural or organic states."[1] In Rastas' mindset, Ital livity's lifestyle comprises practices that provide a cosmic energy commonly known in their communities as "earthforce." Ital livity and earthforce are achievable through a naturalist inclination according to which Rastas structure their lifestyle. Moreover, Rastas' naturalist inclination encompasses spiritual continuity with ancestors. Rastas venerate the teachings of their deceased elders and by extension the biblical prophets. Rastas' spiritual continuity with their ancestors is manifest and embodied in the Ethiopian emperor Haile Selassie. Rastas believe that Haile Selassie is a direct descendant of King David.

Ital livity and earthforce are the incentives of the Rastas' imperative to create an egalitarian relationship with natural artifacts upon their freedom from technological oppression. For Rastafari, an ideal way to conduct oneself would be to sever from the ways of life of the West and to embrace a way of life linked to the Black God in the spiritual, political, social, and cultural senses. In other words, the notion of livity represents a form of liberation in the various senses of the term.[2] It is important to emphasize that Rastas' view of nature is concrete rather than abstract, manifesting itself in important animistic beliefs about natural objects and products. As a creature, man is subject to all the forces mentioned above: God, spirits, the dead, nature.[3]

To elaborate my argument, I start with a discussion of the role of Bedwardite beliefs and the gospel of the founding fathers in defining the theological tenets that shape Rastafari's cosmology and how the academic study of Rastafari cosmology contributed to its acceptance by mainstream Jamaican society. This is the preliminary step to show how Rastafari cosmology eschews the oppressive monolithic theology of traditional Christianity by allowing a tripartite theology that is manifest in the organization of the three mansions of Rastafari. I also elaborate how the belief that adherents should align their lifestyle with the natural order illustrates that Rastas' profound respect for natural artifacts is proof of their resistance to their technological oppression. On the premise of this thesis, I then draw the conclusion that Rastas' ethos of Blackness, which includes the creation of nonoppressive communities for people of African descent, encompasses the freedom of natural artifacts from technological oppression as well. Put differently, in Rastafari cosmology's ethos of Blackness, freedom from oppression for people of African descent is isomorphic with the freedom of natural artifacts from technological oppression.

RASTAS' THEOLOGY AND JAH'S BLACK DIVINITY

It is noteworthy that Rastas' account of God, expressed through their faith in Jah, is informed by the specific social and religious circumstances of Jamaican society during the first half the twentieth century. Their conception of Jah is partially informed by the need for social improvement of the poor and disenfranchised groups of Jamaican society and the necessity to elaborate religious tenets that can accommodate the Afrocentric religious beliefs the practitioners inherited. These needs shaped the taxonomy of their ethical and social practices. The cohesion of this system of cultural and spiritual practices, beliefs, and social norms constitutes Rastafari cosmology. Rastas thus forged their conception of Jah as Black as a corrective theological strategy aimed at redressing the large-scale demoralization among poor and alienated Jamaicans during the postcolonial era. Rastas think that the experience of low self-esteem by some Jamaicans arose as a byproduct of colonialism, specifically from the widespread view of God as a White European entity. From the Rasta perspective, the pervasiveness of low self-esteem among people of African descent is the natural outcome of being unable to conceptualize themselves in the image of the White European God. The inability to view their physical image in the prominent Caucasian depiction of God and Christian theological practices led them to believe that they are invisible to this God and concomitantly that their realities do not fall in the purview of this Caucasian God. The Rastas were in tune with the theological and spiritual basis for the poor self-esteem and the loss of racial pride that afflicted Afro-Jamaicans. They understood that there was a correlation between construing God as white or colorless and having poor self-esteem.[4] Hence, compelling people of African descent to conform to Eurocentric mores informed by this God only leads to their oppression. The Rasta conception of Jah or more specifically Haile Selassie I as the Ethiopian embodiment of Black divinity may be interpreted as the outcome of brokering the demand for social improvement in Jamaica during the postcolonial era and the need to delineate distinctive tenets of Afrocentric spirituality. By means of Rastafari cosmology, Rastas thus fill the need of the poor and disenfranchised to recast their frame of self-conceptualization according to an Afrocentric image of divinity. This reversed the anthropological implication and gave them permission to revalue and view themselves in the light of the divine image of Blackness.[5]

Moreover, the rise of Rastafari was concurrent with the need to elaborate a system of postcolonial social realities that would be cohesive with the African normative heritage of Jamaicans. African normative heritage means the beliefs, practices, and norms that African slaves operated by and transmitted orally or through continuous interaction to their descendants. The advocates of the system of beliefs that inform Rastafari theology in Jamaica espoused Marcus Garvey's Universal Negro Improvement Association's philosophy of autonomy. Supporters of Garveyism—such as Leonard Howell, Robert Hinds, Archibald Dunkley, and Joseph Hibbert—spread the Rasta gospel that Haile Selassie I was the personification of Jah (the Rasta name for God). As founders of Rastafari, they viewed themselves as prophets—much like the Judeo-Christian model—being predestined to preach the liberation gospel to people of African descent. Howell, Hinds, Dunkley, and Hibbert thus assumed the dual role of religious seers and advocates for social improvement among poor and alienated Jamaican communities. Their gospel promoted social improvement for people of African descent on the basis of Afrocentric spirituality. From its beginning, Rastafari cosmology synthesized religious belief and social activism on behalf of the oppressed and marginalized. Another key implication of this dual mission of Rastafari cosmology is that Jah, unlike the aloof European God of Judeo-Christianity, is actively permeating the social dealings of his believers. This approach is akin to Black theology of liberation in the fact that the Christian model remains in Rastafari cosmology with the innovation of Jah, which is conceived in the image of his Black adherents and is actively involved in calling for the end of their oppression. Having one's own God in one's own image was a grand flowering in Rastafari of what had earlier begun in Myal and developed in Zion revivalism and Pocomania, with the hijacking of the oppressor's God in a move that served to discommode the oppressor. The divinity of all Black people—in fact, of all human beings—here becomes the basis for equality, liberty, dignity, mutual respect, and equity in terms of access to economic resources.[6] Howell, Hinds, Dunkley, and Hibbert disseminated their conviction that Emperor Selassie I was the fulfillment of the Messiah who was promised as the liberator of Africans and people of African descent everywhere. The conception of Haile Selassie I was thus remedial to the lingering ills of the transatlantic slave trade. For many, slavery was the manifestation of extreme trauma and the commencement of a process of silencing. From the silence of slavery came the voice of Rastafari.[7] In the minds of Rastas, affirming Haile Selassie I's Black divinity and inventing a system of practices around his holiness present the preliminary steps toward a conception of people of African descent who have transcended the trauma of slavery and social oppression prevalent in Jamaica during the second half of the twentieth century. This conception is a central component of Rastas' ethos of Blackness.

The rise of Rastafari cosmology may thus be read as a postcolonial technology to create the ideal society for people who have inherited African mores and seek to provision the system of norms, spirituality, and sociocultural values to define their Blackness. Accordingly, the founders of Rastafari—Howell, Hinds, Dunkley, and Hibbert—assumed the role of social engineers engaged in envisioning the religious component of this ideal society by supplanting the White European God with Haile Selassie I as both Black Messiah and promised liberator.

The next step called for a massive exodus to Ethiopia, which the founding fathers portrayed to followers as the divinely ascribed location for people of African descent to find redemption. As such, the Rastafari alone carried the logic of Ethiopianism to its ultimate conclusion. They boldly proclaimed that the final turn into the homestretch of the two thousand years of dispensation of our present age, the African Redeemer should come forward as the King of Kings, Lord of Lords, and Conquering Lion of Judah, to rightfully reclaim the Black people's heritage—their former headship among the brotherhood of nations.[8] This claim echoes the necessity to overcome the deep-seated sense of alienation among people of African descent—the need to reclaim Africa as the suitable location to rekindle their preslavery status. The backdrop of the call for African redemption is that, for Rastas, Jamaica and by extension the Americas, and Europe cannot be the natural home of people of African descent. In the mind of Rastas, Jamaica, the Americas, and Europe can only be painful reminders of servitude, genocide, and continuous oppression of people of African descent. The term *Babylon* partially depicts these painful mementos, when it is used by Rastas to refer to the Americas and Europe. Furthermore, the Rastafari message introduced the platform for Jamaicans of all strata to become cognizant of their African heritage, specifically Ethiopia under the reign of Haile Selassie I. For the new recruits, African redemption promises spiritual uplift and social improvement. Rastafari constitute a modern Ethiopianist movement representing a celebration of a return to Africa/Ethiopia/Zion as part of a larger memory of unresolved issues emerging from colonialism and slavery; this is comparable to the Falashas of Ethiopia, who sought a return to Israel after three thousand years of separation.[9]

It is crucial to ponder the aspects of Jamaica's social context that made adherents inclined to Rastafari theology and its postcolonial ethos. From the beginning of the twentieth century until the uprising of 1938, there was a widening gap between rich and poor people in Jamaica. British officials and foreigners controlled the material resources, social infrastructure, and the government. Inadequate housing, malnutrition, and high unemployment beleaguered the poor and disenfranchised groups of Jamaican society. These factors are usually held by historians to be the incentives for the uprising of the Labour Rebellion from late April to June 1938. The causes of the Labour Rebellion were low wages, high unemployment, and the racist attitudes of the Jamaica elite toward working-class and poor Jamaicans. The constellation of these factors and the ensuing Labour Rebellion reinforced Rasta communities' wary outlook on Jamaica as Babylon, a system of corrupt and oppressive colonial institutions. In Rastafari cosmology, Babylon is polysemous, but it is mainly used by Rastafarians to refer to oppressive and corrupt institutions. On the other hand—as the counterbalance to Babylon—Ethiopia, as the Promised Land, came to assume more than just the promise of spiritual salvation. In Rastafari cosmology, Ethiopia stands as a promise of fair and egalitarian social conditions for all oppressed people of African descent; and Haile Selassie I is regarded as fit to correct the inherent inequality of Jamaican society and provide redemption and equality to every person of African descent. Consequently, Jah is at the core of Rastafari cosmology. Haile Selassie I, as the Black personification of divinity, is at the root of Rastafari taxonomy; Jah Rastafari has both social and religious functions. As a socioreligious movement, Rastafari cosmology is constituted around a dualism—namely, Babylon and Ethiopia. Furthermore, these two constituents of Rastafari cosmology are polysemous in the fact that they are used to denote a wide array of Rastas' conceptions. Rastas' elaboration of Jah and the ensuing Afrocentric practices suggests their transcendence of the dilemma inherent in the perception of the African Diaspora as burdened by the need to reconcile conflicting European and African mores. Put differently, the Rastas transcended this postcolonial dilemma by asserting that people of African descent can lead a meaningful spiritual and social existence without European mores. After all, in Rastafari cosmology, European mores and religion are inherently oppressive to people of African descent.

Another meaning of Babylon is its use by Rastas to express their radical skeptical attitude toward Western institutions. Their skepticism holds that the prevailing norms, beliefs, and practices of Western society are oppressive to poor and marginalized communities and their artificiality is proof that they are unnatural. For Rastas, the artificiality and unnatural practices of Babylon are apparent in the robotic bureaucracy of Western institutions and their deliberate strategies to oppress both human beings and natural artifacts. It is in reaction to the technological exploitative bent of Babylon that some Rasta communities devote themselves to small-scale farming. Biological farming for personal sustenance is a deliberate practice by Rastas to maintain equilibrium with natural artifacts, which ought to be consumed while respecting their inherent sanctity. After all, the competence of most Rastas lies in the semiskilled or the marginally skilled occupations. They are mostly prepared to do farm labor but possess no land.[10] The motivation to conceive and elaborate an alternative to Babylon defines the Afrocentric and nature-congenial society that Rasta communities set out to invent. This alternative to Babylon should be in tune with both the humanity of people of African descent and the freedom of natural artifacts from technological overconsumption. For Rastas, their take on natural artifacts via small-scale farming is inherent in the larger vision of people of African descent living according to their African mores and religion.

THE THEOLOGY OF THE RASTA MANSIONS

The Bobo Dread Rastas community's lifestyle and practices are an illustration of this radical skepticism toward Babylon and Rastas' collective attempt to delineate an Afrocentric communal lifestyle while resisting technological oppression of natural artifacts. The invention of an alternative is proof that Rasta communities are simultaneously engaged in resistance while actively seeking an alternative to Babylon—an alternative that allows both people of African descent and natural artifacts to be rid of Western oppression. During his fieldwork among the Bobo Dread community, the Jamaican anthropologist Barry Chevannes described the beliefs and natural environment of the Bobo Dread thus: "According to Prince Emmanuel, the Holy Trinity comprises the three spirits: Prophet, Priest, and King. The King of course is Selassie. The Prophet is Garvey, and the

Priest is Prince Emmanuel himself. . . . The entire compound is a fairly extensive field of gungu peas, covering more than half the compound's two hectares. The are no other cultivated plants, but during the rainy season calalu is planted. Gungu peas are rich in protein, and do not require much watering."[11] The choice of this geographical location suggests the Bobo Dread's commitment to harmonizing their religious beliefs and rituals with a natural setting beyond the compass of Babylon. It is also evidence of the ingenuity of Rastas' reconfiguration of the classic Judeo-Christian trinity. Haile Selassie I reigns as Black divinity, and Marcus Garvey's prophecy disseminates the Black gospel to the Rasta priests in Bobo Dread Rastas' communes. This Afrocentric spiritual trinity is at the helm of the compound's communal dealings.

The growing appeal of the Rastafari cosmology and ethos was a subversive force in Jamaican society and led the Jamaican government to commission a study of the Rastafarian tenets. Three academics from the University of the West Indies—M. G. Smith, Roy Augier, and Rex Nettleford—were assigned to study the taxonomy of Rastafari cosmology. This turned out to be a fortunate event for Rasta communities. The outcome of the study, published in 1961, facilitated the assimilation of Rastafari as a religious movement in lieu of its stereotype as a platform for lazy and undesirable Jamaicans to congregate. The study confirmed the Afrocentric vision and taxonomy of Rastafari cosmology. In sum:

> The study, which in many respects was sympathetic to Rastafari, sought to help Jamaicans rethink policies and perceptions of Rastafari. The report pointed out that there were vast cleavages in Jamaican society, many of which were caused by the colonial

education system. The system trained the middle class, who had matriculated through the secondary school system, to view Jamaica through European eyes. This placed the middle class on a collision course with Rastafari, who viewed life through Afrocentric lenses. The University Report helped middle class Jamaica see that the Rastas were not as unpatriotic as they had originally thought. Their desire to repatriate to Ethiopia was presented as not un-Jamaican but rather was likened to migration of middle-class Jamaicans in search of their destinies. The issuing of the report two weeks after it was commissioned began the process of middle-class Jamaicans attempting to accommodate Rastafari as a way of life.[12]

Moreover, the study surreptitiously exposed the nefarious impact of colonial vestiges on Jamaicans' social, governmental, and cultural institutions. It tacitly confirmed the necessity for the social mission of Rastafari cosmology—namely, to promote Afrocentricity as an alternative ethos during the postcolonial era in Jamaica. Rex Nettleford shared his outlook on the Rastafari mission to promote race consciousness in Jamaica:

> The influence of the movement has been very, very far-reaching and deeply penetrating . . . which you [Rastafari] must take every credit for because you really have been forcing people in Jamaica to accept the fact that they are Black. I have never seen a Blacker country which is afraid of Blackness. One of the marvelous things about the Rastafarian is, people like us are not racist. We are not that unsophisticated to be racist—only *buttos* are racist. But we are not that silly not to be race conscious. And that's a delicate balance of sensibility which I first found among the Rastafarians.[13]

Rex Nettleford's observation is insightful in being sensitive to Rastas' ambition to elaborate an alternative ethos to guide and promote Blackness. It is thus safe to claim that the academic study reveals to the mainstream in Jamaica Rastas' mission to advance a distinctive ethos of Blackness. In the above observation, Nettleford recognizes that Rastafari cosmology was innovative because of their "delicate balance of sensibility" to the need for a distinct ethos of Blackness in Jamaica and that Rastas did not merely recognize such need; they also set out to supply the norms, beliefs, and cultural practices to constitute Blackness as Afrocentric.

The study also contributed to defining a discursive space for Rastafari cosmology in academia while rendering the choice to convert to Rastafari socially acceptable. Moreover, an indirect outcome of the academic study of Rastafari was to have undertaken an assessment of social class relations, infrastructure, distribution of resources, and the wider attitude of Jamaicans toward the British metropolis. The rise of Rastafari cosmology was thus in tune with exposing the inadequacies of these components of Jamaican society and seeking to correct them. The academic report gave the Rastas a stake in Jamaica as it called on the government to provide employment, housing, and other necessities to rehabilitate Rastas into Jamaican society.[14] Through the academic publications of Jamaican anthropologists and sociologists, Rastafari gradually established itself as a legitimate Caribbean religious movement with an Afrocentric taxonomy. The number of Rasta converts increased accordingly as social attitudes become tolerant toward their faith.

However, the academic report only secured discursive space for Rastafari theology. Rastafari's norms, beliefs, cultural practices, and most significantly their assertion of Jah, as their Black divine figure, caused uneasiness in a predominantly Christian

Jamaican society. Predictably, the initial middle-class reaction was very hostile. Some felt betrayed by the sympathetic tone of the university study while many objected to the mission as a waste of taxpayers' money.[15] In Rastafari cosmology, Jamaica as a colonial establishment was essentially irreconcilable with their Afrocentric ethos. From their perspective, people of African descent ended up in Jamaica against their will; Rastas thus perceived themselves as being in exile in Jamaica. They often asserted that "we are Africans who were born in exile in Jamaica." Accordingly, in Rastafari cosmology, repatriation became imperative in order to restore the forlorn children of Africa to their respective home. This belief defines the two geographical components of Rastafari that are framed in biblical metaphors. Babylon (as Jamaica), the Americas, and Europe on the one hand and Ethiopia (as the Promised Land) on the other, delineate the base and zenith of the axis along which Rastafari cosmology manifests its ethos. Rastafari practices, norms, and beliefs are shaped primarily by the urge to avoid reproducing the practices prominent in Babylon while seeking to emulate Ethiopianist practices. This aspiration asserts Ethiopianism as the crux of Rastafari theology.

In striving toward Ethiopianism, Rastafari theology is enacted in a tripartite fashion. The core belief in Haile Selassie I as the embodiment of Black divinity is observed and manifested differently by three Rasta denominations. This tripartite appropriation of Rastafari theology is commonly known as the three mansions of Rastafari: the Twelve Tribes of Israel, Nyahbinghi, and Bobo Dread. It is safe to observe that this tripartite relation to the belief in Haile Selassie I is consistent with the aim of liberating and uplifting people of African descent instead of reinforcing the monolithic approach of European Christianity. For

Rastas, in adopting this trilogy, Rastafari theology thus eschews the inherent oppression of Christianity, which requires a monolithic observation of its theology. Each mansion has the spiritual freedom to appropriate Haile Selassie I's Black divinity according to their ideal religious experience and suitable rituals. For example, members of the Twelve Tribes of Israel believe that the divinity of Jesus Christ became palpable in the person of Haile Selassie I. The reign of Emperor Selassie I illustrated for Rastas the second advent of the Messiah as promised in the Bible. The Hebrew Bible remains an indispensable source of inspiration for Rastafarians (as for Jews), in the same way that the New Testament does for Christians. The Rastaman does make a compromise: at least one wing has long regarded Haile Selassie as the Christ reincarnate, signifying the Second Coming. This explains the prominence of Jesus in the Twelve Tribes of Israel pantheon of divine icons.[16] For members of the Twelve Tribes of Israel, the authenticity of the second advent of the Messiah is fulfilled in Haile Selassie I's Africanness and is providential by restoring Africans and people of African descent to their precolonial greatness. To the Rastaman, Jah, the divine Selassie, lives in much the same way as Christ lives—that is, within one's heart and one's spirit, instead of beyond the clouds.[17] Members of the Twelve Tribes of Israel generally accept Jesus Christ and believe in the authenticity of the Bible. There are basically two different viewpoints: on the one hand, those who believe that Haile Selassie I is the final Christ who represents the second advent of Jesus Christ and, on the other, those who see Selassie as one who embodies the spirit of Jesus Christ and is the representative of Christ's throne on earth.[18] Moreover, members of the Twelve Tribes of Israel behave in Pauline fashion by spreading Rastafari theology and practices via reggae music. Twelve Tribes' practices illustrate the intersection of the aesthetics and ethos inherent in Rastafari theology. The adaptation of Judaic psalms into reggae songs clearly constitutes some form of appropriation, an act of reinterpretation that has religious, political, cultural, and ethnic implications.[19] Furthermore, it is the only mansion that accepts people of non-African descent as converts. This unbridled universalistic emphasis—so typical of the Twelve Tribes' spirit of internationalism, that is, in opening up their door unreservedly to other nations—stands in stark contrast to the heavy particularistic stress on Black redemption that the doctrinal roots of the movement, with its predominantly Garveyite racial fundamentalism, continue to assert.[20]

The Nyahbinghi mansion of Rastafari integrates the theology and musical expression of Rastafari with spirituality. The Nyahbinghi elders articulate their conviction in Haile Selassie I's Black divinity through rhythmic drum techniques. Rasta adherents of the Nyahbinghi mansion coalesce around the ideal of *holy groundation*. The practice of holy groundation has both a communal and a spiritual purpose. Nyahbinghi's holy groundation provides the forum for Rastas to pray, drum, dance, conduct biblical exegetics, and worship Haile Selassie I. The core of Nyahbinghi ceremonies is to invite adherents to participate in the emperor's divinity through drum beats, debating their reflections about biblical scriptures, and smoking marijuana. The positive-minded Rastafarians attempted to learn from the once-discarded tradition that emphasized their African roots. Some even insist that it is only the Rastafarians (their existence, ideas, and performances) that broke through the barriers and prejudices against the hitherto unappreciated Afro-flavored music.[21] The underlying attempt to revel in the divinity of Haile Selassie I, through musical expression, constitutes the mystical characterization often attributed to the Nyahbinghi mansion. Rastas turned to the drumming of the rural Burru men for inspiration. The Burrus originally worked on plantations but relocated to urban centers as agricultural work declined. Considered disreputable by mainstream Jamaicans, the Burrus found fraternity among the equally downtrodden Rastafarians. The music is played continuously throughout Rastafarian groundation ceremonies—also often called reasonings—where believers discuss biblical scripture and philosophy, often sharing a chalice filled with ganja, or marijuana (considered a holy sacrament by many Rastafarians). Nyahbinghi exerted a profound influence on reggae music.[22] The Nyahbinghi rituals promote communal bonds infused with religious mysticism that synthesizes the philosophy of their religious tenets.

The centrality of collective ruminations about biblical scriptures, specifically their original contexts and their suitable applications among Nyahbinghi, defines their mission in Rastafari cosmology as the high council of the Rastafari faith. Through practices akin to the Vatican papacy's tasks to prescribe suitable relations between the Catholic Church and contemporary society, the Nyahbinghi members hash out how biblical scriptures ought to inform and apply to the contemporary experiences of people of African descent. The rich implication of these practices is undeniable when viewed as an inherent process to define a distinctive system of spiritual practices and beliefs of Blackness for the African Diaspora. Nyahbinghi's mysticism, groundations, and aesthetics are thus intrinsic to the racial ideals of Rastas for people of African descent. The movement has touched much of Caribbean and world culture: it encompasses the domain of spirituality but also of music and lifestyle. In addition to an aesthetic, cultural, and spiritual component, an epistemological perspective has done much to affect Caribbean world sensibilities.[23] The rhythms of the drums provide the means for Rastas to bridge their humanity with Haile Selassie's Black divinity. It is important to emphasize the role of marijuana in these spiritual practices. During these rituals, consumption of marijuana functions as a communal and social means to derive cohesion and spiritual synchrony among Rastas. It is important to be sensitive to the function of marijuana in Rastas' circles. Ganja or marijuana serves as a social and spiritual lubricant among Rastas. It is the means by which Rastas achieve the shared communal and spiritual platform to bond. The established outlook on ganja consumption by Rastas as follows:

> The most common reason for using the sacred plant comes from a biblical passage in which, during the sixth day of creation, God declared that he made the grasses and all vegetation for mankind's enjoyment (Genesis 1:29). The Rastafari also believe that ganja is a holy weed that can promote clearer visions of Jah. In effect, the use of ganja is a highly sacramental act that infuses within the body the sacred power of the spirit as it derives from nature. It also opens the mind to the will of Jah and allows for the miraculous and unexpected revelations from the almighty.[24]

This account illustrates the contrast between Rastas' view of ganja consumption and the Jamaican institutions' prevailing view. Rastas regard ganja as a mystic medium to revel in Jah's divinity; their outlook transcends the institutional outlook on ganja as a hallucinogen and narcotic drug. Hence, Rastas' contention with the institutions about ganja revolves around ganja as a means of spiritual uplift and liberation whereas it is deemed a narcotic drug by the status quo. The mystical and medicinal prowess of ganja is praised by Peter Tosh in the lyrics of his famous song "Legalize It." Michael Barnett's following observations reinforce the centrality of ganja and the communal orientation of Nyahbinghi reasoning practices:

> A good example of the collective consensus within Rastafari is in the case of a Rastafari-reasoning, which is based on the notion of the inter-subjectivity of truth, wherein which because all participants possess the higher I as well as the lower I, they all have truth within them, but more importantly only tease this out after interacting with each other. Thus all are capable of arriving at this truth, via consensus, after adequate reasoning. The reasoning tradition of Rastafari is just one example of the collective dimension of Rastafari.[25]

The third mansion, the Bobo Dread Rastas, live in Bull Bay in a tight-knit community nine miles east of Kingston and are traditionally viewed as the strictest community of Rastafari because of their methodical observances of biblical scripture and elaborate system of rituals to demarcate themselves from Babylon. The ultra-traditionalist proclivities of the Bobo Dread Rastas have earned them the reputation as the purist mansion of Rastafari. For them, deliberate distance from Babylon draws them closer to their African roots and Haile Selassie I's divinity. Moreover, given their restrictions on membership and their appeal to rural settings in the Caribbean, Bobo Dread communities have taken root primarily in the Caribbean; they have not made any significant impact outside of Jamaica. For Bobo Dread Rastas, Haile Selassie I 's Black divinity becomes manifest coherently via the methodical organization of their rituals, which provide the tangible arena for manifesting the emperor's divinity. Bobo Dread Rastas' radical rejection of Babylon's institutions and geographical spaces and their relentless striving to structure their daily life according to biblical scripture are proof of Rastafari's yearning to align their social structures and inner realities with Jah's will. The thrust of Bobo Dread Rastas is to render Black divinity palpable in their midst.

The Bobo Dread Rasta community emerged out of the repatriation to Africa project in the 1950s, which was initiated by their leader Prince Emmanuel. The prevailing belief among Bobo Dread Rastas is that people of African descent cannot achieve complete liberation and realize the aspiration of Ethiopianism while living in Babylon. For them, true liberation of people of African descent is achievable only through redemption of the Promised Land. It started with Prince Emmanuel's convention, which was to deal with the question of repatriation. When it was announced, many of those people who came in from the country had allegedly done so expecting to depart for Africa. Following the convention, the prince's followers became more sectarian. They began to attribute divinity to him and separated themselves from other Rastafarians by wearing turbans and robes.[26] It is noteworthy that Bobo Dread Rastas deliberately distance themselves from Babylon's institutions, which they view as a hindrance to their divine union with Haile Selassie I. This separation is motivated by Bobo Dread Rastas' conviction that genuine liberation and fulfillment of Haile Selassie I's ideals for Africans and people of African descent can only be achieved through an African communal model. Even though the Bobo Dread Rastas' repatriation project was not successful, they have managed to organize the geography of their commune according to a simulation of the biblical account of Jesus Christ's travels. Thus, the settlement in Bull Bay they named Mount Temon, where God is supposed to have come from, according to a passage from Genesis.[27] The tripartite enactment of Rastafari theology generates a distinctive spiritual model for people of African descent under Haile Selassie I's Black divinity as a common aegis. The end result is a system of norms, beliefs, and practices at the intersection of the religious, normative, and sociocultural experiences of people of African descent. It is by virtue of this accomplishment that the Rastafari movement elaborates a complex identity for people of African descent. By attributing Black divinity to Haile Selassie I, Rastas simultaneously situate Blackness beyond the Eurocentric normative confines of postcolonialism.

Each Rastafari mansion elaborates a system of beliefs they deem fit for people of African descent to align themselves with the divine ideals of Haile Selassie I. This tripartite theology, rooted in the Hebrew Bible, generates an ethos in prescribing specific practices and attitudes of the adherents toward their social peers and the natural artifacts in their surroundings. Rastafarians use the Bible to address their specific historical, economic, political, and social situation while seeking ways to express and interpret the epoch-making rise of Selassie as a salvific event for Black people.[28] Thus, the distinctiveness of Rastafari cosmology's approach lies in the aim to supply both a theology and an ethos of Blackness for people of African descent to operate in the postcolonial era according to their original African culture. The aspiration to assert African practices as a social compass for people of African descent is a key motif and proof that Rastafari cosmology is more than a culture of resistance. Many researchers regard the lack of formal organizational links in Rastafari as a very positive characteristic of the movement. It allows the various Rasta groups and camps to enjoy a kind of freedom not always encouraged in many organized religious and secular movements; each group defines its own ethos within the broader Rastafarian culture.[29] The three mansions' system of beliefs coalesces around the shared belief that people of African descent's lifestyle, while aligning itself with Haile Selassie I's Black divinity, must also be in harmony with natural artifacts. Consequently, for Rastas, the liberation project is twofold: (1) people of African descent must be freed from colonial oppression; and (2) this liberation project must also extricate natural artifacts from technological exploitation for mass consumption. Moreover, the system of beliefs and norms practiced by the three mansions elaborate a tripartite conception of Rastas' ethos of Blackness. Each mansion of Rastas deliberately organizes the ideal ethos that they believe ought to constitute the Blackness of people of African descent. Therefore, the Rastas' tripartite approach to worshipping Haile Selasssie I transcends both the monolithic approach of Judeo-Christianity and the colonial restrictions on Blackness. Consequently, the prominence of the three mansions of Rastafari cosmology denies any monolithic outlook on Blackness; the subtle claim is that there can be a plurality of Blackness for people of African descent.

RASTAFARI AESTHETICS AND THE ETHOS OF BLACKNESS

Rastas' conception of African culture shapes Rastafari aesthetics and creates a system of symbols, practices, and beliefs that Rastas depend on to distinguish their physical stance from their neighbors in Babylon. The most celebrated expression of Rastafari aesthetics is the lyrics of reggae music, which provide a mouthpiece for the articulation of Rastafari theology and ethos of Blackness. Reggae disseminated the Rastafarian practice of chanting to musical stages in Jamaica and abroad. Reggae concerts are evolving into new Black cultural spaces in which Rastafari's fashion, news, and knowledge are shared, shown off, and exchanged; reggae itself is an important vehicle through which individual ideas about Blackness are articulated and other sensitive social issues are addressed. In these spaces, a growing sense of shared Black identity is discovered and created.[30] Reggae music reconciles and broadcasts the theology of each mansion into a cohesive global message. As such, it is a medium of Rastafari spirituality, a vocal means to critique Babylon, and a medium to expose the plight of the poor and disenfranchised. The potential in reggae is therefore not only in its manifested unification of the inner and outer landscapes of the Rastafari and the African Jamaican experience but also in its humane qualities, which provide an empathetic potential for all who hold the need for liberation, equity, and dignity.[31] The growing demand for social improvement in the United States was congenial to the social revolution that reggae lyrics brought on the local and international scene. Reggae music, along with the positive representation of Blackness and the rhetoric of justice attracted many during the post-1969 period. It promoted antiquity, Black redemption, repatriation, righteous living, and the Godly emperor Haile Selassie I as cornerstones of the identity of those who came into the faith through the late 1960s.[32] As an ambassador of Rastafari theology and its ethos of Blackness, Bob Marley assumed many roles. He disseminated Rastafari aesthetics, spirituality, and rhetoric of social justice. Becoming Rasta involved making connections between many dimensions of one's experience. These connections involved linking an acute awareness of oppression, a recognition of being a member of a maligned group, a realization that there exists a long-standing tradition of positive understandings of Blackness, an awareness that one's cultural heritage has been hidden, and insight into how white cultural hegemony has distorted one's earlier understandings.[33] Bob Marley incarnated the multifarious aspects of being a Rasta. Most importantly, he posed as the Rastafari messenger announcing to the world the resurrection of people of African descent through Ethiopianist theology. Bob Marley was like a psalmist and prophet of his people.[34] His message was that people of African descent ought to transcend colonialism and reinvent themselves around the Black divinity of Haile Selassie I. Moreover, the acceptance of a Black monarch must be seen against the rejection of the traditional English monarchy and the acceptance of an African heaven on earth (Ethiopia).[35] Accordingly, during the 1960s, Rastafari theology, aesthetics, and ethos of Blackness were favorable to many countries that were grappling with the onus of colonialism. His vehement critique of colonialism and oppression, and his assertion of Haile Selassie I's Black divinity are voiced in the lyrics of "Ambush in the Night":

> Protected by His Majesty . . .
> And they just cannot touch us

Furthermore, the theology and practices of the Rastafari mansions coalesce around their endeavor to establish Afrocentricity as an alternative ethos for people of African descent. In the context of Rastafari, the elaboration of this ethos assists them in overcoming their marginalization. It is thus reasonable to think that the purpose of the mansions is reconstructivist; they provide cultural and normative technology to people of African descent to reconceptualize themselves as Black. The creation of a distinctive ethos corroborates Black identity and reconstructs the values, beliefs, and norms that were suppressed by the massive displacement of Africans. Paget Henry provides a robust summary of the Rastafari reconstructive project:

> The history of discursive violence in the region has produced high levels of mutual decentering and interculturation between the African and European worlds, the European and Indian worlds, and the Indian and African Worlds.... Given this heritage of imploded worldviews, three clear tendencies have emerged in Afro-Caribbean art, religion, and philosophy: 1) reconstructive work within these traditions; 2) synthetic work between them; and 3) transformative projects beyond them. Reconstructive work has taken the form of a search for lost origins that has involved reconstituting aspects of shattered Amerindian, Indian, and African worldviews.... As the Rastafarians make clear the Caribbean masses have retained the ability to repair or refashion the integrating totalities of India and Africa, which are able to convey a sense of the absolute and of cosmic integration. This type of spiritual production has been and still is the first line of discursive creativity.[36]

Another key figure who was sensitive to the reconstructive purpose of Rastafari cosmology is Walter Rodney. Rodney's revolutionary quest to improve the plight of poor and disenfranchised people in Jamaica and the Caribbean found an affinity in the Rastafari movement. He perceived in the Rastafari movement the fulfillment of a collective approach suitable for improving the plight of poor and disenfranchised people while uniting them around a shared goal. In Jamaica, he regarded the Rasta communities as a major force in the efforts toward freeing and mobilizing Black minds; and he offered his knowledge and experience to the Rastas and all sections of the Black population who wanted to break with the myths of white imperialism. The history lessons on Africa that he took to all sections of the community brought uneasiness and fear to a pretentious leadership that had never considered itself Black, for Rodney stated simply that being Black was a powerful fact of the society.[37] His affinity for the Rastafari movement is inspired by its elaboration of an Afrocentric ethos to uplift people of African descent and encourage them to accept their Blackness. By means of his teaching, he allied with the Rastas to help them promote the African inheritance of Jamaican society that was suppressed by colonialism. He also moved beyond the university to a variety of spaces where he sought to educate, work with, and, importantly, learn from the masses. In his many speeches, Rodney clarified the ways in which contemporary African history related to the plight of marginalized people and their communities in Jamaica and the liberation of people of African descent across the Caribbean and around the world.[38]

Through his interactions with members of the Rasta communities, he expanded their purview by teaching them the theories inherent in white imperialism and their detrimental implication for people of African descent. Moreover, his alliance with the Rastas was a mutual educational process that taught him suitable approaches and language to communicate with nonacademics while he instructed them about academic theories. Rodney gave lectures in notorious ghetto sections of Kingston, and many Rastafari were his students. He was one of the figures who introduced Rastafari to theories of imperialism and Marxism.[39] It is accurate to think that he honed his ability as an intellectual-activist via his involvement with the Rastas and was in tune with their goal to elaborate a distinctive ethos for people of African descent to assert their Blackness in the postcolonialist era. Therefore, by educating Rastas, he was fulfilling his contribution to the project of defining the ethos of Blackness for the African Diaspora.

NATURAL UNITY AND THE ETHOS OF BLACKNESS

Rastafari cosmology elaborates a set of practices for Rastas to live in unity with natural artifacts. Moreover, for Rastas, living in harmony with the natural order is intertwined with Haile Selassie I's Black divinity. The ubiquity of Haile Selassie I's divinity in nature, which is presupposed in the Rasta notion of earthforce, makes being in harmony with natural artifacts an imperative in Rastafari cosmology.

> The RastafarI emphasize, through their way of life, an environmentally friendly ethos. There is a strong belief in the importance of preserving nature and the environment and the need to maintain a balance between what is taken from and given back to the earth. RastafarI philosophy teaches us that since the earth is a gift from our creator, it is incumbent on all of us to take care of its inhabitants. Land and nature are thus important because it is through communing with and respecting nature and the environment that humans are able to reap the necessary fruits the earth produces to sustain our bodies.[40]

The continuity between the ubiquity of Haile Selassie I's divinity and living in harmony with natural artifacts lies in the consciousness of I-an-I, which consists of "the merging of the individual with all life forces, the realization that all life flows from the same source, and the collapse of the distance between internal and external, subject and object."[41] This mystical symbiosis, which is at the center of Rastafari cosmology, presupposes that natural artifacts, as the external components, ought to be freed from technological exploitation for mass consumption. The issue that the exploitation of natural artifacts poses is that it hinders the harmony between Rastas' inner realities and natural artifacts. The practices through which Rastas structure their lifestyle around respect for natural artifacts thus forge a naturalist ethics as an intrinsic component of Rastas' goal to define the ethos of Blackness. Naturalist ethics consists of the religious, social, and cultural practices through which Rastas reinforce their reverence for natural artifacts and harmony with the natural order. It is the articulation of Rastas' conviction that people of African descent must restore their lost harmony with the natural order. Natural order denotes the balanced relationship between natural artifacts and their use for individual well-being in lieu of the technological exploitation of natural artifacts for mass consumption. Rastas hold the belief that alienation from the natural order has erased the inherent alliance between the inner realities of people of African descent and natural artifacts. For them, this alienation is concomitant with slavery and colonialism.

The erasure of this primordial unity is the outcome of the displacement, enslavement, and colonial indoctrination of Africans on the plantations. Slavery and colonialism eradicated this primordial unity as it turned Africans into mere means of production. Displacement, slavery and colonial indoctrination have put people of African descent at odds with natural artifacts. It is in order to redress this predicament that Rastas abide by the injunction that removing the vestiges of displacement and colonial indoctrination is inseparable from the quest to free natural artifacts from technological exploitation. Overcoming the vestiges of slavery and the quest to restore harmony with natural artifacts constitute a dual goal. This dual goal in Rastafari cosmology dictates that people of African descent's freedom from oppression is not achievable unless natural artifacts are equally free and their primordial connection with nature is restored. The Rastafari believe that the killing of an animal for human consumption does nothing more than promote death, for killing the animal removes from it the life-giving power of Jah that resides within it. Hence, the meat that is cut off from a dead animal is unfit for human consumption because it does not hold Jah's life force. The Rastafari follow a vegetarian diet that incorporates dairy products. They believe that a vegetarian diet is sacred, for it allows one to derive from nature Jah's life-sustaining force.[42]

The belief that Jah's life force pervades animals and natural artifacts is evidence of Rastas' commitment to natural unity. The inherence of Jah's life force in every natural artifact, including human beings, constitutes the intrinsic unity of every component of Rastafari's cosmology. From Rastas' perspective, Jah's life force permeates and unites every component of the natural order. Jah, or Haile Selassie I's Black divinity, is the unifying thread that binds Rastas' inner realities with natural artifacts. Moreover, their belief in the pervasiveness of Jah's life force is coherent with their discourse on Blackness since Jah's Black holiness pervades both people of African descent and natural artifacts. It is on the premise of natural unity that vegetarianism among Rastas is normative; it makes them refrain from partaking in the technological exploitation of natural artifacts. Vegetarianism is thus a means to preserve the divinity of Jah's life force in one's body and to avoid imbibing artifacts that are deprived of their divine link to Jah's life force. Hence, in Rastafari cosmology, the techniques of self-management are continuous with the management of natural artifacts. Consequently, the inherent divinity of the self, Black divinity, and the inherent divinity of natural artifacts are isomorphic in Rastafari cosmology.

The prominence of this fact leads Paget Henry to think that it is impossible to grasp Rastafari cosmology unless we accept the Rastafari conception of the self as "a cosmic, expansive construction of the self with deep roots in material nature and extensive connections with spiritual nature."[43] For Rastas, this is achievable by exhibiting profound respect for natural artifacts, striving to parallel the natural order in their vegetarian diet, adoption of a natural vernacular, sensitive consumption, reverent treatment of natural artifacts, and collective sharing of natural provisions. Michael Barnett explains the incentive of this naturalist and collective bent among Rastas:

> The source of the collectivism of Rastafari is due to several features of the movement: firstly as the outcome of the movement's vehement rejection of capitalism and all the social ills that are associated with it such as greed, selfishness, individualized-materialism and a weakened sense of morality. Secondly as an outcome of the movement's quest for what it refers to as Ital livity; that is their commitment to an earthly organic natural lifestyle. Rastas by and large criticize the West for its departure from naturalness and its commitment to artificiality and passionately advocate a return to nature. In this way Rastas seek to build unindustrialized communities with a natural lifestyle wherever possible.[44]

Moreover, it is noteworthy that striving to live naturally presupposes that there is inherent goodness in nature and that living in harmony with nature makes one a good person. Aligning one's inner realities with nature's intrinsic goodness is thus an ethical imperative. This underlying assumption suggests that Rastas are cognizant of their ethical obligations toward natural artifacts. The fact that Rastas acknowledge that it is their duty to respect natural artifacts and align their ethical taxonomy with the natural order illustrates the prevalence of deontological morality vis-à-vis nature in Rastafari cosmology. In other words, there are unshakable rules to apply in interacting with natural artifacts.

Furthermore, Rastas' naturalist bent thrives on the tacit assumption that Haile Selassie I's Black divinity is manifest in every natural process and artifact. Naturalist ethics is yet another expression of Rastafari theology and proof of the parallelism between Rastas' self-structuring and the inherent order they perceive among natural artifacts. For example, Rastas' view of salt consumption illustrates both a spiritual and a naturalist attitude. It was a prevailing belief among some of the slaves of the New World that salt consumption confines one's spirit to the finite realm and prevents it from reuniting with one's original African ancestors. Accordingly, total salt avoidance was presumed to have the opposite effect—such as facilitating the possession of a higher spiritual force and the requisite harmony with nature in order to be transported back to Africa. Hence, the common Jamaican expression *yu salt* or *im salt* describing a streak of bad luck, preserves this tradition.[45] Avoidance of salt and other staples of the mainstream Jamaican diet illustrates Rastas' Afrocentric and naturalist orientation. For them, nourishing food must be farmed without chemical fertilizers, which they perceive as technological means to mass produce food. Horace Campbell summarizes the naturalism of the Rasta diet or *ital* food thus:

> One of the early manifestations of the new spirit was in the very preparation of food and meals—in the making of ital food. Forced

to live at the barest minimum, the Rastas sought a diet which would ensure a healthy existence, since they knew that the medical infrastructure of the society was prejudiced against the poor and the Rastas. Rastafari were at the forefront of articulating the need for a food policy for the people, for it was never part of the overall objective of the colonial or neocolonial State to provide a proper balanced diet for the people. The post-slavery consumption habits which relied heavily on imported food—especially cod fish and chicken backs for the poor—guaranteed that the tastes and eating habits of the society integrated Jamaica into the North American agricultural/food complex. Rastas embarked on a project to use the fruits, vegetables and plants of the countryside so that they could break the dependence on imported food. Yams, boiled bananas, plantains, callaloo, chocho and a wide range of local foodstuffs, which had been the food of the slaves, were prepared meticulously by the Rastas.[46]

The I-tal diet may be interpreted as a mechanism to redress the colonial and postcolonial strategy to assimilate Africans and people of African descent into the prescribed diet of plantation slavery and colonialism. For Rastas, this methodical dietary assimilation was a form of subjugation in addition to the physical subjugation of Africans and people of African descent. Hence, the I-tal diet was a normative means to undo the systematic dietary integration that people of African descent underwent on the plantations.

Furthermore, Rastas believe that the I-tal diet agrees with the heredity and physiology of people of African descent. It defines a specific dietary identity for the African Diaspora that is grounded in respect for natural artifacts. The I-tal diet is thus a crucial dimension of Rastafari cosmology, given its larger implication for Rastas' ethos of Blackness. It presents a distinctive dietary practice that delineates a normative component of Rastas' ethos of Blackness. This natural diet emphasizes the consumption of organic foods instead of the processed and fertilized foods of the North American dietary institution. It is another technology for restoring autonomy to local and small-scale agriculture. Rastas believe that industrialization thrives by reducing human beings to mere tools in a manner consistent with the enslavement model. In contrast, individual farming promotes self-sufficiency; individual freedom; and a connection between Rastas, as farmers, with the soil as a central natural artifact. Rastas think of natural foods as natural gifts that reinforce *irieness*, meaning harmony, with the natural order and their social neighbors. Ital living also means that Rastas are basically vegetarian, rarely eating meat and strictly prohibiting pork, shellfish, and scaleless fish, especially those that are predators. The strong disapproval of fish that are predators coincides with the belief that eating them would be an implicit approval of their human predator counterparts.[47] Moreover, the I-tal diet may be regarded as a deliberate mechanism by Rastas to reproduce the dietary habits of their African ancestors. It calls for avoidance of salt, meat, and processed food. A vegetarian diet displays Rastas' reverence for natural artifacts. Strong adherents of the faith believe in a life of simplicity with an avoidance of excessive materialism and the embrace of a diet of I-tal foods, those that are pure and free of chemical additives.[48] The I-tal diet is regarded by Rastas as a means of preparation for spiritual uplift. It purifies the body and mind of the artificial impediments that hinder their harmony with the natural order. Its spiritual significance lies in the effort to establish continuity between the spirit of African ancestors and contemporary Rastas. Chevannes elaborates the theological role of the I-tal diet thus:

Rastafari salt avoidance, under the Ital rubric, is probably linked to ideas of spiritual force and repatriation prevailing from the time the earliest Africans were forced across the middle passage into bondage.... The extent, therefore, to which most Jamaicans have become reconciled to adopting the island as their land may be measured in the adoption of 'salt fish,' a slave food imported from Newfoundland, in combination with the slave dish of ackee, a west African fruit, now the national dish.[49]

The I-tal diet is a core component of Rastas' naturalist ethics. It has spiritual prowess for Rastas who depend on it to kindle their latent Black divinity. Central to the ideal of I-tal living is a belief in herbal healing. Rastas believe that the entire universe is organically connected and that the key to both physical and social balance is to live in accordance with organic principles, as opposed to the artificiality that characterizes modern technological society.[50] Thus, the I-tal diet, as a naturalist ethical practice, has many virtues. It provides a normative principle for the African Diaspora, restores harmony with the natural order, and serves as a means to kindle spiritual connection.

Furthermore, Rastas' endeavor to align their religious practices with the natural order may be interpreted as a surreptitious method for overcoming the fragmentation among people of African descent, which resulted from slavery and colonialism. The disconnection of people of African descent results from the loss of the original social, cultural, and religious norms and practices performed in Africa and their coercion to imbibe Western social, cultural, and religious norms and practices on the plantations. Rasta communities are cognizant of the impact of this disunity among people of African descent. They set out to overcome it by proposing an alternative ethos that encompasses the religious, cultural, and ethical experiences for people of African descent. I-tal livity and naturalist ethics are guidelines that Rastas employ to restore their harmony with nature as conceived through an Afrocentric frame.

The aesthetic of Rastas' appearance illustrates another set of naturalist practices. One of the most popular consists of wearing dreadlocks and a long beard; African-inspired jewelry and paraphernalia; and long African robes in gold, red, and green to symbolize the Ethiopian flag. Close scrutiny of the Rasta aesthetic suggests that it consists of a set of African symbols that are deliberately selected to cast Rastas' bodies as Afrocentric and natural amalgams. As an illustration, the famous dreadlocks that identify many proponents of the faith stem from the Rastafarian prohibition against cutting or using chemical products on the hair.[51] Hair growth without the use of chemical products promotes natural growth. According to Rastas, hair straightening and skin bleaching by Black people reflect a yearning for whiteness and are therefore symptomatic of alienation from a sense of their African beauty. Against this backdrop, dreadlocks signify the reconstitution of a sense of pride in one's African characteristics. Ideologically, dreadlocks express the Rastafarian belief in and commitment to naturalness.[52] Dreadlocks, African-inspired jewelry and paraphernalia, and long African robes in gold, red, and green are thus tangible manifestations of the Afrocentric orientation of Rastas. For example, by wearing dreadlocks and Afrocentric clothing, Rastas not only defy and question dominant European aesthetic norms and standards of beauty but also reevaluate and challenge old stereotypes about Blackness. The seemingly unkempt appearance of dreadlocks symbolizes Rastas' categorical rejection of Babylon. Still others believe that, historically, Blacks are the descendants of kings and queens and are therefore of royal pedigree, and their "manes" recall the emperor's honorific title as the Lion of Judah. Moreover, Rastafari thought emphasizes that all things natural and untouched (and many would claim that growing out their locks and beards manifests that belief) are a manifestation of a natural physiognomy that was given to humankind at creation—neither changed by cosmetics nor sculptured by human hands.⁵³

The fact that dreadlocks grow naturally and Rastas' jewelry and paraphernalia are handcrafted natural artifacts are proof of Rastas' attunement with nature. Rastafarians not only cultivate dreadlocks to resemble the head and mane of a lion—the royal symbol of the vigor and enterprise of the Black race—but they also imitate its regal, dignified walk, manifesting to others that despite enslavement and oppression they belong to a princely race with a glorious past. By cultivating deadlocks, Rastas distance themselves from the wider society, at the same time signaling that they have no wish to be accepted if this means conforming to the latter's criteria.⁵⁴

In conclusion, Rastafari cosmology includes harmony with natural artifacts in the quest to provide a distinctive system of social, cultural, ethical, and spiritual norms as the constituents of Blackness for the African Diaspora. The uniqueness of Rastafari cosmology is its cognizance of the demands for self-definition and self-improvement of people of African descent after the systematic destruction of their African heritage by slavery and colonialism. The ethos of Blackness that Rastafari cosmology elaborates is intended to fulfill these demands. Furthermore, Rastafari cosmology unfolds on the premise that the achievement of authentic freedom for people of African descent must be in tandem with the freedom of natural artifacts from the oppression of technological exploitation for mass consumption. Rastafari cosmology pioneered the requests of contemporary environmental ethics while also asserting that human entities' freedom from oppression is inseparable from the freedom of nonhuman entities from technological exploitation. In addition, Rastafari cosmology recognizes and fulfills the need to provide a system of norms, practices, and beliefs for people of African descent to buttress their racial identity as Black people. In doing so, it manages to elaborate an ethos of Blackness, which transcends the oppressive shackles of postcolonial institutions.

4

RASTAFARI'S THEOLOGY OF BLACKNESS

A Eurocentric God Cannot Love Africans and People of African Descent

In this section, I argue that Rastafari cosmology is in tune with the alienating component of orthodox Christianity for Africans and people of African descent—namely, the theological conundrum that a Eurocentric God is unfit to love and guide people of African descent—and that Rastafari cosmology recognizes this theological dilemma and elaborates a Black theology as a solution. Then, on the premise of the discussion of Rastafari Black theology and hermeneutic, I delineate how a messianic model is inherent in Rastas' reception and interpretation of biblical scriptures as it draws continuity between religiosity and the social amelioration of the circumstances of people of African descent. Finally, I show that Rastafari Black theology, on the basis of its advancement of the messianic model, frames Rastas' attitudes toward both their present and future by conditioning Rastas to view them as temporal media for the redemption of the Black Messiah.

The dissemination of Rastafari cosmology was most prominent during the late 1960s and throughout the 1970s. The large number of new converts to the Rastafari movement contributed to the rise of the Twelve Tribes of Israel, which is considered the Rasta mansion that is the most structured, organized, and in unison with the edicts of the movement. The emergence of the Twelve Tribes of Israel during this decade is proof of the unity that the Rastafari movement achieved around specific edicts and practices and its growing recognition as a distinctive socioreligious movement in Jamaica and abroad. Concurrently, there emerged during this decade some major criticisms of Rastafari as it was defining itself. The most ardent criticisms were directed toward its development beyond the confines of religiosity. Rastafari cosmology expanded beyond its Revivalist roots and Afrocentric religious tenets to become a movement that questioned the established sociocultural practices of Jamaican institutions while simultaneously promoting their own as alternatives.

The criticisms of Rastafari revolved primarily around deeming Rastafari religious practices irreverent toward the established Christian orthodoxy, which has historically been the premise of Jamaica's intense religiosity. The subtle aim of deploying these accusations was to sustain the marginalization and trivialization of the movement and to undermine the tenets of Rastas' religious orientation. The consensus among the detractors of Rastafari cosmology was that it is plagued by the lack of a coherent theology. Emphasis on this lack was a surreptitious strategy to portray Rastafari cosmology, along with its sociocultural practices, as an obscure religious sect in hopes that it would be less appealing to Jamaican youth who were joining the movement in large numbers during the 1960s and 1970s.

The attacks on Rastafari cosmology posed a threat to the longevity of the movement. However, among the Rasta mansions, this showed the urgency for Rastas to define both a cohesive religious hermeneutic and an epistemology to address the threat of being undermined by their detractors. Accordingly, the elaboration of a Rastafari theology of Blackness became imperative for the survival of the movement. Another restriction the detractors imposed on the definition of Rastafari theology was that it must be continuous with Christian orthodoxy and fit within the aegis of the Bible. To circumvent its characterization as an obscure religious sect, Rastafari theology had to ground its religious tenets in the Bible while preserving the Afrocentric bent of the movement. It is in response to criticisms, the expectations of their detractors, and the necessity to preserve their Afrocentricity that Rastafari cosmology created a unique theology to advance the ideals of Blackness for people of African descent.

The mansions of Rastafari had already instilled both an intellectual tradition and a vernacular to hash out the details of Rastafari epistemology. This intellectual tradition, called "grounding," consists of lively, energetic debates about racism, identity, Black dignity, and equality. Furthermore, the Afrocentric message of reggae lyrics attest to the dissemination of both the aesthetic and epistemology of Rastafari. Faced with criticisms and detractors, the epistemic aspect of the movement began to merge with its theology as the groundings expanded to include debates about the Bible and to undertake the process of putting Rasta religious beliefs in conversation with the prevailing Christian orthodoxy in Jamaica. The criticisms forced Rastas to begin the practice in which an emerging Caribbean religious tradition was compelled to engage with the dominant religious tradition in order to secure its legitimacy. Accordingly, this catapulted Rastafari cosmology into the power dynamics of religiosity in Jamaica to secure mainstream recognition. It also drove Rastas to elaborate a detailed theology around their Afrocentricity. Rastafari Black theology, then, is Rastas' assertion of their religious power stance vis-à-vis Jamaica's dominant Christian orthodoxy.

Rastafari cosmology was thus shaped by the necessity to fulfill these demands. Moreover, this exigency contributed to

Rastafari's expansion beyond its religious premise into a sociocultural movement. Rastas grappled with the challenge of defining an epistemic framework while simultaneously recasting the religious and sociocultural narratives of Africans and people of African descent against the Eurocentric characterizations ensconced in Christian orthodoxy. Rastas had to navigate within the paradoxical necessity to recast orthodox Christian narratives about people of African descent while grounding their theology in biblical scriptures. Given that Christian orthodoxy remains the umbrella theology and backdrop of Rastafari Black theology, it may be accurate to regard the relationship between Christian orthodoxy and Rastafari Black theology as a friendly antagonism. As a new world religion and sociocultural movement, Rastafari cosmology remained bound to the dominant religion, which fueled slavery while simultaneously redefining the stance of people of African descent within it.

The paradoxical nature of remaining bound to Christian orthodoxy while defining the stance of people of African descent within it sheds light on why Rastafari Black theological tenets are formulated as exhortations, which urge both the transcendence and reconfiguration of the biblical accounts of people of African descent. This system of exhortations ultimately culminates in Rastafari's proposal of Haile Selassie I as the suitable Godhead for people of African descent by virtue of the key premise in Genesis that God's creatures are created in his image. Rastafari's assertion of Haile Selassie I as the Godhead is thus a logical step in the process of advancing Afrocentricity while grounding their theology in Christian orthodoxy. Supplanting the orthodox Christian God with Haile Selassie I is the core premise of the Rastafari theology of Blackness. Rastas' assertion of Haile Selassie I as Jah is coherent with Rastafari being more than a religion. Haile Selassie I stands as a theological necessity in Rastafari cosmology. Haile Selassie I as Jah may be interpreted as the synthesis of Rastafari's response to the criticisms of their detractors and the assertion of a Black Godhead in whose image Africans and people of African descent are created. The transcendence of biblical narratives about people of African descent and grounding of Rastafari Black theology, which is carried out in Rastas' proclamation of Haile Selassie I as Jah, inspired Rex Nettleford to make the following claim:

> The Rastafarians have tuned into a major strategy of demarginalization: religion. Having one's own God in one's own image was a grand flowering in Rastafari of what had earlier begun in Myal and developed in Zion revivalism and Pocomania, with the hijacking of the oppressor's God in a move that served to discommode the oppressor. The slave forebears of Rastafarians understood fully that there are areas of inviolability beyond the reach of the oppressors, and that these are what guarantee survival and beyond. Such exercise of the creative imagination and intellect remains, then, the most powerful weapon against all acts of inhumanity; and that Rastafarians have drawn on the tradition, which was nurtured since the eighteenth century, to cope with and defy the harshness of twentieth-century indulgences.[1]

In his magisterial observation, Nettleford captures the necessity that restrained Rastafari Black theology to remain in its friendly antagonism with Christian orthodoxy. The fact that Rastas' grounded their Black theology in the Bible, which is regarded as the key tool of the oppressors, may be misunderstood as proof that Rastas remained psychologically dependent and religiously colonized despite the attempt to formulate their own Black theology. Nettleford surreptitiously corrects such misreading by drawing out that Rastafari Black theology remains in a friendly antagonism with orthodox Christianity out of the necessity to survive, specifically to thrive as a legitimate religious group instead of being deemed an obscure religious sect. Rastafari could not thrive and overcome the criticisms of its detractors if Rastas did not ground their Black theology in the Bible. Nettleford accentuates correctly that this feat by Rastas is continuous with the long tradition of survival strategy by slaves on the plantations—namely, to borrow and emulate the colonizers' practices as a means to survive. Furthermore, Rastas went farther than merely emulating to survive; they postulated a theology that would be loyal to the Afrocentricity of their adherents.

Despite having to rely on the model of borrowing and emulating Christian orthodox practices to accommodate their theology, Rastafari Black theology remedied a pernicious ill of the biblical accounts of people of African descent. The crowning achievement of Rastafari Black theology's brokering with Christian orthodoxy is the assertion of intrinsic Black divinity in the humanity of people of African descent. The assertion of Haile Selassie I as the Black Godhead transforms Africans and people of African descent as multiplicities of Black divinity. It is by virtue of this novel Afrocentric narrative that Rastafari Black theology provides a panacea to address many of the religious and psychological traumas that slavery and colonialism inflicted on people of African descent. Therefore, Rastafari Black theology, via the assertion of Haile Selassie I as Jah, delineates an ontology for people of African descent. As a logical premise in the elaboration of Rastafari Black theology, Black ontology defines the religious and sociocultural domains for people of African descent to manifest their being as Black divine entities. Furthermore, this ontological legitimacy provides the basis for Rastas to advance their demands for equality, freedom, dignity, mutual respect, and access to economic resources for people of African descent.

The elaboration of Rastafari Black theology merges Rastas' religious experiences with their ontological assertion. The point is that Rastas' postulation of their Black theology provides Africans and people of African descent the platforms to perform their humanity as Black and divine entities. Through the formulation of their Black theology, Rastas transcend the colonial depiction of people of African descent that is reinforced in the biblical scriptures by promoting a novel conceptualization of themselves as divine Black entities who are inseparable from Haile Selassie I's divinity. It is by virtue of this postcolonial self-conceptualization as divine Black entities that Rastas derive the sociocultural worth and conviction to revendicate equality, freedom, dignity, and economic justice for people of African descent. It is on the grounds of their formulation of a distinctive Black theology that Rastas can claim the values advanced by democratic society. The transformative impact of this achievement is more evident among Jamaican institutions and the wider Caribbean where Rastafari cosmology has reshaped the infrastructure and distribution of power and social resources.

Moreover, it is a remarkable feat that Rastafari Black theology situates Haile Selassie I's divinity in the spiritual consciousness of the faithful. Rastas' grounding of Haile Selassie I's presence and their religious experiences in spiritual consciousness rebuke their detractors' requests to legitimate their religious experiences in the oppressors' history and the scrutiny of the historical accuracy of their characterization. It is formulated in response to detractors such as the Reverend Clinton Chisholm who is skeptical about the divinity of Haile Selassie I:

> Some Rastafarians make much of the meaning of Tafari Makonnen's names and titles, especially the name Haile Selassie (Power of the Trinity) and the title *Ras* (head); but since the former emperor had no unique name or title, appreciating the cogency

of the argument for Selassie's prestige or divinity based on his names and titles is difficult. So, the names or titles *Haile, Selassie, Ras* and *Tafari* are not unique to him. Further, perhaps a different view of Haile Selassie's lineage prestige would emerge if the record were set straight concerning the lineage and blood relationship of Ethiopian emperors.[2]

Chisholm abides by the standards of objective historical accuracy to validate religious faith. The underlying premise of his critique in raising doubt about the divinity and prestige of Haile Selassie I is to show that Rastafari Black theology is historically illegitimate.

However, Chisholm overlooks the fact that the Rastas' approach is in tune with the oral tradition of African religions in which religious experiences are manifest in group spiritual experiences and the primacy of the believer's inner experience. Furthermore, as a new world religion, Rastafari manages to eschew the colonialist request to legitimate the divinity of their Godhead and the sanctity of their religious experiences by grounding them in the adherents' inwardness. Rastas' assertion of spiritual experience thus puts Rastafari Black theology in a position of indifference toward the requirement of objective historical artifacts to legitimate religious experiences. Rastas' Black theology thrives on spiritual experiences and the oral tradition practiced in the groundings—where elders debate about biblical scriptures.

It is noteworthy that, in partaking in these religious practices, Rasta elders act as griots who are preserving and disseminating the tenets of Rastafari Black theology. The Rastafarian creed is considered by the brethren to be no less true or theologically legitimate than those of Christianity, whose historicity, by implication, allows for the manifestation of God on earth in a form appropriate to the felt needs of a people.[3] Appealing to a divine authority beyond the social control of the oppressors was, for Rastas, a pragmatic survival strategy. Haile Selassie I embodies Black divinity and the religious means for Rastas to appropriate his divinity inwardly according to the needs of their respective realities. The detractors of Rastafari fail to acknowledge its complexity and the myriad survival strategies it adopted to prevail in a friendly antagonism with Christian orthodoxy. In critiquing and raising doubts about the tenets of Rastafari Black theology, its detractors merely reinforce the colonialist's view that people of African descent are unfit to create sophisticated religions and engage in religious experiences that are authentically their own creations.

RASTAFARI'S AFROCENTRIC HERMENEUTIC

The historical evolution of Rastafari cosmology and more specifically its detractors' criticisms imposed the elaboration of a Black theology as an imperative and a survival mechanism. Rastas had to delineate a theology in the context of a friendly antagonism with Christian orthodoxy in order to avoid being discarded as an obscure religious sect. The theological premise of Rastafari's project to delineate their Black theology is the assertion of Haile Selassie I as their Godhead to secure the divine reflection of people of African descent and to undo the collective experience of religious forlornness that plagued people of African descent as a result of not seeing their reflection in the Eurocentric Godhead. The completion of Rastafari Black theology, thus, calls on them to detail the auxiliary components of their theology. Rastas' groundings and close scrutiny of the Bible provide the auxiliary components of their theology. These auxiliary components of Rastas' theology define their hermeneutic by means of which they appropriate the Bible according to their Afrocentrism. The fact that Rastas appropriate the Bible according to their Afrocentrism encapsulates their friendly antagonism with Christian orthodoxy. I use friendly antagonism to mean Rastas' recasting of Christian orthodoxy according to their Afrocentrism.

Rastas regard the Bible as the central artifact of their religious faith. They routinely cite lengthy biblical scriptures in their oral and written discourses. Biblical passages also often pervade their aesthetic expressions via reggae music and Rasta paraphernalia. The fervency that permeates these practices and the innumerable hours that Rastas spend discussing them during their groundings stem from their conviction that the Bible was written by and for Black people to record and manifest their latent divinity. Rastas' attitude and approach to the Bible undertakes a blatant denial of the Eurocentric primacy on the Bible as a holy book written to celebrate European peoples' inherent superiority. Moreover, the methodical reading and interpretation of their hermeneutic set out to reveal the African origin of key biblical figures. It is, therefore, by virtue of this undertaking that Rastafari Black theology simultaneously supplants and appropriates the Eurocentric theological institution. By undertaking a rigorous Afrocentric interpretation of biblical scriptures, Rastas act as theologians engaged in the process of revealing Haile Selassie I's Black divinity to people of African descent. From their perspective, it is through Rastafari Black theology that Africans and people of African descent can finally ascend to the authentic knowledge of their true Godhead and their inherent Black divinity.

It is pivotal to emphasize that the kernel of Rastafari Black theology revolves around their critical and Afrocentric attitude toward biblical scriptures. Rastas avoid the colonized bent toward the Bible as the dominant source of theological truths and the predilection to imbibe them uncritically. So, the critical and Afrocentric frame of mind that guides Rastas' reading of the Bible constitutes their postcolonial and liberated appropriation of the Bible. This hermeneutical undertaking is coherent with Rastas' injunction that people of African descent must purge their minds of insidious colonial conceptions; mental freedom, as it is applied in Rastas' hermeneutic, consists in revisiting the colonizers' theological, social, and cultural institutions with an Afrocentric and critical gaze. The ideological critique and an associated hermeneutical suspicion, considered so important for liberating exegesis, are already at work in the interpretive approach that Rastafarians adopted toward Christian tradition and the scriptures in particular.[4] The project of achieving religious freedom via a critical and Afrocentric approach is most obvious in the fact that many Rastas are barely literate. However, they are nevertheless keen on casting their critical stance toward the Eurocentric components of the Bible and resisting the disparagement of people of African descent. This skeptical and corrective stance is crucial in Rastafari cosmology because it does not merely reject biblical scriptures; instead, it stipulates a frame of mind that remains vigilant and wary of Eurocentrism while correcting instances which reinforce the subjugation and inferiority of people of African descent. This skeptical hermeneutical approach is both applicable and prescriptive because it spells out Rastas' ideal epistemological approach toward all Eurocentric institutions, which are characterized as Babylon. From Rastas' point of view, the suitable frame of mind vis-à-vis Eurocentric institutions ought to be skepticism and the quest to rectify the position assigned to people of African descent.

Rastas' hermeneutic is committed to the fundamental belief that the prevailing Eurocentric interpretation of biblical scriptures was the ideological strategy used to enslave and justify the enslavement of African people. Eurocentric exegesis was the accompanying ideology without which the enslavement of people of African descent would not have been possible. For Rastas, their hermeneutic aims at correcting the marginalization and disparagement of people of African descent in biblical scriptures, and restoring Africans and people of African descent to their biblical preeminence. After all, Rastas hold the conviction that the Bible was written to provide the suitable ethics and religious rituals to worship their African Godhead.

> To Rastas, the biblical personalities, writers, and common people were all Black, and the books were all written to give a lesson to the Black people of all ages about the proper way to live and worship Jah. But the Europeans, after enslaving the Black man, took his scriptures and attempted to enslave them, even though they hardly understood the language in which they were written—the Amharic language. In so doing, Whites twisted the Scriptures to favor their race at the expense of Black people. White translators and interpreters used the Bible to support their ideology of white superiority and to justify slavery in Babylon (Jamaica and the West). King James the I of Britain, a white man, translated the Bible from Amharic, distorting and confusing its message; but those who, through Ras Tafari, are given inspiration and prophetic insights, the false passages put in by the white man for his own purposes are easily detected.[5]

For Rastas, the Bible is a means for ideological manipulation and provides a platform for the contest of racial superiority. In their minds, it is primarily a racial record that supersedes its apparent religious purpose. It is important to note that Rastas' emphasis on inspiration and prophetic insights are, for them, the media to discover the suppressed presence of Africans and people of African descent in the Bible. So, under the Rasta Black hermeneutical lens, Africans and people of African descent are deeply ensconced in the architectonic and narratives of the Bible. Furthermore, Haile Selassie I or Jah is the only source of inspiration and prophetic insights required to appreciate and exhume the presence of Africans and people of African descent in the Bible. Thus, in the process of formulating their Black hermeneutic in friendly antagonism with orthodox Christianity, Rastas recast the Bible as bearing the ethical guidelines for Africans and people of African descent and as an artifact that records the genealogy and inherent divinity of Africans and people of African descent.

However, Rastas are divided regarding the guiding assumption of the Rasta Black hermeneutic and the racial primacy of Africans and people of African descent in the Bible. The crux of the divide consists in the fact that some Rastas believe that the Bible has intrinsic authority by virtue of bearing the words of God while other Rastas accept the authority of the Bible on the grounds that its validation is conferred by the divinity of Haile Selassie I. This twofold approach suggests that there are two stances on the relation between the Bible and Blackness among Rastas. The difference in biblical approach is most apparent in the Rastas' view of Jesus Christ. Some Rastas regard Haile Selassie I as the fulfillment of the messianic promise and equate his being to Jesus Christ. Haile Selassie I incarnates the deliverance of the promise of redemption through his Africanness as the distinctive feature. Haile Selassie I's coming was akin to Jesus descending into hell to free the captives who had not known about him. The coming of the emperor was to give people in the present age a chance to know the truth. Unlike Jesus, Selassie did not die; rather, he was taken up into the heavens as is described of Jesus in Luke and Acts (Luke 24:50–53; Acts 1:7–11).[6] Rastas believe that they are fit to decipher this hidden truth in the biblical scriptures by virtue of the enlightenment that Haile Selassie I confers on them. The running premise is that divine enlightenment coupled with meticulous readings and faith can allow people of African descent to appropriate biblical scriptures according to their Blackness.

In the alternative approach, Rastas think that race is a secondary component because the Bible is racially neutral and can be appropriated via faith. The racial aspect lies in the realities of the adherents and not in the Bible. This approach is illustrated in the Twelve Tribes' conception—as illustrated by their standard formal greeting to those gathered at official meetings: "In the precious name of our Lord and Saviour Jesus Christ, who has this day revealed Himself to us through the personality of HIM Haile Selassie I"—moved the Rastas' doctrine that much closer in line with Euro-Christian biblical orthodoxy.[7] The stance of Twelve Tribes' Rastas is nuanced and at first may seem not to differ from the view of Haile Selassie I as the Messiah. However, the distinction revolves around the nuanced assumption that Haile Selassie I's divinity differs from Jesus Christ's by virtue of his lineage.

> The prophet Gad of the Twelve Tribes of Israel said in an interview in 1997, in response to a question about the difference in doctrine between Twelve Tribes and other Rasta groups, "Yes, there is a basic difference because we see Christ, that die and rose again, and that die for sin, we see that person. So that is, you know a different teaching, because is not many see this teaching, that Christ is the person. The prophet Gad taught that a person can be saved by no other name but that of Jesus Christ, recognizing that though Haile Selassie is indeed divine, he is really only the custodian of the Davidic throne on earth."[8]

The second stance promotes that people of African descent can appropriate biblical scriptures unless, via inspiration and prophetic insight, they discover the presence of Africans and people of African descent. In essence, the Rastafari Black hermeneutic promotes faith and meticulous study as one alternative to appropriate the Bible. The second option is to appropriate the Bible under the condition that the presence of Africans and people of African descent is made manifest. It is remarkable that, in proposing this dual approach in their Black hermeneutic, Rastafari cosmology avoids Christian orthodoxy's monolith, which posits faith as the only medium to interpret the Bible. Rastas' advancement of a Black hermeneutic on the grounds of resemblance between a Black Godhead and adherents may seem radical. However, it is noteworthy that this is driven by some Rastas' conviction of the impossibility that, having created human beings in his own image, a Eurocentric God could love Africans and people of African descent. The theological dilemma for Rastas who embrace this hermeneutic is inspired by the book of Genesis—namely, that God created human beings in his image. This theological conundrum drives Rastas' debates about this question: How could Africans and people of African descent have been enslaved and oppressed if they were indeed created in God's image?

The pragmatic application of Rastas' Black theology is most evident in their project to promote Black pride. One of the unique aspects of the Rastafari movement is its program to recast the self-conceptualization of people of African descent; more specifically, Rastas emphasize the need to undo the colonial self-conceptualization that people of African descent in both their inner constitution and outer appearance are less desirable and inferior to white people. Via the advancement of a Black theology and broadcasting the primacy of Africans and people of African descent in the Bible, Rastas undertake a correction of the inner sense of worth of people of African descent by asserting that their inherent divinity can be substantiated by meticulous interpretations of the Bible. It is important to bear in mind that, during the decades of the 1960s through the 1980s, the politics of physical appearance in Jamaica and many Caribbean countries were more favorable toward light and white skin as being most desirable and, in contrast, dark skin and physical features of people of African descent were shunned. Rastafari cosmology was fit to promote a positive self-conceptualization of people of African descent's appearance on the assertion of their resemblance to Haile Selassie I's as an African king and Jah. The point is that Rastas' vehement promotion of the adage "Black is beautiful" as another way to claim that Black physical features are valuable and desirable presupposed their Black theological endeavor. Rastas reversed the narrative about Black skin and African features in claiming that it is the primordial skin complexion, given that all life began in Africa. Thus, Rastafari Black theology informed the sociocultural program of casting both positive self-esteem and physical self-conceptualization for people of African descent. Detractors of Rastafari Black theology may raise doubts about the historical accuracy of their Afrocentric appropriation of biblical scriptures. However, its pragmatic accomplishments in providing alternative doctrines to assist people of African descent in overcoming internalized colonialism is undeniable.

> While some traditional interpretations of the Bible saw Blackness as a curse (Noah's curse), Rastas reverse the racial epithet so that Whiteness becomes the world's curse. Human life began in the Horn of Africa, the world's first people were all Black and human. Beings were meant to remain one color, Black. Rastafarians go beyond the identification of Blacks in the biblical text and

the association of the Black experience with those of the ancient Israelites; Rastas go on to "Blacken" biblical peoples and biblical theology. Rastas believe not only that the people of the Bible were Black but that God is also Black and that the name and worship of Jah (God) originated in the Black race.[9]

These constituents of the tenets of Rastafari Black theology are proof that they have managed to appropriate Christian orthodoxy's narratives in order to remedy the colonial ills that afflict people of African descent.

Another poignant aspect of Rastas' Black hermeneutic is their interpretation of the book of Revelation, which entwines biblical interpretation with the promise of liberation from oppression for people of African descent and their ascension to the rank of Jah's chosen people. In light of Haile Selassie I's Black divinity, Rastas deem him both the only suitable one to unlock the concealed mysteries of the book of Revelation and the fulfillment of the book of Revelation. Rastas viewed the major historical events during the reign of Haile Selassie I in Ethiopia—such as Ethiopia's resistance to Italian invasion; the inclusion of Ethiopia in the League of Nations and the United Nations; the modernization of Addis Ababa as the center of the African Union; and the return of Haile Selassie I to power on May 5, 1941, exactly five years after being forced into exile—as a testament of his divinity and fulfillment of the return of the Messiah that is predicted in the book of Revelation.

In addition, for Rastas, it is by virtue of Jah Rastafari's access to the prophetic insights and his reflection in people of African descent that they can come to embrace their primacy as the chosen people. Rastas' interpretation of the book of Revelation delineates the intersection of their Black hermeneutic with the postulation of a theology of liberation. Some detractors may regard this as racial hubris and a mechanism to advance Black supremacy on biblical grounds. However, when read in the context of a new world religion, it becomes evident that the Rastas' interpretation of the book of Revelation is informed by the collective wish to end the oppression and marginalization of people of African descent. The prominence of Christian orthodoxy in Jamaica made it necessary for the message of liberation from oppression to people of African descent to be broadcast in a Christian frame. The fact that Rastas regard the book of Revelation as the central book of the Bible is coherent with their religious mission and their resistance to oppression. The cryptic constitution of the book of Revelation lends itself to myriad interpretations and Rastas' appropriation of it as a promise of the liberation of people of African descent and their return to Africa. In essence, Rastas' reception of the book of Revelation is the lynchpin of the continuity between the Rastafari Black hermeneutic and their theology of liberation.

Another central theological notion that Rastafari Black theology refigures is that of original sin, a major concept in Christian theology. It has been the topic of a plethora of theological debates, especially given its introduction in the first book of the Bible. Some theologians regard it as a lingering concept that subtly permeates every succeeding book in the Bible. Sin is depicted in many ways. Some theologians regard it as an offense against God, disobedience to God's edicts, and the arrogant assertion of human pride. The Catholic priest John Dear thinks that "contemporary theology defines sin as 'any thought, word or deed that deliberately disobeys God's will and in some way rejects the divine goodness and love.' Sin includes any deviation from God and God's way of nonviolent love. Sin is not just passive; it is deliberate infidelity to the will of God."[10] Dear's account is in agreement with the Orthodox Christian characterization of sin.

It privileges and reinforces the notion of sin as an individual and personal state. This view conceives the individual as a detached social entity who is inherently in a state of sin. Humanity is intrinsically sinful.

Furthermore, this conceptualization of sin is in tune with the Augustinian depiction of sin in *The Confessions* as an innate state of human beings vis-à-vis God. For Augustine, no one is free of sin in the eyes of the Lord. Dear's and Augustine's accounts of sin—as illustrations of the orthodox Christian take on original sin—describe sin as a spiritual state because it is strictly in relation to God that the individual is sinful. This echoes the separation of church and state by emphasizing that the individual is sinful only against God. Accordingly, people cannot be deemed sinful against their social peers and social institutions.

Rastafari Black theology departs from the orthodox Christian take on sin. Instead, it proposes that sin is a socio-institutional state of affairs. Sin is an ongoing institutional performance in the West, and Westerners are living in sin as their institutions dehumanize and oppress people of African descent. The reversal consists in the fact that Rastas manage to detach sin from the relation between individual and God and recast it as a political state that everyone under Western institutions (Babylon) partakes in. Thus, sin is a socio-institutional phenomenon that prevails in Babylon, as the sum of these Western social institutions. The Rastaman has been enlightened with the knowledge to recognize the true nature of reality. Human beings live in a world of sin—personal, inherited, and corporate. Perhaps the key sin is corporate sin, which is reflected in a Babylon system that practices racial, economic, and cultural domination, particularly against the African. Overcoming the Babylon system requires not just individual redemption and liberation but also social redemption and liberation.[11] The Rastas' interpretation of sin is a unique aspect of their Black theology because it situates sin in the relationship between state and religion. Moreover, it uproots sin as an inherent state of the individual and situates it in the dynamic of the relationships between Western peoples and their institutions. In other words, from the perspective of Rastafari Black theology, sin is relational because it dwells between Western peoples and their institutions and is not an inner state. The bright side of the Rastafari's account of sin is making the possibility of redemption from sin achievable. Western peoples can be liberated from their sins by undoing the unfair racial, economic, and cultural domination practices performed by Western institutions.

The Rastafari Black theological characterization of sin establishes a duality in their cosmology, consisting of Babylon, on the one hand, and Africa or Afrocentric institutions on the other. And Haile Selassie I as Jah oversees the dealings of his children, while steering them away from Babylon to reach redemption in Africa. Rastas' conceptualization of sin gives proof that striving to be free from sin is concurrent with the liberation of people of African descent from oppression. The goal to free people of African descent from the oppression of Babylon is ensconced in Rastafari Black theology. It is encapsulated in the notion of "Zion" in Rastafari cosmology. Zion is not merely a spiritual idyllic state as depicted in the Bible. Consistent with the Rastafari Black theological account of sin, it is the alternative sociocultural institutions Western peoples will build once they have undone their unfair racial, economic, and cultural domination. The philosopher Lawrence Bamikole makes the following observations regarding Rastas' conception of Zion:

> Thus, it becomes important to revise or reinterpret the notion of Zion to be in consonance with the present realities of the

Rastafari themselves and the spaces they occupy. The notion of Zion was derived from the Bible, which is connected to the Promised Land. The ideal of the Promised Land is a situation where oppression, exploitation, deprivation, and discrimination will cease and where happiness (in Aristotelian terms) will be achieved. This appears to be a secular conception of Zion, and I think it is more reasonable to press this notion; after all, some mansions have interpreted Zion from this perspective.[12]

Rastafari Black theology manages to propose an account of sin and redemption via Zion that accommodates the colonial and postcolonial experiences of people of African descent. Hence, Rastas establish a coherent Black theology that unfolds under a conception of Haile Selassie I as Jah. Rastas' advancement of Jah is concurrently the rejection of a God who is completely outside their experiences in the world. Their commitment to Haile Selassie I as Jah encompasses both the transcendent and immanent nature of people of African descent's ideal Black divinity. Jah's spiritual virtues define his transcendent attributes. For Rastas, these spiritual virtues are expressed tangibly through Haile Salassie I, whom Rastas hold as the embodiment of Jahweh/Jahoviah. By virtue of the spiritual and normative nature of Rastafari Black theology, Rastas are always in communion with divinity as they conceptualize themselves and their immediate natural surroundings.

The Rastafari Black hermeneutical approach imparts valuable lessons about the central importance of restoring the social and religious dignity of people of African descent by pegging the Black self on biblical narratives. The project of restoring the dignity of the self for people of African descent is the dominant incentive for Rastas' meticulous and critical search through the pages of the Bible to recover, rewrite, and validate their experiences. This endeavor serves as a model for carrying out similar reinterpretations of the presence and assertion of the contribution of people of African descent in other Western institutions. As such, Rastafari Black theology serves as a corrective to the physical, mental, and spiritual abuses people of African descent have suffered for many centuries. The Rastafari tradition of resisting the blind acceptance of Eurocentric epistemologies and narrations of history is of direct pedagogical relevance to those students who aspire to emulate the movement's teachings and who feel empowered enough to critically analyze and challenge what is being taught and presented in the materials in mainstream schools.[13] Rastafari Black theology provides an Afrocentric conceptual medium for discussing and thinking about the social and cultural presence of people of African descent. It assists in defining the required autonomy for people of African descent to narrate and manifest their historical and social experiences from a noncolonial perspective.

The emphasis on individual enlightenment and appropriation of the scriptures in Rastas' Black hermeneutical approach makes their theology flexible and dynamic. The fact that Rastafari cosmology does not have a defined book of beliefs to determine their orthodoxy allows each generation of Rastas to appropriate the scriptures according to the social, political, and cultural dynamics of their time. The core religious beliefs of Rastafari—such as the divinity of Haile Selassie I, Zion, Babylon, and the complex ethos of Rastafari—lend themselves to each generation's interpretation of their own circumstances. Rastafari's resistance to hegemonic control of people of African descent and the disparagement of African cultures informs Rastafari Black theology by encouraging each individual to search for the greatness of people of African descent in the Bible. Hence, Rastafari Black theology is inherently in opposition to systematic theology. This opposition consists in the fact that systematic theology's restraints and rigid expectation for adherents to conform to a fixed creed violates Rastafari Black theology's emphasis on each Rasta's enlightenment and fitness to seek biblical truths.

> That Rastafari has no central doctrinal commission, formal or informal, that defines and determines its orthodoxy is not surprising. Its passion for freedom and liberation and its antipathy toward hegemonic control allow individual members of the movement to define personal "reasoning" and "citing up," that is, engaging in appropriate reflection and interpretation of their experience and arriving at personal conviction and conclusion on matters of their belief. The belief system is itself also dynamic; it is responsive to changed circumstances and the emergence of new realities while making needed adjustments. . . . The concept of Messiah is thoroughly biblically based; it is influenced directly by the movement's own interpretation of selected biblical material that deals with messianic promise and hope.[14]

The concept of Messiah is one of the dominant paradigms in Rastafari Black theology that makes it fit to frame each generation of Rastas' social, political, and cultural circumstances. It has remained a consistent concept that most Rastas embrace on the basis of their readings of the Psalms and the book of Revelation. The literary form and poignant poetry of the Psalms and the book of Revelation invite Rastas to latch on to the words and to form convictions around the imagery that suits their present circumstances and their expectations for the future. These features of the Psalms and the book of Revelation define the dynamism of the concept of Messiah as they frame Rastas' attitude toward their present and future simultaneously. This key paradigm is equally relevant to Rastas' collective need to transcend the bounds and oppression of Babylon's institutions by helping them formulate a conception of postcolonial realities as the redemption of the promised Messiah. It is thus fair to observe that a distinctive aspect of Rastafari Black theology is its advancement of continuity between religiosity and the amelioration of the social circumstances of people of African descent. Unlike forms of religiosities that alienate their adherents from social dealings, Rastafari Black theology draws a pathway between religiosity and social involvement.

The link between religiosity and social involvement is evident in the historical lens that Rastas use to interpret biblical scriptures. The Rastafari Black hermeneutic is driven by the emphasis on the historical situation of Africans in the Bible, which they assert as the genealogical premise of Black people's glorious and divine past. Rastas' exegeses are inseparable from a rigorous historical search for the divinity and glory of Africans in the Bible. The restoration of Africans' glory and divinity, via biblical scriptures, is intended to supply an alternative to the disparaging colonialist account of Africans and people of African descent. The Rastafari Black hermeneutic defines a collective platform in which people of African descent engage in reflection on their historical genealogy and how it informs their current sociopolitical and cultural realities. This process constitutes the liberating exegesis of Rastafari Black theology; Rastas' "reasonings" about the scriptures illustrate the rigorous undertakings in which scripture is bent to shed light on the social and economic experiences of people of African descent.

Rastas' search for how historical genealogy informs their current sociopolitical and cultural realties distinguishes Rastafari Black theology from being an abstract spiritual means to seek collective healing. Rastas are unsatisfied with any form of religiosity that does not stretch into the realms of institutional justice for people of African descent. The socioreligious dynamic of Rastafari Black theology is guided by their belief in Haile Selassie I as the Messiah who transcends time in permeating the present and future circumstances of people of African descent. The ubiquity of the Messiah in the present, future, subjectivity, and surroundings of Rastas is articulated in the central expression for self-reference in Rastafari vernacular: "I-an-I." It is important to note that it bears significant import for Rastafari Black theology. I-an-I is a spiritual and linguistic medium that keeps the Black Messiah hovering over Rastas' realities. Each utterance of I-an-I is symbolic of Rastas' perpetual redemption of the Black Messiah. It asserts that the Messiah has come and is always coming. It also serves as a spiritual shield and weapon in Rastas' dealings with the oppressive anti-Black institutions of Babylon. I-an-I will be discussed further in the next chapter.

Rastafari Black theology subverts the orthodox Christian account of heaven as an afterlife idyllic place. Rastas' denial of heaven as an afterlife idyllic location is driven by their belief that it is a means to justify the oppression and subjugation of people of African descent in their current sociopolitical circumstances on the promise of salvation and improvement after death. This feat is opposed to Rastafari Black theology's goal of securing the salvation and social improvement of people of African descent's circumstances in the palpable present. For Rastas, the promise and hope inherent in their messianic approach are fulfilled in the redemption of Africa, more specifically Ethiopia as the Promised Land. Rastafari Black theology does not merely reject heaven; it provides Ethiopia as the suitable alternative to heaven in orthodox Christianity. Claiming Ethiopia to be the realization of Zion as the Promised Land instills a circularity in Rastafari Black theology consisting in the fact that the migration of people of African descent to Ethiopia or Zion is a return to their starting point. Rastas' surreptitious claim is that, as the chosen people, Africans and people of African descent were forced out of their divine location by the transatlantic slave trade. Accordingly, settling in Ethiopia could only be a return to their natural dwelling.

In conclusion, Rastafari Black theology simultaneously subverts and remains in a friendly antagonism with orthodox Christianity in order to secure its survival. It is noteworthy that this twofold approach—subversion and negotiation—expands Christian orthodoxy to make it accommodable to Africans and people of African descent. In essence, for Rastas, the freedom the kingdom of God imparts to humanity must be immanent in the sociopolitical, economic, and cultural circumstances of people of African descent. Rastafari Black theology is unique in the Caribbean because it manages to avoid destroying the colonial religious institution. Its genius consists in the fact that it elaborates a system of Afrocentric beliefs which define the suitable religious discursive space within the colonial religious institution for people of African descent. The messianic approach to the Bible illustrates Rastas' undoing of what they view as a form of religious subjugation and extrapolating from it the gospel that is pertinent to the current sociopolitical circumstances of people of African descent.

5

RASTAFARI I-TALK AND BLACK CONSCIOUSNESS

In the previous chapter, I demonstrated how the constituents of Rastafari cosmology promote an ethos of Blackness for people of African descent. The norms, beliefs, and spirituality, along with dietary, aesthetic, and cultural practices of Rasta communities, encompass Rastafari's ethos of Blackness. In this section, I take up the Rasta vernacular, *I-talk*, which is a pivotal dimension of Rastafari cosmology. I begin by elaborating the intricacies and details of Rasta I-talk to situate it in the context of Jamaican institutions. The discussion of the intricacies of Rasta I-talk outlines the premise for the argument of the chapter—namely, that Rasta I-talk is the sociocultural means for the articulation of Rasta Black consciousness. The account of Rasta Black consciousness complements the definition of Rastas' ethos of Blackness by showing that I-talk is the sociocultural mechanism Rastas use to align their ethos of Blackness with their objective and inner realities. As the medium for the expression of Rastas' Black consciousness, I-talk reconciles Rastas' inner realities with their objective realities. Given that consciousness is polysemous, I am using it in the context of Rasta Black consciousness to mean the congruity of Rastas' realities with their Afrocentricity. The conclusion of the chapter is that

Rasta Black consciousness, via I-talk, stands as the cognitive and spiritual synthesis of Rastas' realities with their Afrocentricity. The following depiction of consciousness by Thomas Metzinger is congenial to the aim of this chapter: "Consciousness is knowing *that* you *while* you know. . . . Consciousness is what binds things together into a comprehensive, simultaneous whole."[1] Furthermore, to render the account of Rasta Black consciousness more salient, I compare and contrast the subjective personal pronoun *I-an-I* in Rastas' I-talk to Descartes's account of *I Think* in the *Meditations on First Philosophy*. This comparison aims to show that the Rastafari account of I-an-I as the linguistic marker of inner realities in Rastafari I-talk, like Descartes's postulation of the I Think emerged as a technology of resistance to existing sociopolitical and religious institutions. In both cases, inner realities encompass the sociopolitical, religious, and epistemological standpoints that constitute the individual subject as an I. The outcome of the comparison is that, despite postulating their markers of inner realities under similar contexts, Descartes's I Think and Rastafari I-an-I are shaped by different sociohistorical circumstances and norms. The chapter concludes by delineating the key distinction between Descartes's account of the I Think and Rastafari I-an-I in asserting that Descartes casts the I Think as a transcendental and formal entity while Rastas promote I-an-I as a spiritual and phenomenal entity.

As this section unfolds, it will become apparent that this comparison is in unison with the claim that Rastafari cosmology proposes an ethos of Blackness. It is important to bear in mind that Rastafari cosmology is the outcome of a twofold endeavor, which arises from the attempt of the Jamaican peasantry and underprivileged communities to legitimate their African heritage within the logic of the dominant Eurocentric institutions of

Jamaica. This quest prompts Rastas to delineate an alternative and competing system of religious beliefs and cultural practices to the prominent Eurocentric norms of Jamaican institutions. The side effect of this twofold process is that Rastafari cosmology influences the sociopolitical institutions by demanding acknowledgment of the African heritage of the Jamaican poor and disenfranchised. Hence, to grasp the influence of Rastafari cosmology beyond Rasta communities, the following questions emerge: What is the social status of the adherents of Rastafari? What is their socioethical profile in Jamaican society? These questions will be addressed throughout this section.

Rastas are often marginalized and their religious tenets are stigmatized by their larger sociopolitical context. Accordingly, their experience of social alienation compels them to rely on the system of values inherent in their ethos for self-validation. They strive to keep their cosmology as the means to regulate their religious, cultural, and social activities. It is on account of this regulating and normative role that Rastafari cosmology supplies a technology of social, cultural, and religious media for Rastas to define themselves as a sociospiritual community. In the context of the experience of Rastas, promoting themselves as sociospiritual entities constitutes the fulfillment of their conviction in Haile Selassie I's Black divinity and that they belong to Africa as the Promised Land. By actively resisting Eurocentric assimilation and asserting that Jamaican institutions are corrupted by Babylon (the Rastafari biblical reference for corruption and evildoings), Rastas serve as major critiques of the status quo. For Rastas, their technology to assert themselves as sociospiritual entities is thus inseparable from being a means of resistance.

Acknowledging the dual role of Africa in Rastafari cosmology sheds light on Rastas' role as critiques of Jamaican establishments. Africa's duality in Rastafari cosmology consists in being religiously symbolic and associated with freedom from Western institutions. Looking first at the religious symbolism of Africa, it is the lynchpin of Rastafari cosmology. On the one hand, Rastas view Africa as an idyllic location promising redemption from their alienation and enslavement in Babylon. As such, it is tantamount to an ideal religious location in both the inner and collective realities of Rasta communities. Rastas thus inherited and endowed Garvey's ideal Africa with spiritual significance. Most critically, this religious take on Africa promises Rastas the redemption of a preslavery glorious past. Africa is rooted in the past and yet critical to shaping the present of Rastas' social attitudes and beliefs. Indeed, this religious view of Africa defines the system of values that regulate Rastas' inner realities and socioethical experiences; Africa—more specifically Ethiopia—is always hovering in Rastafari cosmology. The movement is also heir to an African diasporic tradition, which has looked toward Africa for hope and strength in the midst of white Western domination. One of the most important antecedents of Rastafari is Ethiopianism, a philosophy that glorified Africa, its people, and its past.[2] Ethiopianism encapsulates the existential and religious significance of Africa in Rastafari cosmology. As a system of beliefs that references Ethiopia within the Bible, Ethiopianism shapes the religious and ethical attitudes of Rastas toward Jamaican institutions and supplies the system of values that Rastas deem fit for guidance in their communities.

The second role of Africa in the Rastafari worldview is the association of its geography with freedom from Western institutions. This geographical conception of Africa is an extension of the religious symbolic view of Africa. Rastas' appreciation of the continent itself springs from their religious perception of Africa. In Rastas' minds, the geographical Africa represents the physical basis that corroborates their religious symbolic view of

Africa. For Rastas, geographical Africa bears the testimony of the greatness of preslavery African tribes and is thus the bearer of Africa's former glory. Rastas' view of salt consumption offers an illustration of the impact of their religious view of Africa on Rastafari cosmology. It was a prevailing belief among some of the slaves of the New World that salt consumption hinders the possibility of one's reunion with the ancestral spirits. This belief that salt consumption impedes the spirit, restricting it to the finite realm, is African in origin and many slaves believed that their spirits would be forever prevented from returning to Africa to be with their ancestors. Accordingly, total salt avoidance was presumed to have the opposite effect, facilitating possession of a higher spiritual force such that one might be transported back to Africa. The common Jamaican expression, "yu salt" or "im salt," describing a streak of bad luck preserves this tradition.[3] Here, we see the impact of Africa on Rastafari beliefs and the expansion of these religious beliefs into the activities of daily life. This is how the religious attitude of Rastas shaped their inner realities. By avoiding salt and other staples of the traditional Jamaican diet, Rastas define themselves and are perceived as a distinct segment of Jamaican society. This represents an active attempt to resist assimilation into the mainstream diet and to offer an alternative ethos.

The sociopolitical position of Rastafari in Jamaica was shaped by the growing number of peasants and poor people who migrated to Kingston in search of employment and better living conditions. The majority of Rastas come from a landless and small-cultivator class of peasants.[4] One of the aspects of Rastafari is that it provides a social point of convergence for marginal and poor people to club together. It assists the adherents in overcoming their experience of alienation from the Jamaican institutions by granting them a feeling of belonging that revolves around an

Afrocentric system of values. Bearing this fact in mind, the migration to Kingston is a necessary step toward social improvement. Given the rural origin and character of the early Rastas, it is not surprising that they brought along elements of the outlook of the peasantry.[5] The rural origin of Rastas and their commitment to an Afrocentric system of values are crucial to understanding the sociopolitical impact of Rastafari on Jamaican institutions. There is evidence that the growing number of peasants and poor people in Kingston coincided with the expansion of the Afrocentric ideology in Kingston, the political and social capital of Jamaica, and that the paths leading to Kingston as a final home were direct for some of the founding members of the Rastafari.[6] Rastafari cosmology thus provided a spiritual and ethical alternative for the estranged segments of Jamaican society. Poor people flocked to Rastafari, and Kingston became the gravitational point for rural Jamaicans in search of Afrocentric spiritual and normative guidance.

Furthermore, the migration of peasants and poor people and their embrace of Rastafari ideology compelled Jamaican society to grapple with the Afrocentric system of values they asserted. As they grew in number and developed their ideology, Rastas acquired political and social power in Jamaica. While this did not remove the sense of oppression and the exclusion experience of Black Jamaicans, their ideological standpoint took on political and social relevance.[7] As a defining lifestyle and system of religious beliefs and practices for many Jamaicans, Rastafari imposed some key demands on the Jamaican social and political establishments. However, a paradox ensued—namely, that Rastafari cosmology shaped the very institutions it aimed to resist. In other words, Rastas' deliberate striving to resist Babylon led to their cosmology having social and political relevance to Babylon's institutions. This fact is most apparent in Bob Marley's symbolic gesture onstage during the 1978 One Love Peace Concert in Kingston, which was organized to end political civil war between the Jamaican Labor Party and the People's National Party. In this concert, Bob Marley joined the hands of political rivals Michael Manley and Edward Seaga in a symbolic gesture to signal unity between them. In this instance, the Rastafari movement transcended its usual practice of resistance and operated as a means to unite and end social and political conflicts in Babylon. In the late 1970s, Rastafari cosmology rose as a necessary component of Jamaican society fit to influence Jamaica's political and social establishments.

Another distinctive feature of Rastafari cosmology and ideology of resistance is the Afrocentric interpretation of biblical figures. As members of the African kingdom on earth, the Rastas deem themselves both a chosen and a marginalized community. Indeed, they see their alienation as a natural consequence of their inherent divinity and proof of being the community of God's chosen people in Jamaica. Rastas' deliberate distance from the sociocultural institutions is motivated by these religious convictions. In their minds, their displacement from Africa as the Promised Land and their imminent return are proof that they are God's chosen people. A corollary of their distance from Jamaica's sociocultural institutions is that Rastas validate each other as social and religious agents within their religious communities. In other words, Rastas grant each other the social recognition that Babylon denies them. This mutual practice of recognition entails that a fellow Rasta is both a social and religious agent. The Rastas' approach to recognize and validate each other is more rewarding and consolidates the standing of Rastas in their respective communities. Rastas grant recognition to each other socially on the basis of their shared religious conviction. Thus, their social detachment from Jamaican institutions can be viewed as both willful and a mechanism to reinforce and safeguard the collective dimension of their communities. Rastas' attitude sets the Rastafari movement in direct antagonism to the colonial heritage of Jamaican institutions. Naturally, then, the police paid close attention to frequent Rastafari street meetings, religious as well as political, listening keenly and jotting down notes the Rastafaris referred to as "shorthand."[8]

Furthermore, in this context, the centrality of the Rastafari aesthetic comes into focus. Their dreadlocks, flags, diet, dialect, and marijuana use all drew censure from mainstream Jamaican institutions; thus, Rastas relied on them to mark their distinctive socioreligious identity and promote African culture. Barry Chevannes offered the following comment about the Rastafari anticolonial stance: "Rastafari were known to be anticolonial, and it had not taken the colonial authorities long to realize that ganja offered a good pretext for imprisoning Rastafari. The Youth Black Faith went a step further. It institutionalized ganja as an integral part of the Rastafari reform movement. The reasoning behind this was simple: there was nothing wrong with ganja, so if the government attacked the people because of it, such an attack must be motivated by the desire to suppress the people."[9]

The consumption of marijuana became illegal as a means to marginalize Rastas from Jamaican society. In the context of the antagonism between Rastafari and the Jamaican institutions, the censorship of ganja represents a deliberate strategy aimed at demonizing Rasta communities. The planters associated ganja, Rastas, and the revolt, leading to a revision of the Dangerous Drug Law as a weapon against poor Blacks, especially the Rastafari who suffered periodic raids. The police had discretionary powers over the type of arrest and thousands of Rastas and youths were branded as criminals and imprisoned for possession of an herb that was part of the popular culture.[10] The consumption of marijuana and the perception of it as a means of spiritual uplifting, despite its censorship, is proof of its use as a resistance medium among Rastas.

The Rastafari aesthetic and lifestyle are driven by anticolonialism and the goal of validating their African heritage in the prominent Judeo-Christian tradition prominent in Jamaica. Dreadlocks, facial hair, African clothes, and the staffs they often carry are aspects of the Rastafari aesthetic that express their religious beliefs and believed kinship to the biblical prophets. Their Ethiopian emblem, diet, and use of ganja are means to resist the prominent establishments. Perpetual reinforcement of Afrocentric beliefs and the elaboration of a distinct aesthetic are thus the practices through which Rastafari, as a religious group, carved out their discursive social space in Jamaican society. The dreadlocks, ganja, and the symbolic meaning of the colors red (a reminder of the blood shed for African freedom), gold (representing the wealth of Africa), and green (a symbol of the vegetation of Ethiopia) are intended to inspire awe and unease in the members of the Babylon establishment.

Stigmatized as a "cult of outcasts," the Rastafari movement nevertheless began attracting more attention because of the growing consciousness among Jamaican Blacks of their African heritage. The Rastafari appeal slowly spread into middle-class neighborhoods, as young Blacks became sensitive to their ambiguous place in a sharply divided society and to aspects of white culture that had served to alienate them from the Black masses.[11] In doing so, the Rastas forced the colonial institutions to acknowledge and validate the repressed African heritage of Jamaican society. Dreadlocks, as the hair-symbol of the Rastas, announce that they are outside Jamaican society and do not care to enter under any circumstance other than one of radical change in the society's attitude toward the poor.¹² Rastas affirm African culture and demand validation by Jamaican institutions. The constituents of the Rastafari aesthetic are mechanisms of resistance and symbols of African cultural memory. The Rastafari not only grow dreadlocks to resemble the head and mane of a lion—the royal symbol of the vigor and enterprise of the Black race—but also imitate this animal's regal, dignified walk, manifesting to others that, despite enslavement and oppression, they belong to a princely race with a glorious past. By growing dreadlocks, Rastas distance themselves from the wider society while at the same time signaling that they have no wish to be accepted if it means conforming to the latter's criteria.¹³

I-TALK AS THE FRAMEWORK OF BLACK CONSCIOUSNESS

Ras Iration or I-talk is a core constituent of Rastafari cosmology and Rastas' promotion of their ethos of Blackness. It also has a spiritual function. I-talk is worthy of consideration because it conveys the key aspects of their shared self-conceptualization and their positioning in relation to the social and political institutions. Indeed, I-talk is best understood as Rastas' means to delineate Black consciousness as the epistemological framework of their ethos of Blackness with specific religious and collective practices. It is thus the epistemic framework of Rastas' inner realities that encompass both their religious and communal perspectives. A creation of the Black Faith Youth movement in the 1940s, the dialect is infused with the ideological heritage of Garveyism, Amharic—Ethiopian language, inflections of English vernacular, and biblical references. As a vernacular spoken mainly by uneducated peasants, it does not conform to the grammatical conventions of standard English. According to Leonard Barrett: "[I-Talk] is Jamaican dialect used on the philosophical level, a burden which it was not created to bear; and finally, the Rastafarian speech is almost devoid of subject-object opposition as well as without verbs."[14] In this observation, Leonard Barrett captures the distinctive epistemological import of I-talk. In blurring the difference between subject-object and omitting the use of verbs, I-talk transcends the inherent relationship of domination between the primacy of the subject over the object or between the knower and the known. This reversal inherent in I-talk confers on subject and object, knower and known, equal standing. This reversal of traditional epistemology in I-talk—in which the subject is in unity with its known object—is a pushback against the oppressive relationship that is ensconced in traditional epistemology and accounts of consciousness. Rastas' commitment to this postcolonial epistemology and approach to consciousness is, furthermore, asserted and reinforced in every verbal utterance given its inherence in their vernacular. Rastafarian beliefs are reflected in and given expression in their use of language. In fact, they have developed this language into a keen instrument for defining reality and stating the distinctive Rasta worldview. Word is power.[15]

I-talk articulates the attempt of Rastas to interpret and communicate the various facets of their experience and natural environment through an all-inclusive linguistic medium. Given that linguistic media usually synthesize the subjective and objective outlooks of the speakers, I-talk—as the Rastafari vernacular—bends the sociopolitical context to conform to the history and experience of the peasant class and marginalized communities in Jamaica that do not possess a mastery of standard English as a colonial heritage. Standard English is therefore not natural to the peasant or worker, and his own efforts at expressing himself in it are often quite torturous. The Dreadlocks have taken the language they inherited and, beginning with the Youth Black Faith, have made a deliberate attempt to develop a subdialect.[16]

The central aspect of Rastas' I-talk is the universal use of I-an-I to designate oneself and to articulate Rastas' inner realities. Its centrality lies in its epistemological implication. In Rastas' I-talk, the guiding assumption for refraining from the use of personal pronouns—such as "you," "she," "he," "we," and "they"—is the belief that they violate the all-inclusive and intrinsic divinity of each I. So, using I-an-I is meant to acknowledge and kindle the communal aspect and inherent divinity of each I beginning with oneself. Meanwhile, the designator is also always involved in the experience of the other I or Is to which she refers. Paget Henry summarizes the all-inclusive nature of I-talk: "Among Jamaicans, Rastafaris are unique in their use of the pronoun 'I.' It is substituted for the 'me' and 'my' which represents the old self before awakening to the divinity of Haile Selassie. Thus, all things and persons that have acquired this new identity through mystical participation have 'I' attached to them in some form. The Rastafari individual becomes an 'I.' He becomes 'I-man' or she becomes 'I-woman.' A plurality of Rastafaris produces not a 'we' or a 'you and I,' but, 'I and I.'"[17]

In this observation, Paget Henry surreptitiously captures the unity of divinity, community, and Black consciousness in Rastas' locution. I-talk elaborates a discursive medium to enact the inherent divinity of Blackness in an all-inclusive communal relationship. As Rastas strive to extricate their inner realities and language from the restrictions of postcolonialism and claim the continuity of their divine Blackness with Africa and Emperor Selassie I, I-talk behaves as the means to cement and preserve their accomplishment. Accordingly, for Rastas, this vernacular must be grasped as an indispensable dimension of the ideal Black consciousness. Thus, we see that I-talk articulates the collective basis of identity in Rastafari cosmology; it bears the pluralism inherent in Rastas' worldview. The Rastas' use of I-an-I always implies the "we" borrowing from the West African proverb "I am because we are." As such, I-an-I is never a singular in the Rastafari vernacular but rather an entity in which both collectivity and Black divinity are already always ensconced.

Moreover, the alteration that words undergo as they are inflected and used with I-an-I expresses Rastas' attempt to refigure their sociopolitical context according to their primordial Afrocentric worldview and to delineate an alternative form of consciousness in lieu of the forms of consciousness prevalent in Babylon. I-talk embodies Rastas' ideal of how the self in harmony with its African heritage ought to relate and articulate its relation with divinity, its social milieu, and the natural environment. Thus, the use of I-an-I in the Rastas' vernacular is proof of the attempt to transcend, via a linguistic medium, Western subjugation of the worldview of people of African descent. Hence, the Rastafari dialect stands as a mechanism of resistance to Western worldview and its bifurcation of inner realities and objective experiences. The corrective import of the use of I-an-I instead of we, you, and they is that it simultaneously violates the standard of English grammar while expanding the usual subjective and objective restrictions of the Western tradition's use of the pronoun I. Through the use of I-an-I, the personal pronoun I loses its traditional singularity and Western boundaries to engage in a communion with other selves, natural artifacts, and divinity. This stands as a critique of the individualist nature that colonial institutions impose on the I as the marker of inner realities. Moreover, the spiritual connotation of I-an-I strives to overcome the separation between God and humanity in the Western religious tradition. The Rastafari use of I-an-I articulates a spiritual and metaphysical perspective that stands in opposition to a classical Western philosopher like René Descartes, whose notion of the Cogito or *I Think* advances singular subjectivity as the fundamental principle of social experience and epistemological truth.

The use of I-an-I epitomizes Rastas' attempt to refigure a sociopolitical landscape reflective of their Afrocentric cosmology. Through the use of I-an-I, Rastas strive to minimize difference and articulate their cohesive view of the world. The strict use of I-an-I challenges the traditional distinction between subjects imposed by the use of I, you, she, he, we, and they. I-talk encompasses the collective relationship of the Rastas with each other within their cosmology. The cohesive relationship that it articulates is essentially the unity of inner realities, community, nature, and divinity, which constitutes a pluralist account of Rasta subjectivity.

Moreover, the centrality of I-an-I in Rastafari dialect is paradoxically both biblical and anti–Judeo-Christian. On the one hand, the reference to oneself and others under the category of I-an-I is meant to celebrate universal belonging in the divine status of the Ethiopian emperor Haile Selassie I. Meanwhile, it is a critique of the Judeo-Christian tradition, which restricts its adherents' outlook to a synthetic and singular worldview, because it attributes divinity to all people and attempts to overcome the social and political differences between adherents. Rastas' vernacular is used in a world that is in contradisposition to constituted religion (here symbolized by all branches of the established church), to the establishment and constitute authority with its laws, which, in many instances, run contrary to the Rastafarian preferred way of life, and to a society in which, for a number of social, economic, and historical reasons, Rastas feel they have little stake in.[18] Rastas use I-talk as a hermeneutical tool. In other words, I-talk provides a system of words, as symbols, to promulgate their alternative religion and sociocultural institutions. Thus, by means of I-talk, Rastafari theology simultaneously rejects and recasts their Christian heritage in the light of the intuitive knowledge of Haile Selassie I's Black divinity. This hermeneutical undertaking reveals the extent to which Rastafari thought has both remained within and moved beyond the categorical framework of Christian ideology.[19] The endeavor to recast their appropriation of Christianity suggests that Rastas have been in tune with the necessity to carve out a discursive space for the African heritage of people of African descent in the Judeo-Christian tradition. The resulting outcome is a balanced form of recognition that is not plagued by a radical departure from Christianity altogether. To the extent that I-talk articulates the cosmological penchant of Rasta communities, it broadcasts their assertion of appropriating divinity in the image of the Black emperor and in a communal fashion.

Additional epistemological implications of the Rastas' use of I-an-I emerge through a contrast of this linguistic practice with René Descartes's account of the Cogito or "I Think" in the *Meditations on First Philosophy*. Despite the historical difference between Descartes's seventeenth-century European setting and the Rastas' twentieth-century situation in Jamaica, their common ground lies in the fact that both the account of the *Meditations* and Rastafari I-an-I challenge the established dogmas of their respective contexts. Descartes's formulation of the I Think in the *Meditations* challenges the rule of the dogmas of medieval Christianity, Thomism, and Aristotelianism on seventeenth-century European peoples' inner and objective realities. In formulating the I Think, Descartes strove to introduce an alternative system of beliefs congenial to the methodological approaches of the natural sciences. The institution that Descartes sought to undermine was the popery's regime of truths, the reduction of epistemological experiences to faith, and rigid compliance to papal edicts. As Descartes set out to elaborate a necessary form of skepticism antecedent to all philosophical investigations in the *Meditations*, his underlying goal was to draw out a basis for undertaking an epistemological investigation that was extricated from the tight grip of the papacy's tyrannical control. Inseparable from Descartes's endeavor is its implication for the subjectivity of believers who viewed and conceptualized themselves as subjects of faith and papal edicts. In doing so, he displaced the medieval dogmatic basis of European subjectivity and supplied a scientific and epistemological alternative to the religious model. Though Descartes denied that his doctrines were threatening to the faith, the Jesuits regarded any novelty in either theology or in philosophy as inherently threatening, especially those that concerned the axioms and common opinions of scholasticism.[20]

Similarly, as discussed earlier, Rastafari cosmology resists the oppressive nature of twentieth-century colonial institutions that refuse to validate the humanity of the urban poor and their Afrocentricity. The Rastas' perception of Jamaican institutions as Babylon is thus similar to Descartes's skepticism toward the deceitful nature of the evil genius, which is Descartes's symbol for the papacy's institutions of the seventeenth century. It is noteworthy that the colonial institutions, depicted as Babylon, were the embodiment of a regime of truths and reinforced a form of self-perception that was consistent with colonial norms. When viewed from this premise, Babylon and the institutions of the papacy in Descartes's seventeenth century were equally oppressive toward their subjects. Rastas and Descartes were thus both skeptical of the prominent socioepistemological institutions of their times. In the second *Meditation*, the evil genius, who Descartes posits as the root of deceit and cleverness, is analogous to the colonialist rule of Jamaican institutions—as Babylon from the standpoint of Rastafari cosmology. In both cases, Babylon and the evil genius are metaphors for the oppressive sociopolitical regimes that Rastas and Descartes sought to challenge.

Descartes's aim in the first *Meditation* is to displace certainty in sensory perception as the foundation of epistemological experience. To undermine the dominance of sensory perceptions in seventeenth-century epistemology, Descartes introduced the notion of radical doubt. Indeed, radical doubt is the epistemological attitude on which the I Think stands in its striving for clarity and distinctness of epistemological experience by calling into question the prevalent rules that the medieval tradition, the reign of Thomism, and Aristotelianism established as the epistemological standard. For Descartes, the radical doubt of the I Think is the medium by which seventeenth-century European subjectivity could rid itself of deep-seated medieval prejudices based on faith. It is by virtue of this epistemological accomplishment that Descartes secures his role in the Enlightenment tradition. After all, Enlightenment authors, in their own minds and self-presentations, shared an essential common denominator: they rejected the presumptive authority of the past.[21] Descartes believes that medieval institutions were founded on religious superstitions, not on methodological scientific procedures. This, then, justifies the radical doubt of the I Think: "Although the utility of so extensive a doubt is not readily apparent," he writes, "nevertheless its greatest utility lies in freeing us of all prejudices, in preparing the easiest way for us to withdraw the mind from the senses, and finally, in making it impossible for us to doubt any further those things that we later discover to be true."[22] It is apparent that Descartes's ambition is twofold: first, it is a radical bouleversement of medieval institutions' dogmas. It instantiates a rejection of the senses in exchange for a new scientific approach against scholastic teaching.[23] Second, it heralds a new world order in which a novel cosmology privileges scientific and methodological grounds for European peoples to interpret their inner and objective realities. Descartes's I Think is the foundational existential truth—that is, the first truth about what exists in the universe. It is thus an ontological claim and serves as an insignia of truth. When an idea bears this insignia, Descartes can confidently assert it to be true.[24] Husain Sarkar's observation is insightful in emphasizing Descartes's deliberate postulation of a novel cosmology for the scientific communities of his seventeenth century. Accordingly, it is reasonable to think that the attempt to advance an alternative cosmology to the status quo is a common feature of both Rastafari cosmology via I-an-I and Descartes's I Think in the *Meditations*.

In the second Meditation, Descartes demonstrates the persistence of the I Think's certainty in the face of radical doubt and establishes that the I Think can exist independently of empirical data. By empirical data, Descartes has in mind the beliefs, norms, and practices promoted by the papacy. For Descartes, the central accomplishment of the I Think is its ability to overcome the institution of the papacy as the evil genius attempts to make it doubtful of its conceptual existence. Descartes describes the I Think's mechanism of resistance thus: "But there is some deceiver or other who is supremely powerful and supremely sly and who is always deliberately deceiving me. And let him do his best at deception, he will never bring it about that I am nothing so long as I shall think that I am something. Thus, after everything has been most carefully weighed, it must finally be established that this pronouncement 'I am, I exist' is necessarily true every time I utter it or conceive it in my mind."[25]

In this statement, Descartes acknowledges the deceitful nature of the evil genius as an impediment to clear and distinct epistemic experiences and self-consciousness. As a metaphor for the papacy's institutions and dogmas, the evil genius oppresses the I Think by virtue of the obstacle it poses to its epistemic freedom from dogmas. In this way, Descartes's position resembles the skepticism of the Rastas. In both cases, the evil genius and Babylon stand as impediments to the formulation of the social and epistemological aspects of subjectivity in freedom from oppressive dogmas. They both pose persistent threats to the consciousness of their proponents independently of papacy and colonial dogmas.

Despite this similarity, however, key differences are evident in the responses of Descartes and the Rastas to their respective oppressive institutions. One striking example is that Descartes contemplates the possibility that, after asserting the I Think, he may nevertheless misrecognize it given that he does not yet know the complete nature and inner realities of the I Think when divorced from its usual institutional experiences. The possibility of misrecognizing the I Think is an implication of its nascent theoretical constitution. Bear in mind that, in the second *Meditation*, Descartes's I Think remains strictly cognitive, provisional, defiant; it is ultimately a formal I Think without social and empirical content given that Descartes removes its reliance on the usual institutions of the papacy. Hence, the I Think is merely a sketch of Descartes's ideal subjectivity awaiting to imbibe content. "But what then am I? a thing that thinks. What is that? A thing that doubts, understands, affirms, denies, wills, refuses, and that also imagines and senses."[26] The conceptual nature of the I Think, in the second meditation, makes it necessary for Descartes to investigate the phenomenal nature of truth and falsity and then posit the metaphysical existence of God to substantiate the I Think.

Moreover, the framework of the I Think has some features that make it distinctive and contrast it with the Rastas' account of I-an-I. First, it is undeniable that Descartes's account of the I Think is informed by the social status of its author. The possibility of such radical abstraction to bring forth the bare I Think, as a mere residual epistemic entity separated from empirical content and social circumstances, is evidence of the privileged social status of René Descartes. Expressed differently, the contemplation of the radical doubt of the I Think can only be conceived by a privileged man of letters who belongs to the upper echelon of French society. Meanwhile, the Rastafari I-an-I, the subjective assertion of poor and marginalized members of Jamaican society, does not have the luxury of such radical withdrawal from empirical reality. Indeed, having such radical doubt is unlikely or implausible given Rastas' pressing concerns about the oppressive sociopolitical institutions of Babylon. The inherent aloofness of the I Think's radical doubt toward the sociopolitical context does not suit the pressing and pragmatic agenda of Rasta communities. The underlying rationale is that marginalized and poor subjects cannot afford—literally or metaphorically—a skeptical attitude toward oppressive social institutions. For Rastas, embracing the abstract I Think of Descartes would be escapism—an effort to seek solace by withdrawing from the oppressive institutions of Babylon.

Additionally, the separation of mind from body that Descartes carries out in the second meditation on the basis of the I Think's radical doubt is not feasible for Rastas. Descartes meticulously grants specific attributes to the body to guarantee its scientific visibility and, in doing so, he conflates all human bodies as scientific phenomena. Descartes writes: "Were I perhaps tempted to describe this nature such as I conceived it in my mind, I would have described it thus: by 'body,' I understand all that is capable of being bounded by some shape, of being enclosed in a place, and of filling up a space in such a way as to exclude any other body from it; of being perceived by touch, sight, hearing, taste, or smell; of being moved in several ways, not, of course, by itself, but by whatever else impinges upon it."[27]

In this observation, Descartes's conflation of all bodies under scientific entities is both remarkable and fundamentally distinct from Rastas' view of bodies as phenomenal. For Rastas, the human body is more than a mere scientific entity, it is an inalienable phenomenal dimension of the I-an-I. In contradistinction to the scientific approach to the body that Descartes promotes, the Rastas' view of the body is cognizant of the scars of the transatlantic slave trade, colonialism and postcolonialism. For Rastas, their bodies ought to move through Jamaican society as anticolonial entities and painful reminders of the inhumane treatment of African peoples in the New World. Thus, the body is so vital in Rastafari cosmology that it is included as an inherent manifestation every time that I-an-I is uttered. The emphasis on health and well-being of the body through the I-tal diet illustrates the centrality of the body in Rastafari cosmology.

When Descartes finally deduces the certainty and essence of the I Think, it is strictly formal. For him, the certainty of the I Think is grounded in its ability to think; it is the mere formal substrate of epistemological endeavors. Accordingly, the conviction of the defiant I Think vis-à-vis the evil genius is grounded in its sheer cognitive abilities. It overcomes the deceit of the evil genius—the papacy's institutions—with the confidence that it can think scientifically. In this way, Descartes asserts the I Think as the substrate of its epistemic experiences. It is what is left after the deliberate withdrawal from phenomenal stimuli that leads to knowledge. Thus, the "I" has a transcendental function as foundation: it defines the conditions of the possibility of experience, which it opens up because it precedes experience.[28] By virtue of such a transcendental function, Descartes's Cogito depends on an inferential relationship with the empirical realm to confirm its phenomenal existence. Thinking is the sole modality through which the Descartes's I Think thrives. The Cartesian I Think—as a transcendental entity—is therefore exhausted by the cognitive operations it performs. Descartes ponders about the performance of the I Think in the following passage:

> What about thinking? Here I make my discovery: thought exists; it alone cannot be separated from me. I am; I exist—this is certain. But for how long? For as long as I am thinking; for perhaps it could also come to pass that if I were to cease all thinking I would then utterly cease to exist. At this time I admit nothing that is not necessarily true. I am therefore precisely nothing but a thinking thing; that is, a mind, or intellect, or understanding, or reason—words of whose meanings I was previously ignorant. Yet I am a true thing and am truly existing; but what kind of thing? I have said it already: a thinking thing.[29]

Descartes's assertion "I am therefore nothing" suggests that the I Think is no phenomenal thing but rather a transcendental entity which confirms the empirical realm through a mediated relationship. For Descartes, the self that is allegedly known to continue to exist is a thing in itself, and not the phenomenal self.[30] Descartes is aware that the I Think depends on a methodological relationship to the phenomenal realm for its confirmation as a phenomenal self. Furthermore, his account of thinking allows an observation about the sociopolitical situation of the I Think. When read in the sociopolitical context, the ability of the I Think—a transcendental entity—to cast such radical doubt toward the phenomenal realm presupposes the intellectual and social privilege to disengage from the pressing demands of daily life and social institutions. In this way, as previously noted, the account of the I Think is proof of Descartes's privileged European status and his belonging to the elite Rationalist tradition. The rationalist arguments are all based on the mere thought of oneself as the subject of experiences.[31] In keeping with its privileged intellectual and social station, the Cartesian I Think can choose to withdraw from its external surroundings and the demands of social institutions at will. It has the freedom and privilege to choose the contemplative life or to shut out the empirical domain. This privilege derives from the fact that the Cartesian I Think did not emerge out of slavery and colonialism and that it is not accustomed to being coerced to engage in external realities. Given that the Cartesian I Think did not emerge out of slavery and colonialist contexts, it is always endowed with the freedom of self-determination in its sociopolitical context.

In contrast, while the Cartesian I Think is fundamentally formal, Rastas' I-an-I is phenomenal. Rastas' I-an-I is grounded in the empirically based conviction that Haile Selassie I is Black divinity. Descartes asserts the idea of God as both the means to leverage the certainty of the I Think and the proof of God's existence. Rastas, also, assert Haile Selassie I as the means to reinforce their physical existence as African in origin and divine by nature. The key distinction is that Rastas seek phenomenal certainty in alignment with their take on Blackness. Unlike Descartes's transcendental I Think, the Rastas' I-an-I always claims its phenomenality. This phenomenality is rooted in the fact that the phenomenal self that Rastas assert is historically conditioned by slavery and the strains of sociopolitical oppression. The experience of oppression and marginalization conditioned Rastafari communities to assert the I-an-I always as a phenomenal self and never as a formal entity in order that they might refigure their inner realities and divinity on empirical grounds. In Ras Iration, the intention behind the manipulation of words is usually to establish a kind of identification with the man at the bottom of the social ladder, the suffering Jamaican.[32] The assertion of Haile Selassie I as Black divinity reinforces the phenomenal religious attitude of Rastas. Thus, the Rastas' conception of Haile Selassie I as Jah is logically linked to Rastas' phenomenal account of their inner realities. Rastas' view of Haile Selassie I as Black divinity is consistent with the phenomenal account of subjectivity that Rastas endorse. Hence, by virtue of its phenomenal stance, the I-an-I—unlike Descartes's I Think—is unfit to relate to God as the guarantor of epistemological truth. Instead, God, as the embodiment of truth and goodness, must be manifest. For Rastas, the spoken word as a manifestation of the divine presence and power can be creative or destructive, kill or cure. Words are an ontological phenomenon.[33] Moreover, the purview of the Rastafari I-an-I is always collective and sociopolitical because it encompasses Rastas and their neighbors, the ideal sociopolitical institutions, and Black divinity. As Chevannes observes regarding the Rastas' use of I-an-I: "The religious meaning behind this substitution is that the Rastafari is also part of God, and if God is a visible, living man, it must mean that the Rastafari is another Selassie, another 'I.'"[34]

Thus, the Rastas' utterance of I-an-I articulates their inner realities, which are collective by virtue of the inherent validation of other members of the community it asserts when uttered. Simultaneously singular and plural, I-an-I always broadcasts the collective cosmological outlook the members of the community share. Meanwhile, the certainty of the Cartesian I Think is grounded in the singular and formal conviction of its existence by means of the cognitive process of thinking. The confidence of the I Think vis-à-vis the empirical domain and other selves remains formal and singular. As a formal entity, the epistemological and social experience of the I Think is always mediated by the unity of concepts and representations. But Rastas' I-an-I is immediately collective because it always strives to articulate Black divinity, natural artifacts, and the members of its community. The collective and phenomenal premise of the I-an-I defines the community's epistemological and religious experience. The utterance of I-an-I by Rastas asserts, as previously noted, that "I am" is only possible on the premise that "we are." Accordingly, Rastas see no difference between being, knowing, and doing. This ontology underpins Rastas' theory of knowledge and sense of social responsibility. For one to know, one must be; and for one to do anything effectively, one must know.[35] Ultimately, the Rastafari account includes both its Afrocentric collective tradition and the prevalent ethos of its community, whereas the Cartesian I Think depends on mere cognitive ability to ground its formal subjectivity.

Furthermore, the collective nature of Rastafari I-an-I defines the basis of social recognition and validation that Rastas grant to one another. The practices of recognizing and validating each other are intrinsic to Rastas' inner realities as expressed in their vernacular. Jamaica Creole, the speech of the man in the street and the language of informal interaction in the society, is a creole of English lexicon; the code of Rastafari is an adjustment of the lexicon of either of these languages to satisfy certain requirements of speakers who are sympathetic to the philosophy of Rasta.[36] Another distinctive feature of Rastas' I-an-I is that it articulates its collective nature by granting recognition on the basis of reasonable pluralism. As subjects, Rastas grant recognition and validation to each other on the assumption of shared values and beliefs. Leonard Barrett offers the following comment to illustrate reasonable pluralism among Rastas: "The language of the Rastafaris is a soul language in which binary oppositions are overcome in the process of identifying with other sufferers in the society."[37] As marginalized communities, Rastas share a cosmology, language, and attitudes toward the dominant society that is derived from shared marginalization. These beliefs and cultural practices then operate as the social and religious media that guarantee validation and recognition of Rasta communities' members. This process, inherent in Rastas' I-an-I, provides a well-defined social dynamic in which Rastas behave as social agents and religious adherents to achieve the social worth that the mainstream institutions of Jamaica deny them.

As a religious and social community that is grounded in the experience of Jamaican peasants, Rastafari cosmology provides a system of values that is loyal to the Afrocentric politics and spirituality of its members; and in doing so, it supplies the basis for solidarity among the alienated peasantry of Jamaican society. Thus, via Rastas' I-an-I, Rastafari cosmology defines a space for the integrity of marginalized people's inner realities against the experience of oppression. Broadcasting and asserting their inner realities via the lens of Black divinity, in unity with natural artifacts, and collectivity inherent in I-an-I frames Rastas' distinctive conception of Black consciousness. Accordingly, Rastas' conception of Black consciousness by means of I-an-I supplies the cognitive and spiritual synthesis through which Rastas put their ethos of Blackness into practice. Furthermore, the intrinsic Afrocentricity of I-an-I provides a technology of resistance and calls on Jamaican institutions to acknowledge their African heritage. Besides, the collective nature of Rastas's I-an-I reality runs against the singular form of subjectivity that postcolonial Jamaican institutions inherited from the Cartesian I Think via European colonialist rule. On this view, the system of values inherent in Rastas' I-an-I is innovative because it continuously rejects the intrinsic tyranny of singularity of Western subjectivity and the Cartesian I Think.

In conclusion, both the Cartesian and Rastafari take on the self's inner realities aimed to displace the norms of their institutions and provide alternatives. Cartesian I Think displaced medieval dogmas and beliefs to ground European inner realities on the path of scientific certainty. Accordingly, Descartes shifted the faith relation to God and supplied a deistic alternative. In this formulation, God signifies the thinking thing's apprehension, not of the supreme essence or of the supreme existence but of God.[38] Similarly, Rasta Black consciousness articulated through I-an-I encompasses the repressed constituents of a colonial society that demands acknowledgment and works to create its own sociopolitical domain in Jamaican society. Rasta Black consciousness discloses the repressed dimension of Jamaican institutions with their African past and the scars of slavery.

By transcending the rigid boundaries that Western institutions set around the I as the marker of subjectivity, Rastas I-an-I thus provides an alternative and critique of Descartes's account of subjectivity, reinforced by Western institutions, with the I as the sole marker of subjectivity. Indeed, by asserting an isomorphic relationship between Black divinity, nature, and humanity, Rastas I-an-I overcomes the underlying deism that Descartes proposed in the *Meditations*. The resulting obliteration of boundaries between the I-an-I, other selves, Black divinity, and natural artifacts unsettles the prevailing perspectives of Jamaican institutions. Rasta Black consciousness claims divinity as a phenomenal component of Rastas' experiences. Whereas Descartes's I Think pines for the spiritual and physical confirmation that God exists but settles for a mere skeptic and intellectual experience of Deism, Rasta Black consciousness refuses to settle for anything short of the divine, relocating God's presence by insisting that their Blackness encompasses divinity, nature, and celebrating their fellow humans as well.

In Rastafari cosmology, Rastas' I-an-I functions as a social, theological, and cultural expression of their attitudes toward Babylon and their respective communities. Rastas' vernacular encompasses the core theological and ethical conceptions that Rastas depend on to structure coherent communities. Rastas also use I-an-I deliberately to distinguish Rastas from non-Rastas. I-an-I thus bears Rastas' politics of self-differentiation from the Judeo-Christian institutions. The I-words in Ras Iration thus operate as vehicles for this politics of self-differentiation. The creation of Ras Iration is proof that Rastas grasped the importance of defining a vernacular to assert their distinctive perspective on Western institutions. The implicit message of the Rasta vernacular is that, in order to be Black, people of African descent must disengage from Judeo-Christian ethics and embrace an alternative that is in harmony with their African roots and Black divinity. Every utterance of I-an-I is thus simultaneously a theological edict and a means of social disengagement from Babylon. Through I-an-I and Ras Iration, Rastas assert that they wish to remain free from the social realities that stemmed from colonialism and the enslavement of people of African descent.

The remedial dimension of Rastafari cosmology and the quest to elaborate a distinctive ethos of Blackness are evident through this vernacular, which they deem the suitable means to articulate the Black consciousness of the African Diaspora. Ras Iration provides a discursive arena through which Rastas show their total rejection of Babylon's norms while demonstrating their ability to create a fitting alternative language for the liberation of "Jah people" from Babylon. Out of this I-an-I locution and other

I-words comes a new sense of self that leads to a new vision of values, inclusive of art and beauty as well as power.[39] The theological power of the vernacular is evident in the metaphorical purpose of I-an-I in Rastafari theology; it makes mystical communion with Jah feasible. As I-an-I, each Rasta stands as a chosen manifestation of Jah's divinity. Therefore, Rastas' Black consciousness is reparationist because it rescues people of African descent from the spiritual alienation imposed on them by slavery and Judeo-Christian theology.

6

THE LIMIT OF RASTAFARI COSMOLOGY

Gender Inequality and the Failure to Liberate Rasta Women

Despite its promotion of an ethos of Blackness and the elaboration of a suitable Black consciousness to put it into practice, Rastafari cosmology is plagued by a key shortcoming. My argument in this chapter is that, in their cosmology, Rastas have failed to redress the sexist attitudes and practices toward women which were prominent during colonialism and postcolonialism. I argue that this failure impedes the fulfillment of Rastafari cosmology's ambition to liberate all people of African descent from oppression. In this chapter, I show that male Rastas' sexism toward Rasta women is further reinforced by Jamaican religious institutions—namely, the depiction of women in biblical scriptures and the economic subordination of women during both colonialism and postcolonialism. The chapter concludes with the claim that the persistence of gender inequality impairs Rastafari cosmology's advancement of freedom from oppression for all people of African descent because Rasta women remain oppressed in Rasta communities. Gender inequality stands out as the main practice in colonialism and contemporary Jamaican institutions that Rastas did not endeavor to redress. In essence, the failure to end gender inequality lingers as a major shortcoming in Rastafari's Afrocentric project to uplift all people of African descent and renders Rastafari cosmology susceptible to the accusation that it perpetuates sexism toward women. Thus, I begin by elaborating the communal practices, norms, and beliefs of the Bobo Dread Rastas community to show how sexist practices undermine Rastas' advancement of their ideals of Blackness and Rastafari's endeavor to liberate people of African descent. Then, I discuss the debate in the existing literature on sexism in Rastafari communities in order to point out an alternative root cause of sexism that has been overlooked.

BOBO DREAD RASTAS, RIGHTEOUSNESS, AND BLACKNESS

So far, we have seen that, as a socioreligious movement, Rastafari revolves around two fundamental aspects: resistance to Eurocentric institutions and the elaboration of an Afrocentric cosmology, which defines the Rastafari ethos of Blackness. Another noteworthy dimension of Rastafari cosmology is that these two aspects delineate a distinct set of practices and rely on Afro-Judaism as the central reference point for the sociospiritual memory of Rastas. Lying at the intersection of the Afrocentric values and the Judeo-Christian beliefs that Rastas embrace, Afro-Judaism consists in endorsing the beliefs and customs of the Falashas—an Afro-Judaic community in Ethiopia. The beliefs and practices of the Falashas inform Rastas' efforts to be an authentic and distinct community in the African Diaspora. This Judaic influence defines Rastafari cosmology as a tripartite religious organization. By virtue of the African, Christian, and Judaic influences, Rastafari stands as a unique sociopolitical and religious community that, despite being informed by all three, has managed to combine their influences in a distinctive cosmology. Afro-Judaism is a crucial component of the Rastafari sociospiritual experience; it emphasizes Ethiopia, specifically the lifestyle of the Falashas, as Rastas' ideal social location and the root of Rastafari spiritual guidelines.

The Afro-Judaic influence on Rastafari is obvious in the views and practices of one community of Rastas—namely, the Bobo Dread. Unlike other groups of Rastas who share the same physical and social space as non-Rastas, the Bobo Dread community opted to live in seclusion to assert their commitment to Ethiopianism in order to self-define themselves as an Ethiopian religious community on Jamaican land. For members of the Bobo Dread community, they are an African spiritual community in exile. Thus, seclusion from Babylon is more pressing as a means to preserve their Afrocentric spiritual ties and resist the pernicious influence of Western institutions. This philosophy makes the Bobo Dread community the most exclusive group of Rastas and a fascinating community for investigation because their views and practices remain intact from Jamaican social institutions. Barry Chevannes describes the compound in which Bobo Dread Rastas live: "The compound is entered through an arched gateway under which every Bobo, on leaving and entering, utters a prayer, sometimes in his heart, sometimes aloud. Above the arch in bold characters is painted the name Ethiopian International Congress."[1] This practice delineates the spiritual commitment of the Bobo Dread Rastas and the daily renewal and commitment to the community's spiritual guidelines. Moreover, the painted words above the arch broadcast their spiritual and political stance vis-à-vis non-Rastas. Chevannes observes further that "the world of the Bobo is as close as any Rastafarian can come to that mental state the fundamental Christians call 'being saved.'"[2] Bobo Rastas moved away from Babylon, which they perceive as the world of the profane. Their retreat is a mechanism to distinguish themselves and maintain spiritual and social separation through ritualized distance. This exclusionary stance is consistent with Bobo Dread Rastas' aspiration to gain African redemption and reproduce the original lifestyle of African communities prior to slavery.

For historical contextualization, the Bobo Dread Rastas' community emerged out of the attempt to repatriate to Africa during the early twentieth century and to define their religious community as the kingdom of Jah (Rastas' rendition of God) on earth. Their communal organization and distrust of Jamaican institutions were shaped by Garvey's grand vision to reclaim Africa and his conviction that people of African descent can flourish only in Africa. Refraining from partaking in daily dealings and demarcating their physical space express Bobo Dread Rastas' strong belief that Jamaican society and, by extension, Western society are intrinsically antithetical to the fulfillment of people of African descent. Indeed, in many ways, the Bobo Dread Rastas' community stands as the embodiment of the ideals of Marcus Garvey and the Universal Negro Improvement Association (UNIA) in Jamaica. The Bobo Dread Rastas' endorsement of Ethiopianist tenets suggests that they conceptualize themselves as an Ethiopian community in exile; Bobo Dread Rastas view themselves as prodigal children yearning to reclaim Haile Selassie I's homeland. Moreover, Bobo Dread Rastas identify strongly with the Falashas. This includes the Falashas' semantic use of "we" even when referring to oneself or any single person.[3] It is noteworthy that this linguistic practice influenced Rasta I-Talk and is proof that Falashas' practices pervade Rastafari cosmology.

Ultimately, on the basis of this identification with the Falashas, Bobo Dread Rastas assert that they are the genuine Israelites. To accentuate their commitment to Afro-Judaism, some

Rastas have learned Amharic, the language of the Falashas. Indeed, one of the preoccupations of the Rastafari between the mid-1950s and mid-1970s was learning Amharic, an Ethiopian language. They reasoned that they needed to learn it in order to prepare for repatriation to Ethiopia. This effort further supported their identification as Africans and drew borders that differentiated them from other groups in Jamaica.[4]

Moreover, Bobo Dread Rastas reinforce their Judaic commitment by observing the Sabbath and adopting the I-tal diet—a vegetarian diet, which resembles the Judaic kosher diet organized around collective well-being. This practice is akin to the Falashas' because, "until this very day Falashas follow the economics of 'communal living,' and believe that 'rule by political power is evil.'"[5] Bobo Dread Rastas rely on their embrace of the Falashas' Afro-Judaism to define their spirituality and Blackness. After all, Bobo Dread Rastas hold the belief that "the true Israelite was the black man, not the Israelis who are white imposters. White philosophy could carry the Blackman nowhere, neither Christianity nor 'religion' only righteousness."[6] The notion of righteousness is central to the commitment of Rastafari cosmology to Afro-Judaism; it is a summary of the religious and moral values that Rastas had adopted as their ethical guidelines. Randal Hepner summarizes the tenet of righteousness as follows:

> Until the day that "righteousness covers the earth" symbolized by Zion, Rastas attempt to create "Zionic" conditions within their respective "exodus" communities. This effort takes many forms. In addition to the ritualized practice of "chanting down" Babylon, wherein Rastas signify to themselves and others the rejection of a world based on crass, materialistic values, competition, and racial animosities, Rastas also attempt to identify positive spatial and temporal locations where people can come together

for worship and play, for entertainment and fellowship. Here new identities can form and communal structures and relationships based on traditional norms of reciprocity, sharing, and collective ownership emerge. Here also one finds the strength and support necessary to live a life that goes against the grain of Babylon's competitive materialism, individualism, and nihilism.[7]

The tenet of righteousness presents the crux of moral responsibility in Rastafari cosmology. Righteousness encapsulates the remedial strategies by Rastafari cosmology to build communities with an alternative system of values and to advance the ethos of Blackness according to an Afrocentric worldview freed from the values that were prominent during plantation slavery and prevail in postcolonial Jamaican institutions. Hepner captures the uniqueness of Bobo Dread Rastas' technology of community building and, by extension, Rastafari cosmology by emphasizing that their approach does not stop merely at "the rejection of a world based on crass, materialistic values, competition, and racial animosities." Rastafari cosmology goes further by conceiving and implementing alternative Black communities. It is, thus, plain that the underlying incentive of righteousness is to postulate moral responsibilities for these alternative communities whose practices are corrective to the values and beliefs prominent in Babylon. Such practices aim at defining an alternative identity for the adherents that is grounded in the collective instead of Babylon's individualism. Zionic conditions are the fulfillment of Rastas' alternative communities according to the adage "I am unless we are."

For Rastas, righteousness is the synthesis of their Afrocentric cosmology with the Judaic values and beliefs of the Falashas. They reject Christian moral values, which they view as essentially Eurocentric and antithetical to the primordial constitution of people of African descent. Accordingly, for Rastas, righteousness supplies an alternative for the African Diaspora to guide their Blackness. The practices of righteousness draw out a system of ethical norms and beliefs that are loyal to the Afro-Judaic penchant of Rastafari cosmology. From this viewpoint, Afro-Judaism embodies Rastafari's response to the marginalization of their social and religious experience by Western institutions and ethics. From the perspective of Rastas, righteousness is the fulfillment of their ambition to create norms that define an ethically meaningful life for the African Diaspora.

On the basis of righteousness, Bobo Dread Rastas view themselves as the actualization of Afrocentric mores and authentic Judaism. The postulation of righteousness on the ground of Afro-Judaism is crucial in Rastafari cosmology because it reconciles Rastas' ideals of the virtuous life with their self-realization in the African Diaspora. The uniqueness of Rastafari cosmology consists in the provision of ethical guidelines to demarcate their African heritage and resist assimilation into Western institutions.

The Bobo Dread Rastas' ethical norms and religious beliefs revolve around practicing righteousness and positing Haile Selassie I as the incarnation of this righteousness. For Rastas, leading a righteous life promises African redemption and the means to align themselves with their glorious African ancestors. Accordingly, there is a teleology—an ultimate end in Rastafari's commitment to Afro-Judaic norms and beliefs. This goal is tripartite because it is religious, social, and political. The religious dimension lies in the perception of Haile Selassie I as the divine personification of authentic African heritage and Judaism; Rastas also refer to Haile Selassie I as the Lion of Judah. For Rastas, Haile Selassie I's Black divinity and worthiness to be worshipped is inseparable from his Ethiopian Falasha origin.

Indeed, Ethiopianism provided Black Jamaicans a framework for a racial, moral, religious, and political grounding compatible with the moral economies of Blackness. Ethiopianism thus supplied an alternative to ideas of White supremacy and Black inferiority, both millenarian and messianic in its prediction of the fall of slavery, an end to oppression, and the redemption of Blacks and the continent of Africa.[8] The resistant mechanism inherent in these practices grants Rastas the means to transcend the oppression of Jamaican institutions.

Endeavoring to elaborate a distinctive Afrocentric system of values and norms and to abide by Afrocentric spirituality makes Rastafari cosmology a multifaceted sociopolitical and religious process. The Rastafarian movement is one of the most interesting and difficult of Jamaican religious cults to summarize. This is due in large part to the fact that it is as much a politicoreligious movement as a cult. And while its forms are religious, its purposes are mainly political.[9] The political bent of Rastafari cosmology is informed by Garveyism and Ethiopianism. Garveyist and Ethiopianist principles are the sociopolitical means that Rastas apply to build their ideal communities. Moreover, it is via Ethiopianist and Garveyist principles that Rastafari cosmology fulfills their endeavor to define their Afrocentric Blackness and carry out their mission to liberate people of African descent. Even though Rastafari cosmology sets out to liberate all people of African descent and promote Blackness according to an Afrocentric tenet, it is hampered by a key impediment.

THE STATUS OF WOMEN IN RASTAFARI COSMOLOGY

The position of women in Rastafari cosmology is shaped by both the historical antecedent of women's role during plantation slavery and the contemporary role and treatment of women in postcolonial Jamaican society. Understanding the role of women during plantation slavery and in their contemporary context sheds light on the perception of them and their expected gender role in Rastafari cosmology. Despite the liberation from physical bondage that postcolonialism heralded for all Jamaicans, postcolonialism was nonetheless less favorable toward Jamaican women who, despite their physical freedom, remained confined to poverty and at the lowest rung of Jamaican society. The rampant poverty of women during the postcolonial period stemmed from two key social practices. First, women were circumscribed to the lowest-paying wage labor and small-scale market enterprises. The second social practice is the traditional function of bearing the burden of childcare alone, which deepened their vulnerability and weakened social standing. Accordingly, the predominant image of poor and working-class Jamaican women is that of a single mother who sells goods in the communal market in order to take care of her children. Despite its enterprising virtue, this traditional depiction of women confines them to economic weakness and dependence on men for social improvement.

It is noteworthy that the status of women in postcolonial Jamaica, unlike other aspects of plantation slavery, has not changed. In other words, sexist practices during slavery persisted in postcolonial Jamaican society despite liberation from slavery. Sexist cultural norms that value men's labor and activities more than women's while securing better social and economic rewards for men have continued to thrive in postcolonial Jamaican institutions. Sexism, gender inequality, and poverty lead to gender antagonism. These norms shape the experience of Jamaican women because women from all social strata are expected to defer to the needs of Jamaican men and to comply with their expectations and behaviors. Thus, women remain bound to the sexist attitudes and practices prominent during slavery. Suzanne LaFont depicts the interplay of the socioeconomic aspects that make sexism and gender antagonism rampant in Jamaican society:

> The slave and post-colonial eras left Jamaica a polarized society with a small number of predominantly Euro-Caribbean elites on one end of the economic continuum and the poor African-Caribbean masses on the other. The elites emulated British culture; they adopted their laws, their religion, and other social norms, including ideas about family and gender. The dominant ideology advocated the western model of gender behavior in which the male was installed as the *de facto* head of the household and economic provider. This ideological ideal co-existed with the actual division of labor in which women labored outside the home both during the slave and post-colonial era. The continuation of women's economic activities after emancipation fostered a tradition of female autonomy and independence. At the same time the colonial socioeconomic environment was structured so that poor men lacked access to the resources necessary to realize the ideal of a dominant breadwinner. Thus, the gender roles that accompany the breadwinner/homemaker ideal never actually became the prevalent practice in Jamaican society.[10]

The socioeconomic structure of Jamaica during both slavery and postcolonialism created an insurmountable rift in Jamaican society. The British colonial model of the family as the primordial institution that Jamaica inherited remained at odds with the available economic means for its fulfillment. LaFont's observation suggests that Jamaican working-class and poor people were mired in the contradiction of slavery and the postcolonial infrastructure—namely, they inherited a colonial model of the family but were never granted the economic resources to abide by this model. It is thus reasonable to think that this prominent dimension of Jamaican society is pervasive in Rasta communities. The issue is that Rastafari cosmology—which set out to formulate a corrective system of norms to replace those of slavery and postcolonial Jamaican institutions—failed to rectify the sexism and gender inequality inherent in the colonial family model and the economic challenges of poor and working-class people.

The sexist norms that plagued women during both slavery and the postcolonial period are also informed by religious dogmas. The obduracy and permanence of sexism toward women is grounded in both religious and secular norms. Belief in the superiority of men and the justification of their privileged status as heads of households are buttressed by secular attitudes and biblical scripture. Accordingly, the sexism and social constraints that women have to deal with are rooted in both religious and secular ideologies. This dual restriction, limiting the social betterment of women—viewed as socially inferior to and economically weaker than men—is more acute in Rastafari cosmology, which is informed by it and radicalizes it on the grounds of Afrocentric religious dogmas. Strict biblical interpretations and other cultural beliefs inherent in Rastafarian ideology combine to further institutionalize women's subordinate status. These constraints include the absence of women in leadership positions, proscriptions on ways of dressing, and notions of female pollution.[11] The layered and ritualized proscriptions that male Rastas impose on their female counterparts to conform to Rastafari norms suggests that they have undertaken a new colonization of female Rasta bodies. Colonization of Rasta women's bodies means that they are always validated and regulated by male Rastas' proscriptions, and Rasta women have no autonomy with respect to their dress code or the freedom to determine how their bodies are perceived.

The lynchpin of Rasta men's assertion of their superiority is the conviction that religious and spiritual wisdom is strictly their own privilege. In relying on the biblical depiction of Eve extended to all women as entities who have fallen from grace and the medium through which humankind became sinful, Rasta men cast themselves as both the bearers of biblical and spiritual wisdom and the means by which women may be redeemed from their original sinful status. Also, endorsing the biblical depiction surreptitiously casts women as unfit for spiritual knowledge and wisdom. For Obiagele Lake, the brunt of male Rastas' oppression of women can be summarized by these two beliefs:

> The popular Rastafarian belief that women are not privy to man's wisdom is one reason offered by many Rasta men for restrictions placed on women. Another has to do with the alleged connection between women and pollution. Buba Shanti women are excluded within a restricted area during their menstruation (although I [Obiagele Lake] was told by these women that this area is not small or claustrophobic) and are not permitted to interact with men or 'non-polluted' (free) women during this period. Almost all other Rasta women I spoke with on this topic indicated that they accepted the principle of pollution and enjoyed the reprieve from household duties that this period of seclusion provided.[12]

Lake's observation bears key implications for my project to show that Rastafari cosmology provides a system of religious, social, and cultural practices to uplift all people of African descent; namely, by holding that only men are privy to spiritual wisdom, Rasta men logically commit to the belief that, as guardians of wisdom, only they are spiritually fit to uplift all people of African descent. Furthermore, Rasta women's acceptance of both seclusion and male Rastas' view of menstruation as pollution is in unison with gender war and manipulation in Jamaican society. Poor Jamaicans exhibit remarkable agency in utilizing the dominant gender ideology to manipulate each other. Men assert the privilege of male dominance even though their economic situation prevents from fulfilling the breadwinner role, and women use the ideal of male breadwinner to justify their claims on men's income.[13] In the context of Rasta communities, Rasta women might agree to their seclusion and association of their menstruation with pollution in order to secure economic support and protection of male Rastas. Timothy White made the following observation regarding the treatment of women in Rasta communities:

> The women were usually segregated from the men, particularly if they were menstruating, which the Rastas regarded to be an unclean state. Women's role in Rasta life is clearly a restricted one—they are child bearers, fire-builders, cooks and honored servants. They may wear no makeup but the beaded gleam on their brows and the dust on their necks, their only fragrance that of perspiration; they are not permitted to join in discussions of consequence, nor may they draw from the chillum. Their dress must be modest as dictated by Deuteronomy 22:5: "The woman shall not wear that which pertaineth unto a man, neither shall a man put on a woman's garment: for all that do so are abomination unto the Lord thy God." Rasta women's heads must be covered, as called for in Corinthians 11:5–6: "For every woman that prayeth or prophesieth with her head uncovered dishonoureth her head: for that is even all one as if she were shaven. For if the woman be not covered, let her also be shorn: but if it be a shame for a woman to be shorn or shaven, let her be covered."[14]

White accurately depicts how Rasta men's attitudes toward Rasta women's menstruation are grounded in their interpretation of biblical scriptures. A key implication of Rasta women's exclusion from "discussion of consequence" is that women are inherently unfit to contribute to Rastafari's project of liberating people of African descent, unless they are granted permission and the spiritual means by Rasta men. Moreover, the alienation of women from wisdom and spiritual leadership is complicated by the dress code. Rasta women's dress code marginalizes them vis-à-vis both non-Rasta men and women in their society. Rasta women's dress code, restrictions forbidding exposing their hair and wearing makeup limit their ability to identify with or draw gender solidarity from non-Rasta women.

Rasta males' attempts to portray women under majestic epithets such as "empress" are attacked by critics of the movement who deem it a mechanism to avoid dealing with the implications of Rasta women's subordinate roles. The qualification of Rasta women as empresses reinforces the dominant role of Rasta men, whereas there are no associated privileges for these women. From Obiagele Lake's perspective, male Rastas' reference to Rasta women as empresses is consistent with the erroneous view of a large portion of working-class Jamaican women as matriarchs. Lake thinks it is inaccurate because it conflates the burden of domestic tasks with maternal power and privileges: "In spite of these realities, the myth of the matriarchy in Jamaican society, especially among the lower classes, remains an unsubstantiated normative construct because of what I suggest is a confusion between domestic responsibilities on one hand, and power in male/female relationships on the other, that is, many working-class women are often forced to support their households almost single-handedly. This is a burdensome task which is not to be equated with liberation."[15]

Lake's observation leads us to deduce that, by referring to Rasta women as empresses, male Rastas are merely reinforcing the contradiction between the colonial family model and lack of economic means in Jamaican institutions to delude women into deriving dignity from their oppression. In other words, arguing that poor and working-class Jamaican women are strong matriarchs and referring to them as empresses are a mere subterfuge to make their predicament acceptable and dignifying. The status of women in Rastafari cosmology exposes a gulf between the normative ideals and realities of Rastafari practices. The ideal of uplifting and liberating all people of African descent remains at loggerheads with the actual treatment of Rasta women who are oppressed not empowered by Rastafari cosmology.

Sexism and gender inequality are implications of male Rastas' dominant roles in Rasta communities. The elaboration of an egalitarian cosmology is hindered by male Rastas' domination of and sexism toward female adherents. The upshot is that Rasta practices promote freedom from oppression only for their male practitioners while binding women to male oppression. Consideration of the accounts of the apologetics and critics of Rasta practices shows that Rastafari cosmology ends up creating communities of mighty religious males despite its attempt to resist Western oppression of the African Diaspora.

FEMALE RASTAS: EMPRESSES WITHOUT ROYALTY

Keen observation of Rasta practices—specifically the practices that are prominent among the Bobo Dread Rastas—reveals the main limitation of Rastafari cosmology. The norms and beliefs of the Rasta communities are patriarchal and reinforce male domination of female adherents. In most Rasta communities, male elders stand as both religious leaders and moral authorities, while Rasta women are regarded and treated as subservient and inferior to Rasta men. In all their dimensions, the normative and religious mores of Rasta communities favor the masculine standpoint.

The existing literature tends to refrain from acknowledging and discussing the impact of patriarchy and gender inequality in Rasta communities. Barry Chevannes and Leonard Barrett are among the few scholars of Rastafari who are receptive to the unfavorable position of women in Rasta communities. As Chevannes explains, in the Bobo Dread community, the male patriarch, Prince Emmanuel, assumes the role of Jesus and the other male Rastas act as his prophets. "The compound is organized simply: at the head is Prince Emmanuel, or Jesus himself, and beneath him his followers. Generally speaking, all male Bobo are either 'prophets' or 'priests.' The function of prophets is to reason, the function of priests to 'move around the altar,' that is to conduct the services. . . . The commune is like a large family over which he presides as father. . . . Finally come the women and the children whose places are subordinate to those of the men."[16]

Chevannes depicts both the family structure of the Bobo Dread Rastas community and the paternalistic role of Prince Emmanuel. Prince Emmanuel assumes the dual role of prophet and moral guide. As prophets, Prince Emmanuel and the Rasta men of the community are privileged to "reason" or engage in biblical musings of the Rastafari creed and perform the sacred rituals. Rasta women, like children, are forbidden to partake in biblical debates and rituals. This exclusion perpetuates the homological and male-centered views of Rasta "groundations" or biblical reasonings. Another unfortunate outcome is that Rasta women's religious and philosophical musings, which if included in the biblical reasonings would enrich Rastafari cosmology, are subordinated under the male Rastas' philosophical and religious reasonings. In order to give a respectable status to the idea of reasoning in Rastafari, women should not be excluded. The exclusion of women from reasoning sessions is a reflection of the patriarchalism in the spaces where the Rastafari live.[17] The subordination of Rasta women's philosophical and religious ponderings under the male Rastas' constitutes the spiritual oppression of Rasta women in Rastafari cosmology. Moreover, it is noteworthy that the assignment of communal functions is guided by the inherent hierarchy of Rasta practices. In these practices, the subordination of women is reinforced as an inescapable step in the logic of the religious practices of the Bobo Dread Rastas community. Prince Emmanuel justifies his moral and religious authority in his knowledge and interpretation of biblical scripture. It is thus plain that patriarchy is an unfortunate component of Rastafari cosmology. Its pursuit of an Afrocentric ethos, therefore, reinforces women's inferiority on both religious and moral grounds. Sexism emerges as an inescapable dimension of Rastafari cosmology. It succumbs to one of the shortcomings of Babylon, which is "rather than looking to economic inequality or other historical or societal factors, many low-income Jamaicans hold their partners personally responsible for their own failed expectations. A cycle has developed in which both sexes blame the other for negative gender interaction."[18]

Barry Chevannes reports that Rastas designate an exclusive place within the Bobo Dread Rastas' compound in which women are confined during their menstrual cycle. "The last structure on the right of the path is a sick bay where the women seeing their menses are confined until their two weeks of defilement (calculated by adding twelve days to the duration of the menstrual flow) are over."[19] This practice is noteworthy because it highlights a major shortcoming within Rastafari cosmology; namely, that Rasta women's freedom to mingle with Rasta males is conditional. Also, this practice reveals Rasta women's helplessness in negotiating their social and spiritual standing in Rasta communities. Furthermore, the seclusion of women during their menses points out a contradiction in Rastafari cosmology's embrace and promotion of natural processes. In secluding women during their menses, Rastas refuse to acknowledge women's menstrual cycles as natural biological cycles. For instance, it is a blatant contradiction that, on the one hand, Rastas refrain from shaving body hair and strictly consume foods grown from the earth without chemicals because these are natural processes while perceiving the natural occurrence of women's menstruation as polluting, on the other. Hence, this contradiction illustrates Rasta males' chauvinistic outlook on menstruation as a cycle during which women are soiled and unfit to be in their communal space. This practice binds Rasta women to the chauvinistic ideals of Rasta males and is proof that they are bound in Rastafari cosmology instead of being liberated.

As an Afrocentric socioreligious cosmology informed by Garveyist ideology, Rastafari cosmology set out to create a liberating and uplifting alternative system of norms and beliefs that people of the African Diaspora could depend on to transcend Western social boundaries and oppression. However, confining Rasta women to a reclusive place in the compound suggests that they are allowed to partake in Rastafari practices of freedom and resistance to Eurocentrism on the exclusive condition that they conform to the male adherents' principles. Chevannes elaborates further on the proscriptions placed on women in the Bobo Dread community:

The place of all females is below that of all males, regardless of age. As a "King-man," or "God-man," the male child is held up as being superior to all females even though the latter are often referred to as "empresses." The subordination of women to men is characteristic of the Dreadlocks in general, only the Bobo carry it to a greater length. In the commune all females must cover their legs and arms. Women are confined to looking after the children and performing household chores such as cleaning and washing. Women give deference to men. A woman may serve guests, but may never serve Bobo males. Traditionally, among the peasantry it is the woman who cooks and serves, but among the Bobo it is the men who cook and the men who serve. The women may eat sitting on a bench outside the kitchen or take the meal back to their private quarters.[20]

Chevannes's claim gives evidence that Rastafari cosmology fails to include feminine mores. Thus, the system of beliefs, norms, and practices designed to end the oppression of people of African descent is exclusively male-centered. The systematic subordination of women in Rasta communities reveals the limits of Rastafari cosmology and the extent to which its practices and norms merely replace one patriarchal socioreligious community with another. Rastas' goal to end the oppression of people of African descent and the tyrannical rule of Babylon's institutions culminates in a cosmology that is male-centric and exclusive of feminine-sensitive norms. Expressed differently, the partial inclusion of Rasta women in Rastas' communal dynamics and the failure to include and apply feminine-sensitive norms lead to an imbalance in Rastafari cosmology. The imbalance consists in Rastafari cosmology's failure to recognize and apply feminine-sensitive norms. The logical implication of this bias is that the larger project of liberation of people of African descent seems to be designed only to end the oppression of men of African descent. In light of the male-centrism of Rastafari cosmology, the Rasta motto is not that all people of African descent should be free and spiritually elevated but rather that only men of African descent ought to be free and spiritually enlightened. This reproduction of gender inequality deeply undermines Rastas' goal to end Eurocentrism, oppression, and racism.

In this context, the use of the descriptor "empress" for women in the Rastafari community seems, at first blush, surprising. Upon closer examination, however, it becomes apparent that the term is strictly linguistic and void of the normative inclusion of women in the category of royalty. By establishing a dominant homological ethos that excludes women as equally worthy of freedom and spiritual betterment, Rastafari cosmology thus succumbs to the Eurocentric injustices that they set out to redress. Indeed, in Rasta communities, the roles of women reproduce the oppressive Western view of women as media of reproduction and sexual gratification. Chevannes gives an account of a Bobo Dread Rasta elder whose interaction with his wife is mainly sexually oriented: "[Prophet Stanley] is thirty-seven and has been a Bobo for seven years. During this period he has not slept in the same room as his wife. Whenever he wants, he has sexual intercourse with her and then leaves. Women he says, distract from meditation."[21]

Prophet Stanley's treatment of his wife is reinforced by Rastas' interpretation of the Bible and the treatment of women in Jamaican society. The perception and treatment of women as means of sexual gratification is pervasive in Jamaican society. This pattern has led many Jamaican women to believe that men want to use them sexually but will disregard responsibilities arising from the sex act.[22] Rasta men merely reinforce prevailing sexist attitudes by assigning women such roles in Rasta communities.

Rastafarian biblical doctrine does not provide comfort for women. It states that man is superior to woman; her knowledge of the scripture is a direct copy of man's; she is not allowed to speak in assembly; she is seductive; she bears the stigma of "periodical uncleanliness," which is a restriction placed on her by God.[23] Depicting Rasta women's knowledge of the scripture as a copy of men's knowledge and forbidding them to speak in religious assemblies is confirmation that Rasta men believe women are naturally unfit to reach spiritual knowledge above their own. Moreover, silencing women during religious assemblies and having them as mere auditors amounts to spiritual oppression of Rasta women. These practices are central to understanding the prominence of gender inequality and how it impairs Rastafari cosmology's aim to redress the tribulations and oppression of people of African descent. In Rastafari cosmology, the role of women thus oscillates between maternal care, provision of sexual gratification, and the "period of uncleanliness." It is fair to think that women are confined during their menstruation because they are not sexually available. Accordingly, their social visibility in Rasta communities is intimately linked to their role as sexual providers and mothers. The confinement of women during their menstruation suggests that, from the perspective of Rastafarian males, women ought not to be included in social and communal affairs unless they are sexually available.

The spiritual invisibility of women in Rasta communities and proscription from spiritual upbuilding posit a major challenge to the Afrocentric collectivity that Rastafari aspires to realize. The mission of reinventing Black communities without the ideological oppression of colonialism is undermined by gender inequality, which fragments Rasta communities and erects insurmountable rifts between men and women. Furthermore, the depiction of women as polluted is significant because it lays the groundwork for their elimination from full participation in social, political, and economic spheres.[24] Prophet Stanley's claim that women are a distraction from meditation is akin to the outlook on women as Jezebels. The standpoint on women as distractors and seductresses positions them as threatening to spiritual enlightenment and as media of pleasure; they can mislead and distract as much as they can please. Furthermore, Prophet Stanley's claim that women are distractions delineates Rasta males' guiding assumptions about masculinity and femininity. The depiction of women's presence as a deviation from spiritual ascension suggests that Rasta masculinity is hegemonic. Hegemonic masculinity consists of social and normative performances that oppress women and expect their subordination. This tyrannical masculinity requires the subordination of women and their surrender to male authority. Prophet Stanley's stance reinforces the adage of "real men." Real men are expected to be forceful, analytical, responsible, and willing to exert authority, all qualities that women supposedly lack. The use of women in the construction of masculinity is so widespread that this dimension of hegemonic masculinity seems hidden in plain sight.[25]

Interestingly, Rastas' interpretation of the Bible is also used in recent academic literature about Rastafari to justify gender inequality. "There can be no denying the fact that RastafarI is a patriarchal movement," writes Maureen Rowe, in a representative statement on the inherent logic of the Rastafari cosmology. "The male is at the head, having responsibility for conducting rituals, for interpreting events of significance to the community, and for the care and protection of the family as well as the community. RastafarI is based on the Bible; it therefore follows that its structure in philosophy would pattern that which unfolds in the Bible. To understand RastafarI attitudes toward females it is necessary to understand the role of females in the Bible."[26] Rowe's perspective casts gender inequality as normative in Rasta communities. Gender inequality derives its normative power directly from biblical mandates. Rowe sees Rasta men's perspectives on the social and religious roles of women as rooted in biblical ground. In grounding women's oppression in biblical scripture, Rowe seems to assert that gender inequality and Rastafari cosmology are fundamentally inseparable. This take on the origin of the poor treatment of women privileges the biblical roots of Rastafari and is indifferent to the fact that the oppressive roles for women in Jamaican society inform and reinforce the poor treatment and oppression of women in Rastafari cosmology. If gender inequality is indeed based on Rastafari's biblical interpretation of the role of women, then improving gender relations would require jettisoning the Bible as its holy compass. If that is Rowe's logic, the only avenue for improving gender relations would be a revision of the traditional role of women in the Bible.

Notably though, Rowe and others rule out even this unlikely possibility. Instead, she argues that male domination could in fact be neutralized if female adherents were to fully accept their subordinate role. Essentially, the argument goes that male domination is inherently neither right nor wrong; it is resistance to this domination that makes it problematic. In Rowe's words:

> It should be noted that beliefs and their resulting taboos cannot be realized unless the females understand, accept, and practice them. With the exception of exclusion from the group, there are no ways of enforcing these practices. It is left to the individual to behave in accordance with his or her understandings. This last

point is critical to the understandings of male/female relationship in RastafarI. The concept of male dominance can have no validity where the female understands, accepts, and operates within the parameters of a prescribed role. It is only when the female resists this role that the concept acquires significance.[27]

Rowe is advocating a conciliatory acceptance of gender inequality as the suitable approach to transcend male domination in Rastafari. Accordingly, from Rowe's perspective, there is nothing inherently wrong about gender inequality and chauvinism in Rastafari. A logical implication of this stance is that the experience of oppression by women is fictitious; the crux of the matter is that Rasta women feel that they are oppressed only if and when they challenge male Rastas' treatment and outlook on them.

The absurdity of this argument lies in its denial of the intrinsic injustice of gender inequality. This argument is akin, for example, to the claim that there is nothing wrong with slavery as long as the slaves passively accept their social treatment and status as slaves. As the preceding discussion of the basic tenets of Rastafari reveal, the argument that gender inequality is aligned with the biblical ground of the movement and that Rasta women only feel oppressed when they challenge Rasta males is untenable because it absolves Rastafari cosmology of the responsibility to provide gender-sensitive values, practices, and norms that improve the social and spiritual circumstances of all African Diasporic peoples.

Responses to the critique of gender inequality among Rastas are mixed. Some Rasta women argue that the pervasiveness of women's oppression in Rastafari practices is a direct legacy of colonialism on the social, religious, and political institutions in Jamaica and must be remedied. Meanwhile, apologists hold that Rastas merely reproduce practices of gender inequality that pervade the family structure of Jamaican society. Here again, Rowe's views are instructive: "Gender and family relations within Rastafari, as in the wider society," she writes, "have been shaped by complex attitudes arising out of the synthesis of African and European cultures in Jamaica."[28] Similarly, "The Rastafari are widely described as a male-dominated collectivity," writes Charles Price in a parallel line of argument, "their gender understandings are deeply informed by biblical prescriptions and cultural understandings developed over the century in Jamaica."[29] In this way, Rowe and Price offer surreptitious apologies for the pervasiveness of gender inequality in Rasta communities on the grounds of biblical interpretation and the colonial legacy of Jamaican institutions. They thereby suggest that male Rastas have not deliberated on their attitudes toward women but rather have passively borrowed them from the syncretism of African and European practices in Jamaican institutions. For this camp, gender inequality is a dimension of colonialism that both the Jamaican institutions and Rasta communities have not managed to transcend. However, the issue with their take remains that gender inequality is the main aspect of Jamaican society's colonial legacy that Rastafari cosmology fails to regard as oppressive while it deliberately strives to free people of African descent from all aspects of colonialism. Moreover, given Rastas' rejection of Babylon's social institutions and their insights about why these institutions are oppressive, it is incoherent with their approach that they reproduce gender inequality with no qualms.

On the other side of the debate, the scholar and adherent Imani Tafari-Ama is critical of male Rastas' perspectives on Rasta women. She relies on her personal experience to argue that Rasta males use their biblical interpretation strategically in an effort to control women through the assignment of fixed sexual and domestic roles while reinforcing their privileged socioreligious status. She argues that "in Rastafari the arena of sexuality is fertile ground for the application of normative control of females," then observes that "sistren internalize traditional roles of woman as servant. But my own experience with the Bobo Shanti commune convinced me that I would not choose to be subjected to such severe sanctioning of my sexuality."[30] In this claim, she voices the plight of female adherents as subordinates in Rasta communities mainly on the grounds of sexual roles. Obiagele Lake, another critic of gender inequality in Rastafari, buttresses Imani Tafari-Ama's account in the following observation:

> The Bobo have very strict rules regarding women's behavior. There are proscriptions regarding women's dress and participation in religious and other arenas. These constraints are based on the belief in women's pollution during their menstruation and their alleged inferior status. These beliefs are generally held by all Rastas but are applied more strictly within this group. The ideology of pollution is fundamental to the marginalization of women.... The diversity of Rastas notwithstanding, to varying degrees, they all embrace the following general tenets of RastafarI: 1) a belief in the divine power of Haile Selassie; 2) repatriation to Africa; 3) the sacred power of ganja (marijuana); and 4) women are subordinate to men.[31]

Lake depicts the pervasiveness of gender inequality as the "sacralization of sexism," meaning that gender inequality is enshrined in the sacred beliefs of Rastafari cosmology. Lake confirms that the subordination of women in Rasta communities assumes sacredness on the grounds of biblical interpretation. "Rastafarian women are doubly oppressed compared to other Jamaican women," she goes on to argue, "since they are subject to proscriptions inherent in Christian doctrines and practices inherent to traditional African cultures."[32] Here, Lake offers a subtle response to the apologists' argument of Rowe, Price, and others, positing that the impact of the syncretism of Christianity and African religious practices is more detrimental for Rasta women than it is for the average Jamaican woman in the traditional Jamaican family structure. Thus, Lake rejects the idea of a passive borrowing of gender inequality practices from the Jamaican institutions as an apology and subtle justification. In contrast to Rowe and Price's apology for gender inequality and male dominance on the grounds of the traditional role of women in the Bible, Lake argues a reverse causality—namely, that sexism and chauvinism assume a religious cloak to suppress the resistance mechanism of female adherents. This sacralization of sexism in Rastafari cosmology may appear insurmountable to female adherents.

Thus, critics like Tafari-Ama and Lake reinforce the vestiges of Eurocentricism and chauvinism in Rastafari cosmology. In doing so, they expose the gender selective nature of Rastafari norms and beliefs. The fundamental premise of Rastas' norms and beliefs is their privilege of male Rastas' dominance. Three aspects of Rastafari cosmology illustrate this fact. First, the difference in diet; Rastas deliberately break away from the Western food chain through critical acknowledgment of its detriment to the harmony between natural artifacts and communal welfare. Second, they critique Western subjectivity and Christianity through the use of "I-an-I" and "I-talk." Third, they readily supplant the Eurocentric biblical account of God by positing Haile Selassie I as their divine figure. Together, these aspects demonstrate Rastas' ability to adopt critical stances and break away from the prevailing norms of Western institutions. It is therefore reasonable to infer that Rastas' failure to redress the oppressed instances of women in biblical scriptures is inconsistent with their relentless endeavor to correct the intrinsic wrongs of Western institutions. This failure seems to suggest instead that Rastas' commitment to the traditional role of women in the Bible is rooted in promoting male Rastas' privileged status. By virtue of this blindside, Rastas' resistance to Western institutions can thus be deemed only partial because their cosmology is bent toward the production of dominant males vis-à-vis subordinate and inferior female adherents. Nathaniel Murrell elaborates on the selective nature of the Rastafari ethos by observing that "Rastas did not see women's liberation and equality as their movement's priority. . . . violence, economic disadvantage, discrimination, and racism were more pressing issues than sexism and patriarchy during the long night of the African American struggle."[33]

For critics like Tafari-Ama and Lake, the promise of freedom from oppression, the postulation of liberating Afrocentric norms, and spiritual enlightenment cannot be fulfilled as long as female adherents are oppressed on the grounds of biblical scriptures and prevailing domestic practices among Jamaican families. Tafari-Ama's and Lake's stances are corrective to Rastafari cosmology because, in critiquing Rasta males' domination, they shed light on the aspect of Rastafari cosmology that is wanting for the fulfillment of its promise to improve the circumstances of people of African descent. Accordingly, their critiques are thus best understood as constructive. For Tafari-Ama, Lake, and Rasta women, Babylon crumbles only if Rasta women's roles are refigured as equally worthy of self-determination and freedom from oppression. Royalty can be restored to "empresses" provided that Rasta men acknowledge Rasta women as fundamentally equal.

Tafari-Ama's and Lake's critiques thus provide strong reasons to reject the perspectives of Rowe and Price, which assert that Rastafari blindly inherited gender inequality from the colonial legacy of Jamaican institutions and their interpretation of the traditional roles of women in the Bible. While Rowe and Price fail to justify the enduring patriarchy of Rastafari, its prevalence is unsurprising given the movement's roots. Diane Austin-Broos draws the following critique of Rowe's apology for Rasta males' oppression of Rasta females from her field studies of Rastafari practices in Jamaica: "Rowe details a number of modifications to this doctrine among Rastafarians with whom she is familiar. Now why should this be so when in the case of Pentecostalism a hostile code does not preclude women rising to prominence in particular spheres at least." She goes on to further refute Rowe's account:

> In the context of variable mating patterns and a high incidence of matrifocal households, Rastafarianism became an attempt to raise male status in lieu of a stable position in the household. The issue of African manhood in the neighborhood context is thus articulated through sexual and domestic relations; Rastafarianism comes to complement a more diffuse cultural concern with the social, sexual and political efficacy of the black peasant and working-class male. This concern with male efficacy is seen nowhere more clearly than in the symbolism of Rastafarianism.[34]

Austin-Broos deals the final blow to the apologists for male Rastas' oppression of Rasta women by suggesting that Rasta males' emasculation in the matrifocal households compel them to oppress Rasta women. In other words, Rasta men oppress Rasta women as a means to alleviate their sense of emasculation and elevate their social status in Rasta communities.

The pervasiveness of gender inequality in Rastafari cosmology could also be viewed as a logical implication of its commitment to Garveyist ideology and Jamaican Revivalism. Garveyism's failure to include a clear agenda for the contribution of women to its pan-African endeavors and promoting egalitarian gender relations has been passed down to Rastafari cosmology, as the meeting point of Garveyism and Revivalism. Furthermore, whereas Rastas have been critical of Christianity, there is no record in the literature that shows a critical assessment of Garvey, whom they consistently hail as a prophet. Moreover, the zealous bent of the Jamaican Revivalists is congenial to Rastas' literal interpretation of women's role in the Bible. The Revivalists' approach to the Bible is a literal Afrocentric rendition, which emphasized African presence in biblical scriptures and preserved the traditional roles of women. Thus, gender inequality in Rasta communities is linked to the legacy of Garveyism and Revivalism. Despite Garveyism and Rastafari cosmology's keen awareness of racism, they did not address prevailing practices and ideologies among Black communities that reinforce oppression. While racism remains a significant problem, there is also a need to rethink ideologies, family practices, and traditions that emerged out of racial oppression and are now enshrined as part of Black culture.[35]

Furthermore, male dominance legitimates the homogeneity of norms and beliefs in Rasta communities. The proscriptions on Rasta women's contributions to spiritual practices and debates about Rasta norms prevent Rastafari from being a heterogeneous cosmology. Unfortunately, this socioreligious uniformity Rastafari cosmology imposes is conducive to male supremacy in Rasta communities. Indeed, Rasta masculinity is grounded on the subordination of Rasta women and the male centric norms that privilege Rasta men. Asserting and performing Rasta masculinity thus depends on endorsing and reinforcing female adherents as subordinates. Consequently, the social and religious presence of female adherents presents an arena of projection for Rasta masculinity. The invisibility of Rasta women, on grounds of their subordination, turns them into socioreligious mirrors that always reflect the expected gaze of male Rastas.

In conclusion, gender role ideology stands as a major shortcoming in Rastafari cosmology's attempt to create a system of Afrocentric norms and values as an alternative to Babylon's Western institutions. Essentially, despite its noble ambition to liberate and furnish a distinctive system of norms, beliefs, and cultural practices, Rastafari cosmology is impaired by a male-centric and homogeneous tenet. This limitation may be a direct inheritance from Garveyism, which, like most pan-African crusades, emphasizes racial injustice but overlooks gender inequality as a form of oppression. This oversight by Garveyism persists in Rastas' failure to establish an egalitarian relationship with Rasta women. Another probable cause of gender inequality in Rastafari cosmology is the rampant poverty in Rasta communities and the financial inadequacy of Rasta males. The material poverty that plagues Rasta communities and the inferiority complex that it instills in male Rastas compels them to seek refuge from their emasculation in the assurance and comfort of female subordination. Meanwhile, on an individual level, Rastafari subjective realities are impaired by a radical masculinity that excludes femininity from Rastafari cosmology.

To use the last stanza of Bob Marley's poetic and prophetic song, "Zion Train," which calls on people of African descent to catch the train heading to the station of liberation:

Oh, children, Zion train is comin' our way, get on board now!
They said the Zion train is comin' our way

The train to liberation that Rastafari cosmology heralds will not deliver its promise unless Rasta women, as equal to Rasta men, have tickets as well.sw

NOTES

PREFACE

1. Ennis B. Edmonds, "The Structure and Ethos of Rastafari," in *Chanting Down Babylon: The Rastafari Reader*, ed. Nathaniel S. Murrell, William D. Spencer, and Adrian A. McFarlane (Philadelphia: Temple University Press, 1998), 354.

1. RESISTANCE TO BRITISH COLONIALISM AND THE RISE OF TWO FORMS OF SUBJECTIVITY IN "YAMAYE"

1. Philip Sherlock and Hazel Bennett, *The Story of the Jamaican People* (Kingston, Jamaica: Ian Randle, 1998), 2.
2. Charmaine Nelson, *Slavery, Geography, and Empire in Nineteenth-Century Marine Landscapes of Montreal and Jamaica* (New York: Routledge, 2016), 197.
3. Trevor Burnard, *Mastery, Tyranny, and Desire: Thomas Thistlewood and His Slaves in the Anglo-Jamaican World* (Chapel Hill: University of North Carolina Press, 2009), 118.
4. Trevor Burnard, *Jamaica in the Age of Revolution* (Philadelphia: University of Pennsylvania Press, 2020), 56.
5. Rex Nettleford, *Caribbean Cultural Identity: The Case of Jamaica* (Los Angeles: University of California Press, 1979), 301.
6. Nelson, *Slavery, Geography, and Empire*, 253.

7. Burnard, *Mastery, Tyranny, and Desire*, 22–23.
8. John Hearn, "Landscape with Faces," *Caribbean Quarterly* 54, nos. 1–2 (2008): 111.
9. Burnard, *Mastery, Tyranny, and Desire*, 26.
10. Burnard, *Jamaica in the Age of Revolution*, 73.
11. Sherlock and Bennett, *Story of the Jamaican People*, 86.
12. Nelson, *Slavery, Geography, and Empire*, 236.
13. Orlando Patterson, *The Sociology of Slavery: Black Society in Jamaica, 1655–1838* (Cambridge, MA: Polity Press, 2022), 261–265.
14. Patterson, *Sociology of Slavery*, 265.
15. Patterson, *Sociology of Slavery*, 275.
16. Burnard, *Jamaica in the Age of Revolution*, 242–243.
17. Patterson, *Sociology of Slavery*, 185, 188–189.
18. Barry Chevannes, "Rastafari and the Coming of Age: The Routinization of Rastafari in Jamaica," in *Rastafari in the New Millennium*, ed. Michael Barnett (Syracuse, NY: Syracuse University Press, 2012), 17–18.

2. THE GENEALOGY OF RASTAFARI COSMOLOGY AND ITS DISTINCTIVE ETHOS OF BLACKNESS

1. Gad Heuman, *"The Killing Time": The Morant Bay Rebellion in Jamaica* (London: Macmillan Caribbean, 1994), 4–5.
2. Charles Price, *Becoming Rasta: Origins of Rastafari Identity in Jamaica* (New York: New York University Press, 2009), 22.
3. Price, *Becoming Rasta*, 27.
4. William David Spencer, "The First Chant: Leonard Howell's *The Promised Key*," in *Chanting Down Babylon: The Rastafari Reader*, ed. Nathaniel S. Murrell, William D. Spencer, and Adrian A. McFarlane (Philadelphia: Temple University Press, 1998), 361.
5. Spencer, "First Chant," 363.
6. Spencer, "First Chant," 368–369.
7. Tommy L. Lott, ed., *African-American Philosophy: Selected Readings* (Hoboken, NJ: Pearson Education, 2002), 86.
8. Horace Campbell, *Rasta and Resistance: From Marcus Garvey to Walter Rodney* (Trenton, NJ: African World Press, 1987), 57.

2. THE GENEALOGY OF RASTAFARI COSMOLOGY ⊗ 191

9. Lott, *African-American Philosophy*, 87.
10. Lott, *African-American Philosophy*, 89.
11. Lott, *African-American Philosophy*, 88.
12. Lott, *African-American Philosophy*, 88.
13. Amy Jacques Garvey, *The Philosophy and Opinions of Marcus Garvey: Or, Africa for the Africans*, 2 vols. (Baltimore, MD: Majority Press 1989), 1:44.
14. Randall Burkett, *Garveyism as a Religious Movement* (New York: Scarecrow Press and American Theological Library Association, 1978), 46.
15. Tony Martin, *Race First: The Ideological and Organizational Struggles of Marcus Garvey and the Universal Negro Improvement Association* (Cambridge, MA: Majority Press, 1970), 69–70.
16. Ernle Gordon, "Garvey and Black Liberation Theology," in *Garvey: His Work and Impact*, ed. Rupert Lewis and Patrick Bryan (Trenton, NJ: Africa World Press, 1991), 141.
17. Lott, *African-American Philosophy*, 89.
18. Lott, *African-American Philosophy*, 89.
19. C. James Boyd, *Garvey, Garveyism and the Antinomies in Black Redemption* (Trenton, NJ: Africa World Press, 2009), 78.
20. Adolph Edwards, *Marcus Garvey: 1887–1940* (London: New Beacon, 1967), 7.
21. Rupert Lewis, "Marcus Garvey and the Early Rastafarians: Continuity and Discontinuity," in Murrell, Spencer, and McFarlane, *Chanting Down Babylon*, 151.
22. Ikael Tafari, *Rastafari in Transition: The Politics of Cultural Confrontation in Africa and the Caribbean (1966–1988)* (Kingston, Jamaica: Miguel Lorne, 2001), 277.
23. Derek Bishton, *Black Heart Man* (London: Chatto and Windus, 1986), 86.
24. Tafari, *Rastafari in Transition*, 33.
25. Tafari, *Rastafari in Transition*, 289.
26. Nicole Plummer, "Untold Stories: Using Oral History to Explore the Coral Gardens 'Incident,' 1963," in *Encyclopedia of African-American Culture and History*, 2nd ed., vol. 5, ed. Colin A. Palmer (Detroit, MI: Macmillan Reference, 2006), 347.
27. Harold Cruse, *The Crisis of the Negro Intellectual: A Historical Analysis of the Failure of Black Leadership* (New York: Quill, 1984), 119.

28. Barry Chevannes, *Rastafari: Roots and Ideology* (Syracuse, NY: Syracuse University Press, 1995), 108–109.
29. Lewis, "Marcus Garvey and the Early Rastafarians," 146.
30. Leonard E. Barrett, *The Rastafarians* (Boston: Beacon Press, 1997), 106.
31. Anthony B. Pinn, ed., *African American Religious Cultures* (Santa Barbara, CA: ABC-CLIO, 2009), 2:342.
32. Theodore G. Vincent, *Black Power and the Garvey Movement* (Berkeley, CA: Ramparts Press, 1971), 37–38.
33. Cary D. Wintz, ed., *African-American Political Thought, 1890–1930: Washington, Du Bois, Garvey, and Randolph* (New York: M. E. Sharpe, 1996), 122.
34. Leslie G. Desmangles, Stephen D. Glazier, and Joseph M. Murphy, "Religion in the Caribbean," in *Understanding the Contemporary Caribbean*, ed. Richard S. Hillman and Thomas J. D'Agostino (Boulder, CO: Lynne Rienner 2009), 315.
35. Lawrence Bamikole, "Rastafari as Philosophy and Praxis," in *Rastafari in the New Millenium*, ed. Michael Barnett (Syracuse, NY: Syracuse University Press, 2012), 130.
36. Barrett, *Rastafarians*, 106.
37. Kojo Nartey, *Dreadlocks, Marijuana, and Rastafari* (Accra, Ghana: Roots Society, 1999), 18.
38. Chevannes, *Rastafari*, 109.
39. Campbell, *Rasta and Resistance*, 43.
40. Chevannes, *Rastafari*, 109.
41. Chevannes, *Rastafari*, 118.
42. Chevannes, *Rastafari*, 154.
43. Patrick Manning, *The African Diaspora: A History Through Culture* (New York: Columbia University Press, 2009), 305.
44. E. David Cronon, *Black Moses: The Story of Marcus Garvey and the Universal Negro Improvement Association* (Madison: University of Wisconsin Press, 1969), 144.
45. Ennis B. Edmonds, "Dread 'I' In-a-Babylon: Ideological Resistance and Cultural Revitalization," in Murrell, Spencer, and McFarlane, *Chanting Down Babylon*, 24.
46. Chevannes, *Rastafari*, 145.
47. Barrett, *Rastafarians*, 174.

48. Paget Henry, *Caliban's Reason: Introducing Afro-Caribbean Philosophy* (New York: Routledge, 2000), 211.
49. Michael Barnett, "Rastafari in the New Millenium: Rastafari at the Dawn of the Fifth Epoch," in Barnett, *Rastafari in the New Millenium*, 17.
50. Molefi Asante, *The Afrocentric Idea* (Philadelphia: Temple University Press, 1998), 49.

3. RASTAFARI COSMOLOGY, NATURAL ARTIFACTS, AND THE ETHOS OF BLACKNESS

1. Ennis Edmonds, "The Structure and Ethos of Rastafari," in *Chanting Down Babylon: The Rastafari Reader*, ed. Nathaniel S. Murrell, William D. Spencer, and Adrian A. McFarlane (Philadelphia: Temple University Press, 1998), 354.
2. Lawrence Bamikole, "Rastafari as Philosophy and Praxis," in *Rastafari in the New Millenium*, ed. Michael Barnett (Syracuse, NY: Syracuse University Press, 2012), 136.
3. Barry Chevannes, *Rastafari: Roots and Ideology* (Syracuse, NY: Syracuse University Press, 1995), 26–27.
4. Anthony B. Pinn, ed., *African American Religious Cultures* (Santa Barbara, CA: ABC-CLIO, 2009), 2:342.
5. Joseph Owens, *Dread: The Rastafarians of Jamaica* (Kingston, Jamaica: United Co-Operative Printers, 1995), 58.
6. Rex Nettleford, "Discourse on Rastafarian Reality," in Murrell, Spencer, and McFarlane, *Chanting Down Babylon*, 315.
7. Jahlani Niaah, "Nettleford and Rastafari's Inner Landscape," *Caribbean Quarterly* 57, nos. 3–4 (2011): 50.
8. Ikael Tafari, *Rastafari in Transition: The Politics of Cultural Confrontation in Africa and the Caribbean (1966–1988)* (Kingston, Jamaica: Miguel Lorne, 2001), 8.
9. Jahlani Niaah, "The Rastafari Presence in Ethiopia: A Contemporary Perspective," in Barnett, *Rastafari in the New Millenium*, 88.
10. Leonard E. Barrett, *The Rastafarians* (Boston: Beacon Press, 1997), 8.
11. Chevannes, *Rastafari*, 173, 179.
12. Pinn, *African American Religious Cultures*, 2:344.

13. Rex Nettleford, "From the Cross to the Throne: Rastafari in the New Millennium," keynote address, Folk Filosofi symposium, University of the West Indies, Mona, Jamaica, 1999, 35.
14. Ennis B. Edmonds, *Rastafari: From Outcasts to Culture Bearers* (New York: Oxford University Press, 2003), 86.
15. Barry Chevannes, "Rastafari and the Exorcism of Racism and Classism," in Murrell, Spencer, and McFarlane, *Chanting Down Babylon*, 63.
16. Nettleford, "Discourse on Rastafari Reality," 320.
17. Nettleford, "Discourse on Rastafari Reality," 318.
18. Monique Bedasse, "The Theology of the Twelve Tribes of Israel," *Journal of Black Studies* 40, no. 5 (2010): 9.
19. Joseph Thompson, "From Judah to Jamaica: The Psalms in Rastafari Reggae," *Religion and the Arts* 16 (2012): 328.
20. Tafari, *Rastafari in Transition*, 317.
21. Yoshiko Nagashima, *Rastafarian Music in Contemporary Jamaica: A Study of Socioreligious Music of the Rastafarian Movement in Jamaica* (Tokyo: Institute for the Study of Languages and Cultures of Asia and Africa, 1984), 55.
22. Jace Claton, "Nyahbinghi," in *Africana: The Encyclopedia of the African and African American Experience*, 2nd ed., ed. Kwame Anthony Appiah and Henry Louis Gates Jr. (Oxford: Oxford University Press, 2007), 883.
23. Michael Barnett, "Rastafari in the New Millenium: Rastafari at the Dawn of the Fifth Epoch," in Barnett, *Rastafari in the New Millenium*, 1.
24. Leslie G. Desmangles, Stephen D. Glazier, and Joseph M. Murphy, "Religion in the Caribbean," in *Understanding the Contemporary Caribbean*, ed. Richard S. Hillman and Thomas J. D'Agostino (Boulder, CO: Lynne Rienner, 2009), 317.
25. Michael Barnett, "Rastafari Dialectism: The Epistemological Individualism and Connectivism of Rastafari," *Caribbean Quarterly* 48, no. 4 (2002): 57.
26. Chevannes, *Rastafari*, 173.
27. Chevannes, *Rastafari*, 174.
28. Nathaniel S. Murrell and Lewin Williams, "The Black Biblical Hermeneutics of Rastafari," in Murrell, Spencer, and McFarlane, *Chanting Down Babylon*, 328.
29. Edmonds, "Structure and Ethos of Rastafari," 349.

3. COSMOLOGY AND NATURAL ARTIFACTS ⊛ 195

30. Katrin Hansing, "Faith: Rastafari," in *Cuba*, vol. 1, ed. Alan West-Durán (New York: Charles Scribner's Sons, 2012), 314.
31. Niaah, "Nettleford and Rastafari's Inner Landscape," 59.
32. Charles Price, *Becoming Rasta: Origins of Rastafari Identity in Jamaica* (New York: New York University Press, 2009), 211.
33. Price, *Becoming Rasta*, 64.
34. Thompson, *From Judah to Jamaica*, 341.
35. Velma Pollard, *Dread Talk: The Language of Rastafari* (Montreal: McGill-Queen's University Press, 2000), 22.
36. Paget Henry, *Caliban's Reason: Introducing Afro-Caribbean Philosophy* (New York: Routledge, 2000), 15–16.
37. Horace Campbell, *Rasta and Resistance: From Marcus Garvey to Walter Rodney* (Trenton, NJ: Africa World Press, 1987), 129.
38. Cadence Wynter, "Rodney and Rastafari: Cultural Identity in 1960s Jamaica," in Barnett, *Rastafari in the New Millenium*, 307.
39. Price, *Becoming Rasta*, 92–93.
40. Adwoa Ntozake Onuora, "Exploring RastafarI's Pedagogic, Communicative, and Instructional Potential in the Caribbean: The Life and Works of Mutabaruka as a Case Study," in Barnett, *Rastafari in the New Millenium*, 155.
41. Carole D. Yawney, "Lions in Babylon: The Rastafarians of Jamaica as a Visionary Movement" (Ph.D. diss., McGill University, 1978), 201.
42. Desmangles, Glazier, and Murphy, "Religion in the Caribbean, 317.
43. P. Henry, *Caliban's Reason*, 60.
44. Barnett, "Rastafari Dialectism," 57.
45. Chevannes, *Rastafari*, 35.
46. Campbell, *Rasta and Resistance*, 107.
47. Edmonds, "Structure and Ethos of Rastafari," 354.
48. Emily Allen Williams, "Rastafarians," in *Encyclopedia of Latin American History and Culture*, ed. Jay Kinsbruner and Erick D. Langer, 2nd ed. (New York: Charles Scribner's Sons, 2008), 5:495.
49. Chevannes, *Rastafari*, 57.
50. Edmonds, "Structure and Ethos of Rastafari," 354.
51. Williams, "Rastafarians," 495.
52. Ennis B. Edmonds, "Dread 'I' In-a-Babylon: Ideological Resistance and Cultural Revitalization," in Murrell, Spencer, and McFarlane, *Chanting Down Babylon*, 32.

53. Desmangles, Glazier, and Murphy, "Religion in the Caribbean," 317.
54. Peter B. Clarke, *Black Paradise: The Rastafarian Movement* (Wellingborough: Aquarian Press, 1986), 90.

4. RASTAFARI'S THEOLOGY OF BLACKNESS: A EUROCENTRIC GOD CANNOT LOVE AFRICANS AND PEOPLE OF AFRICAN DESCENT

1. Rex Nettleford, "Discourse on Rastafarian Reality," in *Chanting Down Babylon: The Rastafari Reader*, ed. Nathaniel S. Murrell, William D. Spencer, and Adrian A. McFarlane (Philadelphia: Temple University Press, 1998), 315.
2. Clinton Chisholm, "The Rasta-Selassie-Ethiopian Connections," in Murrell, Spencer, and McFarlane, *Chanting Down Babylon*, 173.
3. Nettleford, "Discourse on Rastafarian Reality," 320.
4. Nathaniel Murrell and Burchell Taylor, "Rastafari's Messianic Ideology and Caribbean Theology of Liberation," in Murrell, Spencer, and McFarlane, *Chanting Down Babylon*, 395.
5. Nathaniel Murrell and Lewin Williams, "The Black Biblical Hermeneutics of Rastafari," in Murrell, Spencer, and McFarlane, *Chanting Down Babylon*, 327.
6. Anna Kasafi Perkins, "The Wages of (Sin) Is Babylon," in *Rastafari in the New Millenium*, ed. Michael Barnett (Syracuse, NY: Syracuse University Press, 2012), 245.
7. Ikael Tafari, *Rastafari in Transition: The Politics of Cultural Confrontation in Africa and the Caribbean* (1966–1988) (Kingston, Jamaica: Miguel Lorne, 2001), 314.
8. Perkins, "Wages of (Sin) Is Babylon," 245.
9. Williams and Murrell, "Black Biblical Hermeneutics," 332–333.
10. John Dear, *The God of Peace: Toward a Theology of Non-Violence* (New York: Orbis Books, 1994), 60–61.
11. Perkins, "Wages of (Sin) Is Babylon," 252.
12. Lawrence Bamikole, "Rastafari as Philosophy and Praxis," in Barnett, *Rastafari in the New Millenium*, 135.
13. Adwoa Ntozake Onuora, "Exploring RastafarI's Pedagogic, Communicative, and Instructional Potential in the Caribbean: The Life and

Works of Mutabaruka as a Case Study," in Barnett, *Rastafari in the New Millenium*, 155.
14. Murrell and Taylor, "Rastafari's Messianic Ideology," 391.

5. RASTAFARI I-TALK AND BLACK CONSCIOUSNESS

1. Thomas Metzinger, *The Ego Tunnel: The Science of the Mind and the Myth of the Self* (New York: Basic Books, 2010), 26.
2. Katrin Hansing, *Rasta, Race and Revolution* (Piscataway, NJ: Transaction, 2006), 79.
3. Barry Chevannes, *Rastafari: Roots and Ideology* (Syracuse, NY: Syracuse University Press, 1995), 35.
4. Chevannes, *Rastafari*, 44.
5. Chevannes, *Rastafari*, 77.
6. Chevannes, *Rastafari*, 75.
7. Chevannes, *Rastafari*, 49.
8. Chevannes, *Rastafari*, 137.
9. Chevannes, *Rastafari*, 157.
10. Horace Campbell, *Rasta and Resistance: From Marcus Garvey to Walter Rodney* (Trenton, NJ: Africa World Press, 1987), 108.
11. Stephen King, *Reggae, Rastafari, and the Rhetoric of Social Control* (Jackson: University Press of Mississippi, 2002), 33.
12. Leonard E. Barrett, *The Rastafarians* (Boston: Beacon Press, 1997), 138.
13. Peter B. Clarke, *Black Paradise: The Rastafarian Movement* (Wellingborough: Aquarian Press), 90.
14. Barrett, *Rastafarians*, 143.
15. Anna Kasafi Perkins, "The Wages of (Sin) Is Babylon," in *Rastafari in the New Millenium*, ed. Michael Barnett (Syracuse, NJ: Syracuse University Press, 2012), 239.
16. Chevannes, *Rastafari*, 167.
17. Paget Henry, "Rastafari and the Reality of Dread," in *Existence in Black: An Anthology of Black Existential Philosophy*, ed. Lewis Gordon (New York: Routledge, 1997), 161.
18. Velma Pollard, *Dread Talk: The Language of Rastafari* (London: McGill-Queens University Press, 2000), 15.
19. P. Henry, "Rastafari and the Reality of Dread," 161.

20. Roger Ariew, "Descartes and Scholasticism: The Intellectual Background to Descartes' Thought," in *The Cambridge Companion to Descartes*, ed. John Cottingham (Cambridge: Cambridge University Press, 1999), 65.
21. Alan C. Kors, "Just and Arbitrary Authority in Enlightenment Thought," in *Modern Enlightenment and the Rule of Reason*, ed. John C. McCarthy (Washington, DC: Catholic University of America Press, 1998), 22.
22. René Descartes, *Meditations*, trans. Donald A. Cress (Indianapolis, IN: Hackett, 1993), 12.
23. Boyce Gibson, *The Philosophy of Descartes* (New York: Russell and Russell, 1967), 79.
24. Husain Sarkar, *Descartes' Cogito: Saved from the Great Shipwreck* (Cambridge: Cambridge University Press, 2003), 91.
25. Descartes, *Meditations*, 18.
26. Descartes, *Meditations*, 20.
27. Descartes, *Meditations*, 18–19.
28. Jean-Luc Marion, *On the Ego and On God: Further Cartesian Questions* (New York: Fordham University Press, 2007), 4.
29. Descartes, *Meditations*, 19.
30. Andrew Ward, *Kant: The Three Critiques* (Cambridge, MA: Polity Press, 2006), 84n.
31. Ward, *Kant*, 105.
32. Pollard, *Dread Talk*, 71.
33. Perkins, "Wages of (Sin) Is Babylon," 239.
34. Chevannes, *Rastafari*, 167.
35. Adrian McFarlane, "The Epistemological Significance of 'I-an-I' as a Response to Quashie and Anancyism in Jamaican Culture," in *Chanting Down Babylon: The Rastafari Reader*, ed. Nathaniel S. Murrell, William D. Spencer, and Adrian A. McFarlane (Philadelphia: Temple University Press, 1998), 117.
36. Pollard, *Dread Talk*, 71.
37. Barrett, *Rastafarians*, 144.
38. Albert Balz, *Descartes and the Modern Mind* (New Haven, CT: Harden Books, 1967), 188.
39. McFarlane, "Epistemological Significance," 107.

6. THE LIMIT OF RASTAFARI COSMOLOGY: GENDER INEQUALITY AND THE FAILURE TO LIBERATE RASTA WOMEN

1. Barry Chevannes, *Rastafari: Roots and Ideology* (Syracuse, NY: Syracuse University Press, 1995), 172.
2. Chevannes, *Rastafari*, 188.
3. Yosef Ben-Jochannan, *We the Black Jews* (Baltimore, MD: Maryland Black Classic Press, 1983), 95.
4. Charles Price, *Becoming Rasta: Origins of Rastafari Identity in Jamaica* (New York: New York University Press, 2009), 170.
5. Ben-Jochannan, *We the Black Jews*, 90.
6. Chevannes, *Rastafari*, 179–80.
7. Randal L. Hepner, "The Belly of the Beast: The Rastafarian Movement in the Metropolitan United States," in *Chanting Down Babylon: The Rastafari Reader*, ed. Nathaniel S. Murrell, William D. Spencer, and Adrian A. McFarlane (Philadelphia: Temple University Press, 1998), 210–211.
8. Price, *Becoming Rasta*, 38.
9. Chevannes, *Rastafari*, 194.
10. Suzanne LaFont, "Gender Wars in Jamaica," *Identities: Global Studies in Culture and Power* 7, no. 2 (2000): 5.
11. Obiagele Lake, *Rastafari Women: Subordination in the Midst of Liberation Theology* (Durham, NC: Carolina Academic Press, 1998), 72.
12. Lake, *Rastafari Women*, 74.
13. LaFont, "Gender Wars in Jamaica," 12.
14. Timothy White, *Catch a Fire: The Life of Bob Marley* (New York: Macmillan, 2006), 225–226.
15. Lake, *Rastafari Women*, 77.
16. Chevannes, *Rastafari*, 174–175.
17. Lawrence Bamikole, "Rastafari as Philosophy and Praxis," in *The New Millenium*, ed. Michael Barnett (Syracuse, NY: Syracuse University Press, 2012), 138.
18. LaFont, "Gender Wars in Jamaica," 12.
19. Chevannes, *Rastafari*, 173.
20. Chevannes, *Rastafari*, 176–177.

21. Chevannes, *Rastafari*, 177.
22. LaFont, "Gender Wars in Jamaica," 7.
23. Leonard E. Barrett, *The Rastafarians* (Boston: Beacon Press, 1997), 269.
24. Lake, *Rastafari Women*, 94.
25. Patricia Hill Collins, *Black Sexual Politics: African Americans, Gender, and the New Racism* (New York: Routledge, 2005), 188.
26. Maureen Rowe, "The Woman in RastafarI," in Barnett, *Rastafari in the New Millenium*, 178.
27. Rowe, "Woman in RastafarI," 182.
28. Maureen Rowe, "Gender and Family Relations in RastafarI: A Personal Perspective," in Murrell, Spencer, and McFarlane, *Chanting Down Babylon*, 72.
29. Price, *Becoming Rasta*, 214.
30. Imani Tafari-Ama, "Rastawoman as Rebel: Case Studies in Jamaica," in Murrell, Spencer, and McFarlane, *Chanting Down Babylon*, 98.
31. Lake, *Rastafari Women*, 65.
32. Lake, *Rastafari Women*, 93.
33. Nathaniel S. Murrell, *Afro-Caribbean Religions: An Introduction to Their Historical, Cultural, and Sacred Traditions* (Philadelphia: Temple University Press, 2010), 302.
34. Diane J. Austin-Broos, "Pentecostals and Rastafarians: Cultural, Political, and Gender Relations of Two Religious Movements," *Social and Economic Studies* 36, no. 4 (1987): 19–20.
35. Shirley A. Hill, *Black Intimacies: A Gender Perspective on Families and Relationships* (Lanham, MD: Rowman and Littlefield, 2005), 204.

BIBLIOGRAPHY

Adams, Marianne. *Core Processes of Racial Identity Development*. In *New Perspectives on Racial Identity Development: A Theoretical and Practical Anthology*, ed. Charmaine L. Wijeyesinghe and Bailey W. Jackson III, 209–242. New York: New York University Press, 2001.

Akbar, Maysa, John Chambers Jr., and Vetta L. Sanders Thompson. "Race Identity, Afrocentric Values, and Self-Esteem in Jamaican Children." *Journal of Black Psychology* 27, no. 3 (2001): 341–358.

Allen, Richard. *The Concept of Self: A Study of Black Identity and Self-Esteem*. Detroit, MI: Wayne State University Press, 2004.

Alleyne, Mervyn. *The Construction and Representation of Race and Ethnicity in the Caribbean and the World*. Mona, Jamaica: University of the West Indies Press, 1988.

Alleyne, Mervyn. *Roots of Jamaican Culture*. London: Pluto Press, 1988.

Allport, Gordon. *The Individual and His Religion: A Classic Study of the Function of Religious Sentiment in the Personality of the Individual*. New York: Macmillan, 1950.

Ariew, Roger. "Descartes and Scholasticism: The Intellectual Background to Descartes' Thought." In *The Cambridge Companion to Descartes*, ed. John Cottingham, 58–90. Cambridge: Cambridge University Press, 1999.

Asante, Molefi. *The Afrocentric Idea*. Philadelphia: Temple University Press, 1998.

Atkinson, Robert. *The Life Story Interview*. Thousand Oaks, CA: SAGE, 1998.

Austin-Broos, Diane. "The Anthropology of Conversion: An Introduction." In *The Anthropology of Religious Conversion*, ed. Andrew Huckster and Stephen Glazier, 1–12. Lanham, MD: Rowman and Littlefield, 2003.

Austin-Broos, Diane. *Jamaica Genesis: Religion and the Politics of Moral Orders*. Chicago: University of Chicago Press, 1997.

Austin-Broos, Diane J. "Pentecostals and Rastafarians: Cultural, Political, and Gender Relations of Two Religious Movements." *Social and Economic Studies* 36, no. 4 (1987): 1–39.

Baker, Lee. *From Savage to Negro: Anthropology and the Construction of Race, 1896–1954*. Berkeley: University of California Press, 1998.

Balz, Albert. *Descartes and the Modern Mind*. New Haven, CT: Harden Books, 1967.

Bamikole, Lawrence. "Rastafari as Philosophy and Praxis." In Barnett, *Rastafari in the New Millenium*, 125–141.

Banks, William. *Black Intellectuals: Race and Respectability in American Life*. New York: Norton, 1999.

Barnett, Michael. "Rastafari Dialectism: The Epistemological Individualism and Connectivism of Rastafari." *Caribbean Quarterly* 48, no. 4 (2002): 54–61.

Barnett, Michael, ed. *Rastafari in the New Millennium*. Syracuse, NY: Syracuse University Press, 2014.

Barnett, Michael. "Rastafari in the New Millenium: Rastafari at the Dawn of the Fifth Epoch." In Barnett, *Rastafari in the New Millenium*, 1–12.

Barrett, Leonard. *The Rastafarians: Sounds of Cultural Dissonance*. Boston: Beacon Press, 1988.

Barrett, Leonard E. *The Rastafarians*. Boston: Beacon Press, 1997.

Bartlett, Lesley, and Dorothy Holland. "Theorizing the Space of Literacy Practices." *Ways of Knowing* 2, no. 1 (2002): 10–22.

Beckwith, Martha. *Black Roadways: A Study of Jamaican Folk Life*. 1929. Reprint, New York: Negro Universities Press, 1969.

Bedasse, Monique. "The Theology of the Twelve Tribes of Israel." *Journal of Black Studies* 40, no. 5 (2010): 960–973.

Ben-Jochannan, Yosef. *We the Black Jews*. Baltimore, MD: Black Classic Press, 1983.

Bilby, Kenneth. "Ethnogenesis in Guiana and Jamaica: Two Maroon Cases." In *History, Power, and Identity: Ethnogenesis in the Americas, 1492–1992*,

ed. Jonathan David Hill, 119–141. Iowa City: University of Iowa Press, 1996.
Bishton, Derek. *Black Heart Man*. London: Chatto and Windus, 1986.
Bogues, Anthony. *Black Heretics, Black Prophets: Radical Political Intellectuals*. New York: Routledge, 2003.
Bogues, Anthony. "Shades of Black and Red: Freedom and Socialism." *Small Axe* 1 (1997): 65–75.
Boison, Anton. *Exploration of the Inner World: A Study of Mental Disorder and Religious Experience*. New York: Harper and Bros., 1936.
Bones, Jah. "Language and Rastafari." In *The Language of Black Experience*, ed. David Sutcliffe and Ansel Wong, 37–51. New York: Basil Blackwell, 1986.
Booth, William. "On the Idea of Moral Economy." *American Political Science Review* 88, no. 3 (1994): 653–667.
Bowels, Samuel, and Herbert Gintis. "The Moral Economy of Communities: Structured Populations and the Evolution of Pro-Social Norms." *Evolution and Human Behavior* 19, no. 1 (1998): 3–25.
Boyd, James, C. *Garvey, Garveyism and the Antinomies in Black Redemption*. Trenton, NJ: Africa World Press, 2009.
Brathwaite, Edward. *The Development of Creole Society in Jamaica, 1770–1820*. Oxford: Oxford University Press, 1971.
Brathwaite, Edward. "Rebellion: Anatomy of the Slave Revolt of 1831/32 on Jamaica." *Jamaican Historical Society Bulletin* 8, no. 4 (1981): 80–96.
Brooks, A. A. *The History of Bedwardism, or the Jamaican Native Baptist Free Church, Union Camp, August Town, St Andrew, JA, B.W.I.* Saint Andrew, Jamaica: Gleaner, 1917.
Brown, Beverly. "George Liele: Black Baptist and Pan-Africanist, 1750–1826." *Savacou*, no. 11–12 (1975): 58–67.
Brown, Samuel. "Treatise on the Rastafarian Movement." *Caribbean Studies* 6, no. 1 (1967): 39–40.
Bryan, Patrick. *The Jamaican People, 1880–1902: Race, Class, and Social Control*. Mona, Jamaica: University of the West Indies Press, 2000.
Burkett, Randall. *Garveyism as a Religious Movement*. New York: Scarecrow Press and American Theological Library Association, 1978.
Burnard, Trevor. *Jamaica in the Age of Revolution*. Philadelphia: University of Pennsylvania Press, 2020.

Burnard, Trevor. *Mastery, Tyranny, and Desire: Thomas Thistlewood and His Slaves in the Anglo-Jamaican World*. Chapel Hill: University of North Carolina Press, 2009.

Burton, Richard. *Afro-Creole: Power, Opposition, and Play in the Caribbean*. Ithaca, NY: Cornell University Press, 1997.

Campbell, Horace. *Rasta and Resistance: From Marcus Garvey to Walter Rodney*. Trenton, NJ: Africa World Press, 1987.

Carnegie, Charles. "The Fate of Ethnography: Native Social Science in the English-Speaking Caribbean." *New West Indian Guide* 66, no. 1–2 (1992): 5–25.

Carnegie, Charles. "Garvey and the Black Transnation." *Small Axe*, no. 5 (1999): 48–71.

Cashmore, Ernest E. "More Than a Version: A Study in Reality Creation." *British Journal of Sociology* 30, no. 3 (1979): 307–321.

Cassidy, Frederick. *Jamaica Talk: Three Hundred Years of the English Language in Jamaica*. London: Macmillan Educational, 1971.

Cattell, Maria, and Jacob Climo. "Introduction: Meaning in Social Memory and History: Anthropological Perspectives." In *Social Memory and History: Anthropological Perspectives*, ed. Jacob Climo and Maria Cattell, 1–38. New York: Alta Mira Press, 2002.

Césaire, Aimé. *Discourse on Colonialism*. New York: Monthly Review Press, 2000.

Cha-jua, Sundiata K. "C. L. R. James, Blackness and the Making of a Neo-Marxist Diasporan Historiography." *Nature, Society, and Thought* 11, no. 1 (1998): 53–89.

Charles, Christopher. "Skin Bleaching, Self-Hate, and Black Identity in Jamaica." *Journal of Black Studies* 33, no. 6 (2003): 711–728.

Chesters, Graeme, and Ian Welsh. *Complexity and Social Movements: Multitude at the Edge of Chaos*. New York: Routledge, 2006.

Chevannes, Barry. "Jamaican Diasporic Identity: The Metaphor of Yaad." In *Nation Dance: Religion, Identity, and Cultural Difference in the Caribbean*, ed. Patrick Taylor, 129–137. Bloomington: Indiana University Press, 2001.

Chevannes, Barry. *Rastafari: Roots and Ideology*. Syracuse, NY: Syracuse University Press, 1995.

Chevannes, Barry. "Rastafarianism and the Class Struggle: The Search for a Methodology." In *Methodology and Change: Problems of Applied Social*

Science Research Techniques in the Commonwealth Caribbean, ed. L. Lindsay, 9–46. Working paper no. 14. Mona, Jamaica: Institute of Social and Economic Research, University of the West Indies, 1978.

Chevannes, Barry. "Rastafari and the Coming of Age: The Routinization of Rastafari in Jamaica." In Barnett, *Rastafari in the Millenium*, 13–34.

Chevannes, Barry. "Rastafari and the Exorcism of Racism and Classism." In Murrell, Spencer, and McFarlane, *Chanting Down Babylon*, 55–71.

Chevannes, Barry. "The Repairer of the Breach: Reverend Claudius Henry and Jamaican Society." In *Ethnicity in the Americas*, ed. Frances Henry. Chicago: Aldine, 1976.

Chevannes, Barry. "Revival and Black Struggle." *Savacou*, no. 5 (1971): 27–39.

Chisholm, Clinton. "The Rasta-Selassie-Ethiopian Connections." In Murrell, Spencer, and McFarlane, *Chanting Down Babylon*, 166–177.

Clarke, Peter B. *Black Paradise: The Rastafarian Movement*. Wellingborough: Aquarian Press, 1986.

Claton, Jace. "Nyabinghi." In *Africana: The Encyclopedia of the African and African American Experience*, 2nd ed., ed. Kwame Anthony Appiah and Henry Louis Gates Jr., 23–41. Oxford: Oxford University Press, 2007.

Coe, George. *Psychology of Religion*. Chicago: University of Chicago Press, 1917.

Collins, Patricia Hill. *Black Sexual Politics: African Americans, Gender, and the New Racism*. New York: Routledge, 2005.

Cone, James H. *God of the Oppressed*. New York: Seabury Press, 1975.

Cornell, Stephen, and Douglas Hartmann. *Ethnicity and Race: Making Identities in a Changing World*. Newbury Park, CA: Pine Forge Press, 1998.

Craton, Michael. *Searching for the Invisible Man: Slaves and Plantation Life in Jamaica*. Cambridge, MA: Harvard University Press, 1978.

Cronon, E. David. *Black Moses: The Story of Marcus Garvey and the Universal Negro Improvement Association*. Madison: University of Wisconsin Press, 1969.

Cross, William, Jr. "Black Families and Black Identity Development: Rediscovering the Distinction Between Self-Esteem and Reference Group Orientation." *Journal of Comparative Family Studies* 12, no. 1 (1981): 19–49.

Cross, William, Jr. "In Search of Blackness and Afrocentricity: The Psychology of Black Identity Change." In *Racial and Ethnic Identity: Psychological Development and Creative Development*, ed. Herbert Harris, Howard Blue, and Ezra H. Griffith, 33–51. New York: Routledge, 1993.

Cross, William, Jr. "The Negro-to-Black Conversion Experience." *Black World* 20, no. 9 (1971): 13–27.

Cross, William, Jr. "The Psychology of Nigrescence: Revising the Cross Model." In *The Handbook of Multicultural Counseling*, ed. Joseph Ponterotto, J. Manuel Casas, Lisa Suzuki, and Charlene Alexanders. Thousand Oaks, CA: SAGE, 1995.

Cross, William, Jr. *Shades of Black: Diversity in African American Identity*. Philadelphia: Temple University Press, 1991.

Crumley, Carole. "Exploring Venues of Social Memory." In *Social Memory and History: Anthropological Perspectives*, ed. Jacob Climo and Maria Cattell, 39–52. New York: Alta Mira Press, 2002.

Cruse, Harold. *The Crisis of the Negro Intellectual: A Historical Analysis of the Failure of Black Leadership*. New York: Quill, 1984.

Curtin, Philip. *The Atlantic Slave Trade: A Census*. Madison: University of Wisconsin Press, 1969.

Curtin, Philip. *Two Jamaicas: The Role of Ideas in a Tropical Colony, 1830–1865*. Westport, CT: Greenwood Press, 1955.

Dallas, Robert Charles. *History of the Maroons: From Their Origin to the Establishment of Their Chief at Sierra Leone*. Vol. 1. 1903. Reprint, London: Cass, 1968.

Dear, John. *The God of Peace: Toward a Theology of Non-Violence*. New York: Orbis Books, 1994.

De Greene, Kenyon. "Field Theoretic Framework for the Interpretation of the Evolution, Instability, Structural Change, and Management of Complex Systems." In *Chaos Theory in the Social Sciences: Foundations and Applications*, ed. Douglas Kiel and Euiel Elliot, 273–294. Ann Arbor: University of Michigan Press, 1997.

Descartes, René. *Meditations*. Trans. Donald A. Cress. Indianapolis, IN: Hackett, 1993.

Desmangles, Leslie G., Stephen D. Glazier, and Joseph M. Murphy. "Religion in the Caribbean." In *Understanding the Contemporary Caribbean*, ed. Richard S. Hillman and Thomas J. D'Agostino, 63–78. Boulder, CO: Lynne Rienner, 2009.

Drake, St. Clair. *The Redemption of Africa and Black Religion.* 1970. Reprint, Chicago: Third World Press, 1991.

Du Bois, W. E. B. *The Souls of Black Folk.* 1903. Reprint, New York: New American Library, 1969.

Edmonds, Ennis B. "Dread 'I' In-a-Babylon: Ideological Resistance and Cultural Revitalization." In Murrell, Spencer, and McFarlane, *Chanting Down Babylon*, 23–35.

Edmonds, Ennis B. *Rastafari: From Outcasts to Culture Bearers.* New York: Oxford University Press, 2003.

Edmonds, Ennis B. "The Structure and Ethos of Rastafari." In Murrell, Spencer, and McFarlane, *Chanting Down Babylon*, 349–360.

Edwards, Adolph. *Marcus Garvey: 1887–1940.* London: New Beacon, 1967.

Eisner, Gisela. *Jamaica, 1830–1930: A Study of Economic Growth.* Manchester: Manchester University Press, 1961.

Elkins, W. F. *Street Preachers, Faith Healers, and Herb Doctors in Jamaica, 1890–1925.* New York: Revisionist Press, 1977.

Erskine, Noel. *From Garvey to Marley: Rastafari Theology.* Gainesville: University Press of Florida, 2005.

Fahim, Hussein, and Katherine Helmer. "Themes and Counterthemes: The Berg Wartenstein Symposium." In *Indigenous Anthropology in Non-Western Countries*, ed. Hussein Fahim, 9–23. Durham, NC: Carolina Academic Press, 1982.

Fanon, Frantz. *Black Skin, White Masks.* New York: Grove Press, 1967.

Fanon, Frantz. *The Wretched of the Earth.* New York: Grove Press, 1963.

Fisher, Humphrey. "Conversion Reconsidered: Some Historical Aspects of Religious Conversion in Black Africa." *Africa* 43, no. 2 (1973): 27–40.

Forsythe, Dennis. *Rastafari: For the Healing of the Nation.* Kingston, Jamaica: Zaika, 1983.

Fredrickson, George. *Black Liberation: A Comparative History of Black Ideologies in the United States and South Africa.* New York: Oxford University Press, 1995.

Freire, Paulo. *Pedagogy of the Oppressed.* New York: Continuum, 1970.

Frey, Sylvia, and Betty Wood. *Come Shouting to Zion: African American Protestantism in the American South and British Caribbean to 1830.* Chapel Hill: University of North Carolina Press, 1998.

Garvey, Amy Jacques, ed. *The Philosophy and Opinions of Marcus Garvey: Or, Africa for the Africans.* 2 vols. Baltimore, MA: Majority Press, 1989.

Garvey, Marcus. 1937. "The Failure of Haile Selassie as Emperor." *Black Man*, March/April 1958.
Gayle, Clement. *George Liele: Pioneer Missionary to Jamaica*. St. Ann, Jamaica: Jamaica Baptist Union, 1982.
Gerlach, Luther, and Virginia Hine. *People, Power, Change: Movements of Social Transformation*. New York: Bobbs-Merrill, 1970.
Gibson, Boyce. *The Philosophy of Descartes*. New York: Russell and Russell, 1967.
Gillespie, V. Bailey. *Religious Conversion and Personal Identity*. Birmingham, AL: Religious Education Press, 1979.
Gilroy, Paul. *The Black Atlantic: Modernity and Double Consciousness*. Cambridge, MA: Harvard University Press, 1992.
Glazier, Stephen. *Being and Becoming a Rastafarian: Notes on the Anthropology of Religious Conversion*, ed. Werner Zips, 103–117. Kingston, Jamaica: Ian Randle, 2006.
Goerner, Sally. "Chaos and Deep Ecology." In *Chaos Theory in Psychology*, ed. Frederick D. Abraham and Albert R. Gilgen, 83–92. Westport, CT: Praeger, 1995.
Goffman, Erving. *Stigma: Notes on the Management of Spoiled Identity*. New York: Simon and Schuster, 1963.
Gomez, Michael A. *Exchanging Our Country Marks: The Transformation of African Identities in the Colonial and Antebellum South*. Chapel Hill: University of North Carolina Press, 1998.
Gordon, Ernle. "Garvey and Black Liberation Theology." In *Garvey: His Work and Impact*, ed. Rupert Lewis and Patrick Bryan, 116–129. Trenton, NJ: Africa World Press, 1991.
Gosner, Kevin. *Soldiers of the Virgin: The Moral Economy of a Colonial Maya Rebellion*. Tucson: University of Arizona Press, 1992.
Gray, Obika. *Radicalism and Social Change in Jamaica, 1960–1972*. Knoxville: University of Tennessee Press, 1991.
Greenbaum, Susan. *More Than Black: Afro-Cubans in Tampa*. Gainesville: University Press of Florida, 2002.
Hall, Stuart. "Introduction: Who Needs an 'Identity'?" In *Questions of Cultural Identity*, ed. Stuart Hall and Paul Du Gay, 1–17. Thousand Oaks, CA: SAGE, 1996.
Hall, Stuart. "Negotiating Identity." *New Left Review* 209 (1995): 3–14.

Hannah, Barbara M. Blake. "The Meaning of Rastafari for World Critique: Rasta Within a Universal Concept." In *Rastafari: A Universal Philosophy in the Third Millennium*, ed. Werner Zips, 45–63. Kingston, Jamaica: Ian Randle, 2006.

Hansing, Katrin. "Faith: Rastafari." In *Cuba*, vol. 1, ed. Alan West Duran, 179–192. New York: Charles Scribner's Sons, 2012.

Hansing, Katrin. *Rasta, Race and Revolution*. Piscataway, NJ: Transaction, 2006.

Harding, Susan. "Convicted by the Holy Spirit: The Rhetoric of Fundamentalist Baptist Conversion." *American Ethnology* 14, no. 1 (1987): 167–181.

Harrison, Faye. "Introduction: Expanding the Discourse on Race." *American Anthropologist* 100, no. 3 (1998): 609–631.

Hawkins, Mike. *Social Darwinism in European and American Thought, 1860–1945: Nature as Model and Nature as Threat*. Cambridge: Cambridge University Press, 1997.

Hearn, John. "Landscape with Faces." *Caribbean Quarterly* 54, nos. 1–2 (2008): 101–129.

Hefner, Robert W. "Introduction: World Building and the Rationality of Conversion." In *Conversion to Christianity: Historical and Anthropological Perspectives on a Great Transformation*, ed. Robert W. Hefner, 3–46. Berkeley: University of California Press, 1993.

Heirich, Max. "Change of Heart: A Test of Some Widely Held Theories About Religious Conversion." *American Journal of Sociology* 83, no. 3 (1977): 653–680.

Helms, Janet. "Introduction: Review of Racial Identity Terminology." In *Black and White Racial Identity: Theory, Research, and Practice*, ed. Janet Helms, 148–161. Westport, CT: Greenwood Press, 1990.

Helms, Janet. "An Update of Helms's White and People of Color Racial Identity Models." In *The Handbook of Multicultural Counseling*, ed. Joseph Ponterotto, J. Manuel Casa, Lisa Suzuki, and Charlene Alexander, 22–29. Thousand Oaks, CA: SAGE, 1995.

Henderson, Walter. *The Silver Bluff Church: A History of Negro Baptist Churches in America*. Washington, DC: Press of R. L. Pendleton, 1910.

Henry, Beresford. *The Growth of Corporate Black Identity Among Afro-Caribbean People in Birmingham, England*. PhD diss., University of Warwick, 1982.

Henry, Paget. *Caliban's Reason: Introducing Afro-Caribbean Philosophy*. New York: Routledge, 2000.

Henry, Paget. "Rastafari and the Reality of Dread." In *Existence in Black: An Anthology of Black Existential Philosophy*, ed. Lewis Gordon, 157–164. New York: Routledge, 1997.

Hepner, Randal L. "Chanting Down Babylon in the Belly of the Beast: The Rastafarian Movement in the Metropolitan United States." In Murrell, Spencer, and McFarlane, *Chanting Down Babylon*, 117–134.

Heuman, Gad. *"The Killing Time": The Morant Bay Rebellion in Jamaica*. London: Macmillan Caribbean, 1994.

Hill, Jonathan. "Introduction: Ethnogenesis in the Americas, 1492–1992." In *History, Power, and Identity: Ethnogenesis in the Americas, 1492–1992*, ed. Jonathan Hill. Iowa City: University of Iowa Press, 1996.

Hill, Robert. *Dread History: Leonard P. Howell and Millenarian Visions in the Early Rastafari Religion*. Chicago: Research Associates School Times / Frontline Distribution International, 2001.

Hill, Shirley A. *Black Intimacies: A Gender Perspective on Families and Relationships*. Lanham, MD: Rowman and Littlefield, 2005.

Hillman, Richard, and Thomas D'Agostino, eds. *Understanding the Contemporary Caribbean*. Boulder, CO: Lynne Rienner, 2009.

Hobson, Fred. *But Now I See: The White Southern Social Conversion Narrative*. Baton Rouge: Louisiana State University Press, 1999.

Holland, Dorothy, and William Lachicotte. "Vygotsky, Mead and the New Sociocultural Studies of Identity." In *The Cambridge Companion to Vygotsky*, ed. Harry Daniels, Michael Cole, and James Wertsch. Cambridge: Cambridge University Press, 2007.

Holland, Dorothy, William Lachicotte, Deborah Skinner, and Carole Cain, eds. *Identity and Agency in Cultural Worlds*. Cambridge, MA: Harvard University Press, 1998.

Holland, Dorothy, and Jean Lave. *History in Person: Enduring Struggles, Contentious Practice, Intimate Identities*. Santa Fe, NM: School of American Research, 2001.

Holt, Thomas C. *The Problem of Freedom: Race, Labor, and Politics in Jamaica and Britain, 1832–1938*. Baltimore, MD: Johns Hopkins University Press, 1992.

Holt, Thomas C. *The Problem of Race in the Twenty-First Century.* Cambridge, MA: Harvard University Press, 2000.

Homiak, John. "Dub History: Soundings on Rastafari Livity and Language." In *Rastafari and Other African-Caribbean Worldviews*, ed. Barry Chevannes, 169–185. New Brunswick, NJ: Rutgers University Press, 1998.

Homiak, John. "Movements of Jah People: From Sounds Capes to Media Scape." In Pulis, *Religion, Diaspora, and Cultural Identity*, 42–59.

Homiak, John. "The Mystic Revelation of the Rasta Far-Eye: Visionary Communication in a Prophetic Movement." In *Dreaming: Anthropological and Psychological Interpretations*, ed. Barbara Tedlock, 58–73. Santa Fe, NM: School of American Research, 1987.

Hopkins, Elizabeth. "The Nyabinghi Cult of Southwestern Uganda." In *Rebellion in Black Africa*, ed. Robert Rotberg, 9–27. New York: Oxford University Press, 1971.

Hornstein, Donald. "Complexity, Theory, Adaptation, and Administrative Law." *Duke Law Journal* 54, no. 4 (2005): 913–960.

Horton, Robin. "African Conversion." *Africa* 41, no. 2 (1971): 85–108.

Horton, Robin. "On the Rationality of Conversion." *Africa* 45, no. 3 (1975): 219–235.

James, William. *Varieties of Religious Experience.* New York: Random House, 1929.

James, Winston. *Holding Aloft the Banner of Ethiopia: Caribbean Radicalism in Early Twentieth Century America.* New York: Verso Books, 1999.

Jasper, James. *The Art of Moral Protest: Culture, Biography, and Creativity in Social Movements.* Chicago: University of Chicago Press, 1997.

Kebede, Alem Seghed. "Decentered Movements: The Case of the Structural and Perceptual Versatility of the Rastafari." *Sociological Spectrum* 21, no. 2 (2001): 175–205.

Kebede, Alem Seghed, and J. David Knotterus. "Beyond the Tales of Babylon: The Ideational Components and Social Psychological Foundations of Rastafari." *Sociological Perspectives* 41, no. 3 (1998): 499–517.

Kebede, Alem Seghed, Timothy Shriver, and J. David Knotterus. "Social Movement Endurance: Collective Identity and the Rastafari." *Sociological Inquiry* 70, no. 3 (2000): 313–337.

Keith, Nelson, and Novella Keith. *The Social Origins of Democratic Socialism in Jamaica.* Philadelphia: Temple University Press, 1992.

King, Stephen. *Reggae, Rastafari, and the Rhetoric of Social Control.* Jackson: University Press of Mississippi, 2002.

Kitzinger, Sheila. "Protest and Mysticism: The Rastafari Cult of Jamaica." *Journal for the Scientific Study of Religion* 8, no. 2 (1969): 240–262.

Kitzinger, Sheila. "The Rastafarian Brethren of Jamaica." *Comparative Studies in Society and History* 9, no. 1 (1966): 34–39.

Klein, Herbert. *The Middle Passage: Comparative Studies in the Atlantic Slave Trade.* Princeton, NJ: Princeton University Press, 1978.

Kors, Alan C. "Just and Arbitrary Authority in Enlightenment Thought." In *Modern Enlightenment and the Rule of Reason*, ed. John C. McCarthy, 22–39. Washington, DC: Catholic University of America Press, 1998.

LaFont, Suzanne. "Gender Wars in Jamaica." *Identities: Global Studies in Culture and Power* 7, no. 2 (2000): 233–260.

Lake, Obliagele. "The Many Voices of Rastafari Women: Sexual Subordination in the Midst of Liberation." *New West Indian Guide* 68, no. 3/4 (1994): 235–258.

Lake, Obliagele. *Rastafari Women: Subordination in the Midst of Liberation Theology.* Durham, NC: Carolina Academic Press, 1998.

Lewis, Rupert. "Garvey's Forerunners: Love and Bedward." *Race and Class* 28, no. 3 (1987): 29–40.

Lewis, Rupert. "Marcus Garvey and the Early Rastafarians: Continuity and Discontinuity." In Murrell, Spencer, and McFarlane, *Chanting Down Babylon*, 145–159.

Lewis, William F. *Soul Rebels: The Rastafari.* Long Grove, IL: Waveland Press, 1993.

Lott, Tommy L., ed. *African-American Philosophy: Selected Readings.* Hoboken, NJ: Pearson Education, 2002.

Mack, Douglas. *From Babylon to Rastafari: Origin and History of the Rastafari Movement.* Chicago: Research Associates School Times, 1999.

Manning, Patrick. *The African Diaspora: A History Through Culture.* New York: Columbia University Press, 2009.

Marion, Jean-Luc. *On the Ego and On God: Further Cartesian Questions.* New York: Fordham University Press, 2007.

Martin, Tony. *Race First: The Ideological and Organizational Struggles of Marcus Garvey and the Universal Negro Improvement Association.* Cambridge, MA: Majority Press, 1970.

McFarlane, Adrian. "The Epistemological Significance of 'I-an-I' as a Response to Quashie and Anancyism in Jamaican Culture." In Murrell, Spencer, and McFarlane, *Chanting Down Babylon*, 107–124.
McPherson, Everton S. P. *The Culture-History and Universal Spread of Rastafari: Two Essays*. New York: Black International Iyabinghi Press, 1996.
Meeks, Brian. *Narratives of Resistance: Jamaica, Trinidad, the Caribbean*. Mona, Jamaica: University of the West Indies Press, 2000.
Metzinger, Thomas. *The Ego Tunnel: The Science of the Mind and the Myth of the Self*. New York: Basic Books, 2010.
Murrell, Nathaniel S. *Afro-Caribbean Religions: An Introduction to Their Historical, Cultural, and Sacred Traditions*. Philadelphia: Temple University Press, 2010.
Murrell, Nathaniel S. "The Rastafari Phenomenon." In Murrell, Spencer, and McFarlane, *Chanting Down Babylon*, 1–22.
Murrell, Nathaniel S., William D. Spencer, and Adrian A. McFarlane, eds. *Chanting Down Babylon: The Rastafari Reader*. Philadelphia: Temple University Press, 1998.
Murrell, Nathaniel, and Burchell Taylor. "Rastafari's Messianic Ideology and Caribbean Theology of Liberation." In Murrell, Spencer, and McFarlane, *Chanting Down Babylon*, 390–412.
Murrell, Nathaniel S., and Lewin Williams. "The Black Biblical Hermeneutics of Rastafari." In Murrell, Spencer, and McFarlane, *Chanting Down Babylon*, 326–348.
Mutabaruka. "Rasta from Experience." In *Rastafari: A Universal Philosophy in the Third Millennium*, ed. Werner Zips, 115–137. Kingston, Jamaica: Ian Randle, 2006.
Nagashima, Yoshiko. *Rastafarian Music in Contemporary Jamaica: A Study of Socioreligious Music of the Rastafarian Movement in Jamaica*. Tokyo: Institute for the Study of Languages and Cultures of Asia and Africa, 1984.
Nartey, Kojo. *Dreadlocks, Marijuana, and Rastafari*. Accra, Ghana: Roots Society, 1999.
Nelson, Charmaine. *Slavery, Geography, and Empire in Nineteenth-Century Marine Landscapes of Montreal and Jamaica*. New York: Routledge, 2016.
Nettleford, Rex. *Caribbean Cultural Identity: The Case of Jamaica*. Los Angeles: University of California Press, 1979.

Nettleford, Rex. "Discourse on Rastafarian Reality." In Murrell, Spencer, and McFarlane, *Chanting Down Babylon*, 311–325.

Nettleford, Rex. "From the Cross to the Throne: Rastafari in the New Millennium." Keynote address, Folk Filosofi symposium. University of the West Indies, Mona, Jamaica, 1999.

Nettleford, Rex. *Identity, Race and Protest in Jamaica*. New York: William Morrow, 1972.

Niaah, Jahlani. "Nettleford and Rastafari's Inner Landscape." *Caribbean Quarterly* 57, nos. 3–4 (2011): 49–63.

Niaah, Jahlani. "The Rastafari Presence in Ethiopia: A Contemporary Perspective." In Barnett, *Rastafari in the New Millenium*, 66–88.

Olusanya, G. O. "Garvey and Nigeria." In *Garvey, Europe, the Americas*, ed. Rupert Lewis and Maureen Lewis, 41–53. Trenton, NJ: Africa World Press, 1994.

Onuora, Adwoa Ntozake. "Exploring RastafarI's Pedagogic, Communicative, and Instructional Potential in the Caribbean: The Life and Works of Mutabaruka as a Case Study." In Barnett, *Rastafari in the New Millenium*, 142–158.

Owens, Joseph. *Dread: The Rastafarians of Jamaica*. (Kingston, Jamaica: United Co-Operative Printers, 1995).

Patterson, Orlando. *The Sociology of Slavery: Black Society in Jamaica, 1655–1838*. Boston: Polity Press, 2022.

Payne, Anthony. *Politics in Jamaica*. New York: St. Martin's Press, 1994.

Perkins, Anna Kasafi. "The Wages of (Sin) Is Babylon." In Barnett, *Rastafari in the New Millenium*, 239–254.

Phillipo, James. *Jamaica: Its Past and Present State*. 1843. Reprint, Freeport, NY: Books for Libraries Press, 1971.

Pierson, Roscoe. "Alexander Bedward and the Jamaica Native Baptist Free Church." *Lexington Theological Quarterly* 4, no. 3 (1969): 65–76.

Pinn, Anthony B., ed. *African American Religious Cultures*. Vol. 2. Santa Barbara, CA: ABC-CLIO, 2009.

Plummer, Nicole. "Untold Stories: Using Oral History to Explore the Coral Gardens 'Incident,' 1963." In *Encyclopedia of African-American Culture and History*, 2nd ed., vol. 5, ed. Colin A. Palmer, 333–354. Detroit, MI: Macmillan Reference, 2006.

Pollard, Velma. *Dread Talk: The Language of Rastafari*. Montreal: McGill-Queen's University Press, 2000.

Post, Ken. *Arise Ye Starvellings: The Jamaican Labour Rebellion of 1938 and Its Aftermath*. Boston: Martinus Nijhoff, 1978.

Price, Charles. *Becoming Rasta: Origins of Rastafari Identity in Jamaica*. New York: New York University Press, 2009.

Price, Charles. "'Cleave to the Black': Expressions of Ethiopianism in Jamaica." *New West Indian Guide* 77, no. 1/2 (2003): 31–64.

Price, Charles. "Political and Radical Aspects of the Rastafari Movement in Jamaica." *Nature, Society, and Thought* 13, no. 2 (2001): 155–180.

Pulis, John. "Bridging Troubled Waters: Moses Baker, George Liele, and the African American Diaspora to Jamaica." In *Moving On: Black Loyalists in the Afro-Atlantic World*, ed. John Pulis, 111–137. New York: Garland, 1999.

Pulis, John, ed. *Religion, Diaspora, and Cultural Identity: A Reader in the Anglophone Caribbean*. New York: Gordon and Breach, 1999.

Pullen-Burry, Bessie. *Ethiopia Revisited: Jamaica in Exile*. London: T. F. Unwin, 1971.

Purcell, Trevor. *Banana Fallout: Class, Color, and Culture Among West Indians in Costa Rica*. Los Angeles: Center for Afro-American Studies, University of California, Los Angeles, 1993.

Robotham, Don. "The Development of a Black Ethnicity in Jamaica." In *Garvey: His Work and Impact*, ed. Rupert Lewis and Paul Bryan. Trenton, NJ: Africa World Press, 1994.

Rodney, Walter. *Groundings with My Brothers*. Chicago: Research Associates School Times, 1996.

Rowe, Maureen. "Gender and Family Relationships in RastafarI: A Personal Perspective." In Murrell, Spencer, and McFarlane, *Chanting Down Babylon*, 72–88.

Rowe, Maureen. "The Woman in Rastafari." In *Caribbean Quarterly Monograph: Rastafari*, ed. Rex Nettleford, 13–21. Mona, Jamaica: Caribbean Quarterly, University of West Indies, 1985.

Rowe, Maureen Rowe. "The Woman in RastafarI." In Barnett, *Rastafari in the New Millenium*, 177–189.

Sarkar, Husain. *Descartes' Cogito: Saved from the Great Shipwreck*. Cambridge: Cambridge University Press, 2003.

Savishinsky, Neil. "Rastafari in the Promised Land: The Spread of a Jamaican Socioreligious Movement Among the Youth of West Africa." *African Studies Review* 37, no. 3 (1994): 19–50.

Schuler, Monica. *Alas, Alas, Kongo: A Social History of Indentured African Migration into Jamaica, 1841–1865.* Baltimore, MD: Johns Hopkins University Press, 1980.

Scott, William. "And Ethiopia Shall Stretch Forth Its Hands: The Origins of Ethiopianism in Afro-American Thought." *Umoja* 2, no. 1 (1978): 1–13.

Shepperson, George. "Ethiopianism: Past and Present." In *Christianity in Tropical Africa: Studies Presented and Discussed at the Seventh International Seminar, University of Ghana, April 1965,* ed. C. G. Baëta, 163–185. New York: Oxford University Press, 1968.

Sherlock, Philip, and Hazel Bennett. *The Story of the Jamaican People.* Kingston, Jamaica: Ian Randle, 1998.

Simpson, George Eaton. "The Ras Tafari Movement in Jamaica: A Study of Race and Class Conflict." *Social Forces* 34, no. 2 (1955): 167–171.

Smith, M. G., Roy Augier, and Rex Nettleford. *The Rastafari in Kingston, Jamaica.* Mona, Jamaica: Institute of Social and Economic Research, University of the West Indies, 1960.

Smith, Robert T. *Jamaica Genesis: Religion and the Politics of Moral Orders.* Chicago: University of Chicago Press, 1997.

Spencer, William David. "The First Chant: Leonard Howell's *The Promised Key.*" In Murrell, Spencer, and McFarlane, *Chanting Down Babylon*, 361–389.

Tafari, Ikael. *Rastafari in Transition: The Politics of Cultural Confrontation in Africa and the Caribbean (1966–1988).* Kingston, Jamaica: Miguel Lorne, 2001.

Tafari-Ama, Imani. "Rastawoman as Rebel: Case Studies in Jamaica." In Murrell, Spencer, and McFarlane, *Chanting Down Babylon*, 89–106.

Taylor, Patrick. "Perspectives on History in Rastafari Thought." *Studies in Religion* 19, no. 2 (1990): 191–205.

Thomas, Deborah. *Modern Blackness: Nationalism, Globalization, and the Politics of Culture in Jamaica.* Durham, NC: Duke University Press, 2004.

Thompson, Joseph. "From Judah to Jamaica: The Psalms in Rastafari Reggae." *Religion and the Arts,* no. 16 (2012): 328–356.

Thwaite, Daniel. *The Seething African Pot: A Study of Black Nationalism, 1882–1935.* London: Constable, 1936.

Tucker, Jeremy. *The Role of Cosmology in Societal Change: The Development of Indigenous Agricultural Technology Within the Rastafari Movement in Jamaica.* Master's thesis, York University, Ontario, Canada, 1991.

Turner, Mary. *Slaves and Missionaries: The Disintegration of Jamaican Slave Society, 1787–1834*. Champaign: University of Illinois Press, 1982.
van Dijk, Frank. *JAHmaica: Rastafari and Jamaican Society, 1930–1990*. Amsterdam, Netherlands: ISOR, 1993.
van Dijk, Frank. "Sociological Means: Colonial Reactions to the Radicalization of Rastafari in Jamaica, 1956–1959." *New West Indian Guide* 69, no. 1/2 (1995): 67–101.
Vincent, Theodore G. *Black Power and the Garvey Movement*. Berkeley, CA: Ramparts Press, 1971.
Walters, Anita. *Race, Class, and Political Symbols: Rastafari and Reggae in Jamaican Politics*. Piscataway, NJ: Transaction, 1989.
Walzer, Michael. *Exodus and Revolution*. New York: Basic Books, 1985.
Ward, Andrew. *Kant: The Three Critiques*. Cambridge, MA: Polity Press, 2006.
White, Timothy. *Catch a Fire: The Life of Bob Marley*. New York: Macmillan, 2006.
Williams, Emily Allen. "Rastafarians." In *Encyclopedia of Latin American History and Culture*, 2nd ed., ed. Jay Kinsbruner and Erick D. Langer, 5:235–257. New York: Charles Scribner's Sons, 2008.
Wilmot, Swithin. *Freedom in Jamaica: Challenges and Opportunities, 1838–1865*. St. Ann, Jamaica: Jamaica Information Services, 1997.
Wintz, Cary D., ed. *African-American Political Thought, 1890–1930: Washington, Du Bois, Garvey, and Randolph*. New York: M. E. Sharpe, 1996.
Wynter, Cadence. "Rodney and Rastafari: Cultural Identity in 1960s Jamaica." In Barnett, *Rastafari in the New Millenium*, 300–309.
Yawney, Carole D., "Lions in Babylon: The Rastafarians of Jamaica as a Visionary Movement." Ph.D. diss., McGill University, 1978.
Yawney, Carole D. "Moving with the Dawtas of Rastafari: From Myth to Reality." In *Arise Ye Mighty People! Gender, Class and Race in Popular Struggles.*, ed. Terisa Turner, 63–89. Trenton, NJ: Africa World Press, 1994.
Yawney, Carole D. "Only Visitors Here: Representing Rastafari into the 21st Century." In Pulis, *Religion, Diaspora, and Cultural Identity*, 153–188.

INDEX

ackee, 97
aesthetics, Rastafari, 60, 63; as anticolonial, 134, 135; dreadlocks in, 59, 60, 98, 134, 135–36; and ethos of Blackness, 85–90, 135; naturalism of, 98–99; reggae and, 85–86, 103; sexism in, 169, 170
Africa: belonging to, 129, 133; duality of, 129–30; geography of, 130–31; preslavery ties to, 2, 6–7, 22–24, 70, 130–31, 133, 160; return to, 52, 54, 70–71, 83, 118, 125–26
African culture, 41, 44, 48, 89, 108; food in, 96, 97; redemption of, 44–45, 52–53. *See also* West African societies
African normative heritage, 68
African slaves: *vs.* Creole slaves, 8–9, 18–20, 22; spirituality of, 22–28. *See also* slavery, resistance to
Afrocentric normativity, vii–viii, xi, 58, 61–63, 68, 158, 164; aesthetics and, 87–88, 135; and the Bible, 48–50, 103, 106–7; Jamaican establishment grappling with, 132–33; in language, 139, 152–54; and nature, 72–73, 74; in postcolonial Jamaica, 74–77, 84, 131–32; righteousness and, 163
Afro-Jamaican subjectivity, 89; children socialized in, 20; colonizers' awareness of, 8–9; communal ties of, ix, 9, 17, 29–31; Garveyism and, 46–47; heterogeneity of, 7; and I-talk, 127–28; Maroons and, 20; Rastafari cosmology and, 2, 20, 28, 33–34; religious communities nurturing, viii–ix, 9, 19–20, 34–35; and resistance to slavery, 2, 3, 14, 18–20, 27–28
Afro-Judaism, 158–59, 160–63

Amharic, 112, 136, 161
ancestors, spiritual continuity with, 65
ancestral knowledge, 23
Anglo-Jamaican subjectivity, 2, 3, 8, 9, 13; of Creole slaves, 19, 22; Maroons and, 20; slaves' resistance to, 13–14
animals, eating, 92
animism, 66
Arawak people, 15
Asante, Molefi, 63
assimilation: dietary, 95, 131; of Jamaican elites, 166; resisting, 129, 131, 136
Augier, Roy, 74
Augustine, 119
Austin-Broos, Diane, 185

Babylon, 46, 83, 86; Blackness opposing, 63; in Bobo Dread, 82–83, 159–60, 161–62; colonialism as, 27, 57–58, 59–60, 63, 129, 142–43, 146; definition of, 59–60, 70; *vs.* Ethiopia, 71–72; I-talk and, 154–55; Jamaica as, 77, 129; liberation from, 119–20, 123–24, 125, 161–62; nature oppressed by, 72–73, 74; Rastafari aesthetics and, 85, 98; Rastas' relevance to, 132–33; sexism of, 173, 176, 181, 184; sin and, 119–20; slavery associated with, 70
Baker, Moses, 49
Bamikole, Lawrence, 120–21
Barnett, Michael, 62, 82, 93

Barrett, Leonard, 137, 151–52, 172
Bedwardites, 48, 49, 51, 56, 66
Ben-Jochannan, Yosef, 161
Bennett, Hazel, 5–6, 12–13
the Bible: authority of, 113–15; Eurocentric readings of, 110, 111–12; Hebrew, 78, 81, 84; messianic model of interpreting, x, 53–54, 101, 113–14, 117, 123–24, 126; people of African descent in, x, 55, 78, 104–7, 110–14, 115–18, 121–22, 124; Psalms, 123; Revelation, 117–18, 123; slavery and, 112; translation of, 112. *See also* the Bible, Afrocentric appropriation of; hermeneutics, Rastafari
the Bible, Afrocentric appropriation of, 57–58, 103–6, 109–11, 112–13, 114–15, 133; "Blackening" the Bible, 116–17; in Bobo Dread, 82; Haile Selassie I and, 53–54; identity rooted in, 121–22; in Nyahbinghi, 79, 80, 81; by Revivalists, 48, 50, 186; women in, 157, 169–70, 173, 178–79, 181–83, 185, 186. *See also* hermeneutics, Rastafari
Black Codes, 13
Black communities. *See* collectivism
Black consciousness, I-talk and, x–xi, 127–28, 135–39, 152–55
Black Jamaicans: future of, x, 101, 123–24, 125; in image of God, 56, 61, 67–68, 69, 104–7, 115, 121

Black liberation theology, 69
Black Messiah. *See* Haile Selassie I, divinity of
Blackness: academic discussion of, xi; aesthetics of, 98–99; African citizenship reduced to, 12, 13; and collective identity, 29–32, 33–34, 43, 86, 87–89, 134, 138–39, 162; as curse, 116; defining, vii–viii, xii; dehumanization of, 13; internalized fear of, 75, 89; nature and, 90; plurality of, 85; reggae and, 86; three mansions' approaches to, 85. *See also* Blackness, divinity of; theology of Blackness
Blackness, divinity of, 55, 67–70; and God's image, 56, 61, 67–68, 69, 104–7, 115–17, 121; I-talk and, 133, 138–39, 141, 149–51, 153–54; restoration of, 78, 97, 121–24. *See also* Haile Selassie I, divinity of
Black Power, 47
Black pride, 115–16
Bobo Dread, 73–74, 77, 82–83; Afro-Jewish influence on, 159, 160–62; Babylon in, 82–83, 159–60, 161–62; Black divinity in, 82–83; emergence of, 83; righteousness and, 161, 163; seclusion of, 74, 82–83, 159–60; structure of, 172, 175; women in, 158, 168, 171–75, 182
the body: Afrocentric, 98; Cartesian view of, 146–47; female, 167–70, 173–74, 177, 182;

marijuana and, 81; nature and, 90, 92–93, 95–97, 174; as part of the I-an-I, 147. *See also* food
Bogle, Paul, 30–31, 34, 35
Brazil, slave revolts in, 18
the British. *See* colonialism; colonizers
Burkett, Randall, 43
Burnard, Trevor, 7, 20–21
Burrus, 80

Campbell, Horace, 94–95
capitalism, rejection of, 93
Chevannes, Barry: on aesthetics, 60; on Bobo Dread, 73–74, 159, 172, 173–75, 176; on diet, 96–97; on I-an-I, 150; on origins of Rastafari movement, 26–27, 58; on women, 172, 173–75, 176; on Youth Black Faith, 58, 134
childcare, 165
Chisholm, Clinton, 107–8
Christianity, 58, 61, 66, 140, 154; alienating nature of, x, 101, 104, 155, 162–63; Descartes's relationship with, 141–42, 143–45, 153–54; divine-human separation in, 139; heaven in, 125; monolithic, resistance to, 66, 77–78, 85, 115; Myal reinterpreting, 49; Rastafari cosmology bound to, 104, 108–9, 118, 126, 141; Rastafari cosmology challenging, 76–77, 102, 103–4, 109–10, 125, 140–41; sexism in, 157, 183; sin in, 118–19
Code Noir, 13

collectivism, 123–25, 139–40, 150–53, 161–62; in Garveyism, 39–41, 44; nature and, 93; in reasoning, 80, 82; slave revolts depending on, 17–18; women excluded from, 177–78, 181. *See also* I-an-I

colonialism: Afrocentric normativity contesting, 58, 63, 67–70, 111, 122, 139; aims of, 3; and diet, 95, 97; distrust of institutions of, 57–58, 63; Ethiopian resistance to, 55; extractive, 3, 9–11; gender inequality in, 157–58, 166–67, 177–78, 179, 180, 185; and Indigenous people, 6; internalized, 67, 111, 115–16, 121–22; and land appropriation, 6–7; low self-esteem caused by, 67; reconstruction in wake of, 88–89; sin and, 119–20. *See also* colonialism, Jamaican resistance to; colonizers

colonialism, Jamaican resistance to, 1–4, 13–14, 20–21, 142; Garvey consolidating, 56; in language, 139; marijuana as form of, 134–35; spiritual, 22–28, 48–52, 53–54, 57–58

colonizers, 1, 10; Anglo-Jamaican subjectivity as goal of, 3, 8–9; laziness of, 12; mores of, 58, 67–68, 72; religion of, 24, 48–49, 60–61, 69, 87, 104–6, 109–10; wealth of, 11, 12. *See also* Christianity

color symbolism, 135

consciousness, x–xi, 127–28, 153, 154–55

cosmology, Rastafari, 1, 4, 14; Africa in, 129–30; Afro-Jamaican subjectivity and, 2, 20, 28, 33–34; and Black identity, viii–ix, xii, 30; Christian discomfort with, 76–77, 102, 103; criticisms of, 102, 107–9; dissemination of, 101–2; dualism at heart of, 71–72, 120; "earthforce" in, ix, 34, 65, 66, 90; founding of, 68–69; Garveyism and, viii, 45–46, 47, 50, 51–52, 59, 160, 164, 187; holy living in, 35–36, 65; Howell and, 34–36, 68–69; Jewish influence on, 158–59; Judeo-Christian establishment and, 58, 61, 66, 140, 154; lack of institutional strictures in, 84; millenarian aspect of, 52; nature in, 90–92, 99–100; "orthodoxy" and, 122–23; pluralism inherent in, 139; as postcolonial technology, 70; prophets of, 68–69; reconstructive project of, 88–89; Revival movement and, viii–ix, 26–27, 29, 62–63; righteousness in, 161–63; self-differentiation in, 154–55; social activism at core of, 68–69; three mansions of, 66, 77–78, 83–85; uniformity of, 186–87; White God rejected by, x, 33–35, 61, 67–70, 101, 109,

115, 183. *See also* I-talk; women in Rastafari cosmology
cosmology, West African, 7
Creole English, 7, 151
Creole slaves, 8–9, 18–20, 22

dance, 25
Dangerous Drug Law, 134–35
Dear, John, 118–19
Descartes, René, 128, 140; aims of, 141–42, 143–44; "evil genius" in, 142–43, 144–45; privileged status of, 146, 149; on radical doubt, 143–44, 146, 148–49; rationalism of, 146–49. *See also* epistemology, Rastafari; I-talk
diet. *See* food
disunity, 39–40, 97–98
divinity. *See* Blackness, divinity of; Haile Selassie I, divinity of
dreadlocks, 59, 60, 98, 134, 135–36
drumming, 79–80, 81
Du Bois, W. E. B., 52
Dunkley, Archibald, 34, 45, 68–69, 70

"earthforce," ix, 34, 65, 66, 90. *See also* Ital livity
elders, 65, 108, 172
Emmanuel, Prince, 73–74, 83, 172, 173
English Baptist Church, 30
enslaved persons. *See* African slaves; Creole slaves; slaves
epistemology, Cartesian. *See* Descartes, René

epistemology, Rastafari, vii, 80–81, 102, 103; and Cartesian epistemology, 145–47, 152–53; *vs.* colonial epistemology, 108, 137, 152; I-talk and, 136–37, 138, 141, 152–53
ethics, 112, 154, 163; naturalist, 91–98, 99–100;
postemancipation void of, 35–36
Ethiopia: *vs.* Babylon, 71–72; colonialism resisted in, 55; Falashas of, 50, 71, 158–59, 160–61, 162; flag of, 98; God of, 41–42, 45–46, 47; invasion of, 55, 117; mass migration to, 70, 71, 75, 77, 161; as Promised Land, 71–72, 77, 83, 125–26, 129. *See also* Haile Selassie I
Ethiopianism, 71, 77, 164; of Bob Marley, 87; in Bobo Dread, 83, 160; definition of, 130; Garvey and, 43, 45, 46, 164
exodus imagery, 70–71, 77

Falashas, 50, 71, 158–59, 160–61, 162
family, British model of, 166–67, 175, 181
Fanon, Frantz, 1
farming, 72–73, 94, 96
fatalism, 32
First Maroon War, 21
food, 92, 93, 94–96, 134, 183; cooking and serving of, 175; processed, 96, 174; salt consumption and, 94, 96–97, 131; vegetarian, 92, 93, 96

ganja. *See* marijuana
Garvey, Marcus: on African culture, 41, 44–45, 130, 160; on autonomy, 45, 68; on Black disunity, 39–40; deportation of, from U.S., 47, 54, 59; Du Bois on, 52; on Ethiopia, 42–43, 47; on Haile Selassie I, 47, 52–53, 56; materialism of, 41–42, 43, 45, 57; as Moses or Prophet, 50–51, 53, 73, 74; on organizing, 40–41, 44–45; Rastafari movement and, 57, 186; on religion, 38, 41–43, 47, 56; on self-improvement, 38–39, 40, 41–42, 57
Garveyism, viii, 29, 61; appeal of, 46–48, 50–52; as militant nationalism, 39, 48, 50; Native Baptist Church intersecting with, 46, 52, 60, 62; prophetic reception of, 50–51; Rastafari cosmology and, viii, 45–46, 47, 50, 51–52, 59, 160, 164, 187; shortcomings of, 45; women in, 186, 187
gender inequality, colonial, 157–58, 166–67, 177–78, 179, 180, 185
gender inequality, Rastafari, xi; Garveyism influencing, 186, 187; as injustice, 176, 180, 187; and in Jamaican society generally, 180–81, 182–83, 186; women's responses to, 179–80. *See also* women in Rastafari cosmology
genocides, 6

God, Eurocentric: Garvey rejecting, 42–43; Native Baptist Church rejecting, 33–34; Rastafari rejection of, x, 33–35, 61, 67–70, 101, 105, 109, 115, 183. *See also* Christianity; Jah
Gordon, George William, 30, 34
griots, elders acting as, 108
groundation and groundings, 79, 103; Bible discussion in, 103, 108, 109–10; women excluded from, 172–73, 186
gungu peas, 74

Haile Selassie I, 33, 34–35, 36–37, 50; critique of Rasta teachings on, 107–8; Garvey on, 47, 52–53, 56; history of, 53–57, 117; Judaism and, 163; as king, 73, 74, 87, 116; League of Nations speech of, 55; as liberator, 70, 71, 72, 113, 120; as Lion of Judah, 70, 99, 163
Haile Selassie I, divinity of, x, 54–58, 65, 74, 125, 183; awakening to, 71, 138; and biblical hermeneutics, 113–14, 117; Black Jamaicans in image of, 56, 61, 67–68, 69, 104–7, 115, 121; and Black pride, 116; drumming in worship of, 79–80, 81; I-talk and, 140, 141, 149–50; and Jesus Christ, 113–14; in nature, 90, 92, 94; and Rasta identity, 54, 87, 129; redemption through, 36–37, 69–70, 72, 120; and rejection of

the White God, 33, 34–35,
109–10, 121; and Second
Coming, 78, 113–14, 117;
theological necessity of, 104–5,
109; in the three mansions,
77–85. *See also* Jah
healing, 23, 27, 36
heaven, 87, 125. *See also* Ethiopia;
Zion
Henry, Paget, 88, 93, 138
Hepner, Randal, 161–62
herbs, 23–24, 27. *See also* marijuana
hermeneutics, Rastafari, x;
"Blackening" of Bible in, 116–17;
and dignity of Black self,
121–22; disagreements in, 113–15;
Eurocentric interpretation
corrected by, 111–13; Haile
Selassie I and, 113–14, 117; I-talk
as tool of, 140–41; messianism
of, 123–24; of Revelation, 117–18
Hibbert, Joseph, 34, 45, 68–69, 70
Hinds, Robert, 34, 45, 68–69, 70
holy living, 35–36
Holy Trinity, 73–74.
Howell, Leonard, 34–36, 45, 70;
ethics prescribed by, 35–36, 38;
on Haile Selassie, 36–37, 68–69;
social improvement lacking in,
37, 38

I-an-I, 90–91, 138; Black Messiah
and, 125, 149; *vs.* Descartes's I
Think, 128, 140, 141, 144, 145–47,
149–54; divinity represented by,
138, 139, 149–50, 154–55;

phenomenal nature of, 128, 147,
149–51, 153; social status and,
140–41, 146, 149–52, 154
Indigenous people, 4–5; Arawak,
15; in Maroon communities, 7,
15; Taino, 6, 7, 9–10
individualism: in Christian notion
of sin, 118–20; in Western
worldview, 93, 139–40, 162
industrialization, 93, 96
irieness, 96
Ital diet, 94–97, 147, 161. *See also* food
I-talk, x–xi, 127; and Babylon,
154–55; and Black consciousness,
x–xi, 136, 138–39, 153–55; and
divinity of Blackness, 133,
138–39, 141, 149–51, 153–54; and
epistemology, 136–37, 138, 141,
152–53; Falashas and, 160; Haile
Selassie I and, 140, 141, 149–50;
as hermeneutical tool, 140–41;
and Jamaican institutions, x, 127,
128–29, 142; self-differentiation
and, 154–55; *vs.* Standard
English, 137–38; structure of,
136–37; subject and object in, 137,
139; as technology of resistance,
128, 149–50. *See also* I-an-I
Ital livity, ix, 54, 93; definition of,
ix, 65; as liberation, 65, 66, 98

Jah, 53, 58, 67, 72, 78; activity of, in
human affairs, 69; Blackness of,
67, 104–5, 117, 121; Christian
discomfort with, 76–77; I-talk
and, 154–55; life-force of, 92–93

Jamaica, 8, 9–10; colonial administration of, 12–13; colonial wealth of, 11, 12; colorism in, 116; hybrid identity of, 5–6, 7–8; physical environment of, 6–7, 10, 18–19; political violence in, 133; postcolonial, ix, 71–72, 74–76; race consciousness in, 75–76; Rastafari cosmology studied by, 74–77; Spanish rule of, 15; urbanization in, 52; women in, generally, 164–65, 170, 179, 182–83. *See also* poverty

Jamaican institutions: Africa opposed to, 129–30; educational, 74–75, 89; I-talk and, x, 127, 128–29, 142; medical, 95; Rastafarian distance from, ix, 133–36; Rastafarian impact on, 132–33, 135–36

Jesus Christ, 78, 83, 113–14

Judaism. *See* Afro-Judaism; Falashas

justice: gender, 176, 180, 187; and the Morant Bay Rebellion, 31; spirituality as instrument of, ix, 25–26, 31–32, 86–88, 124–26

Kingston, 51–52, 131–32
Kumina, 33

Labour Rebellion, 71
Lafont, Suzanne, 166–67, 173
Lake, Obiagele, 168, 170–71, 182–83, 184–85

land, 6–7, 73, 96. *See also* nature
language, 7, 150. *See also* I-talk
"Legalize It" (song), 81–82
Leile, George, 49
Lewis, George, 49
Lewis, Rupert, 47
liberation, 68–69; and Black hermeneutics, 117–18, 124–26; of nature, ix–x, 85, 91–92, 99–100; orthodoxy opposed to, 123; women excluded from, xi, 170–71, 174–76, 177–78, 181, 184, 187–88
lions, mane of, 98–99, 136
literacy, 111
livity. *See* Ital livity
Long, Edward, 8

Manley, Michael, 133
Manning, Patrick, 59
marijuana, 80, 81; sacramental use of, 81–82, 135; state outlawing, 134–35
Marley, Bob: "Ambush in the Night," 87; at One Love Peace Concert, 132–33; Rastafari aesthetics disseminated by, 86–87; "Redemption Song," 1; "Zion Train," 187–88
Maroons, 3–4, 15, 20–21; Indigenous people among, 7, 15; perceptions of, 21–22; slave revolts suppressed by, 21
Martin, Tony, 43
matriarchy, myth of, 170
men: dominant roles of, 169–70, 171–72, 179–81, 183–84, 186;

emasculation of, 185–86, 187;
and hegemonic masculinity, 178,
186–87; superiority of, 167–69,
175, 177
menstruation, 168, 169, 170, 173–74,
177, 182
messianism, x, 53–54, 101, 113–14,
117, 123–25, 126
Metzinger, Thomas, 128
Morant Bay Rebellion, ix, 29,
30–32, 61, 62
Moses, Garvey as incarnation of,
50–51
Mount Temon, 83
Murrell, Nathaniel, 112, 116–17, 123,
184
Myalism, 20, 24, 25–27, 33, 49, 69,
105
mysticism, 79–80, 90–91

Native Baptist Church, ix, 29–31,
32, 34, 61, 62–63; Garveyism
intersecting with, 46, 52, 60, 62;
origins of, 32–33; Revivalism
and, 29, 52, 53, 62
nature, 33–34, 84, 85; alienation
from, 91; cultivating, 72–73, 74;
divinity of, 92–93; goodness of,
93–94; liberation of, 85, 91–92,
99–100; oppression of, ix–x, 65,
66, 72–73, 93; and Rastafari
aesthetics, 98–99, 174; unity
with, ix, 90–100; and women,
174, 183
Negro Jurisprudence, 12–14
Negro World (newspaper), 52

Nettleford, Rex, 9, 74, 75–76,
105–6
New World, 4–5
Nyahbinghi, 77, 79–82; the Bible in,
79, 80, 81; drumming and, 79–80,
81; marijuana and, 80, 81–82

Obeah, 16, 20, 24–26, 27, 32
One Love Peace Concert, 132–33
Onuora, Adwoa Ntozake, 90
"open secrecy," 26

Patterson, Orlando, 16, 18–19,
24–25
Perkins, Anna Kasafi, 114
Pinn, Anthony B., 74–75
Plummer, Nicole, 49
Pocomania, 69, 105
poison, 16–17
poverty: and food, 95; Garveyism
addressing, 50, 56–57; gendered,
165–66, 169, 173, 187; Howell
addressing, 35, 37; and
Rastafari's appeal, 34, 47, 51–52,
67–73, 74–76, 88, 129, 131–32;
and self-esteem, 67–68
Price, Charles, 32, 181, 183, 185
progress, 39, 40–41, 43, 44–45
Promised Key, The (Howell), 35–37
Promised Land. *See* Ethiopia;
Zion
Psalms, 123

racial identity, 30–32
racialization, 11–13, 22. *See also*
Blackness; Whiteness

radical doubt, 143
Rasta mansions, 73–74. *See also* Bobo Dread; Nyahbinghi; Twelve Tribes of Israel
Rastas: as antiestablishment, 60; community of, ix, 131–32, 133–34, 150–52; converts among, 76, 79, 86–87; police persecution of, 134–35; political and social power of, 132–33; prophetic role of, 60–61; Rodney and, 88–90; social status of, 34, 47, 51–52, 67–76, 88, 129–32, 134–36, 151–52, 187; stereotype of, 74
reasoning, 54, 80, 82, 124; of women, subordination of, 172–73
rebellion, conceptual, 34
reggae, 59, 78–79; biblical quotations in, 110; and Rastafari aesthetics, 85–86, 103
religion: conceptual rebellion in, 34–35, 61, 67; demarginalization through, 105; Garvey's skepticism toward, 37, 38, 41–42; historical accuracy of, 108, 109, 116; and justice, ix, 25–26, 31–32, 88, 124–26; as prop for identity, 43; segregation in, 30; sexism in, xi, 157, 167–70, 176–77, 182–83. *See also* syncretism
Revelation, 117–18, 123
Revivalism, viii–ix, 9, 20, 26–27, 29, 46, 102; Afrocentric appropriation of the Bible in, 48, 50, 53, 105; colonial heritage of, 56, 58–59; nationalism in, 51; Native Baptist Church and, 29, 52, 53, 62; origins of, 48–49; women in, 186
righteousness, 161–63
Rodney, Walter, 88–90
Rowe, Maureen, 178–80, 181, 183, 185

the Sabbath, 161
salt consumption, 94, 96–97, 131
salt fish, 97
Samuel Sharpe's Baptist War rebellion, 31–32, 35, 37, 61, 62
Sarkar, Hussein, 144
Seaga, Edward, 133
the self, 93, 121–22, 139, 153; Descartes on, 148–49; triune constitution of, 26–27
sex and sexuality, 176–77, 181–82, 185
sexism. *See* gender inequality, colonial; gender inequality, Rastafari; women in Rastafari cosmology
the shadow, 27
Sharpe, Samuel, 31–32, 34, 35
Sherlock, Philip, 5–6, 12–13
sin, 118–21
slavery: alienation caused by, 91–92, 97–98, 126, 155; biblical justifications of, 112; and Creole slaves, 8–9, 18–20, 22; ending, 3, 22; industrialization linked to, 96; Maroons benefiting from, 21, 22; psychological oppression of, 24, 39–40; and reenslavement, 31; and salt

consumption, 94, 97, 131; scars of, 147, 153; and subjectivity, viii; theodicy of, 115; trauma of, transcending, 69–70; women under, 164–66, 167
slavery, resistance to, ix, 1–2, 3, 14–20; among African vs. Creole slaves, 18–19; as collective power, 17; covert, 15–16; evasion of work as, 15–16; individual violence as, 16–17; and Jamaica's geography, 18–19; Maroons', 20–22; Maroons suppressing, 21; and mass suicides, 15, 16; mass violence as, 17–19; overt, 15, 16–19; postcolonial struggles tied to, 68; property targeted in, 15; and slave revolts, 14, 17–19, 31–32; spiritual, ix, 22–28, 32–33, 49, 106
slaves, 1–2, 10, 15, 16–17; African vs. Creole, 8–9; 4appropriating physical environment, 6–7. See also African slaves; Creole slaves
Smith, M. G., 74
social improvement, 37–38
spirits, 33
Stanley, Prophet, 176, 178
subjectivity, viii, 1–2; Cartesian, 141–42, 145–46, 151, 152–54; pluralist, 139–40, 151–54. See also Afro-Jamaican subjectivity; Anglo-Jamaican subjectivity; I-an-I; I-talk
sugar production, 10–12, 15
suicide, 15, 16
syncretism, 7, 23–25, 33, 49, 181; with Christianity, 32–33, 48–51, 53–54, 183; with West African religions, 23–25, 33, 183
systematic theology, 122–23

Tafari-Ama, Imani, 181–82, 183, 184–85
Taino people, 6, 7, 9–10
Taylor, Burchell, 123
theology of Blackness, x, 101; the Bible and, 105–7; and Black pride, 115–16, 121–22; heaven in, 125–26; as inwardly grounded, 108, 109; need for, 102, 105, 109; sin in, 118–21. See also Blackness, divinity of; Haile Selassie I, divinity of
three mansions, 66, 77–78. See also Bobo Dread; Nyahbinghi; Twelve Tribes of Israel
Tosh, Peter, 81–82
Trelawny, Edward, 21
Twelve Tribes of Israel, 77, 78; biblical hermeneutics of, 114; emergence of, 101–2; reggae and, 78–79
Twi-Asante, 7

United States, social improvement in, 86
Universal Negro Improvement Association (UNIA), 37, 38, 40, 52; on Africa, 44; on autonomy, 45, 68; Bobo Dread and, 160; Haile Selassie I and, 56; plans of, for Jamaica, 46, 56, 59. See also Garvey, Marcus; Garveyism

vegetarianism, 92, 93, 96
Vincent, Theodore, 51–52

West African societies, 7; ancestral knowledge of, 23, 32–33; syncretism of, 23–25, 33
White, Timothy, 169
white cultural hegemony, 87
white imperialism, 89
Whiteness: assimilation to, 9, 56, 95, 131, 163; British colonial definition of, 11–12; as curse, 116; Ethiopianism opposed to, 164; and white aesthetics, 98. *See also* Afro-Jamaican subjectivity; God, Eurocentric
Williams, Lewin, 112, 116–17
women in Rastafari cosmology, xi, 157–58; as "empresses," 170–71, 175, 176; as inferior, 167, 172–73, 178–80, 182, 183–84, 186–87; lacking autonomy, 167–68, 169–70, 173–74; patriarchy internalized by, 179–80, 182; "pollution" of, 167, 168, 169, 173–74, 177, 178, 182; postcolonial influence on, 165–67; religious dogmas influencing, 167–70, 176–77, 178–79, 181–82; sex and, 176–77, 181–82, 185; slavery and, 164–66, 167; spiritual oppression of, 177
work, 12, 15–16
World War II, 55

Yamaye, 9–10
Yawney, Carol D., 90
Youth Black Faith, 58–59, 62, 136, 138

Zion, 120–21, 125–26, 161–62
Zion revivalism, 69

GPSR Authorized Representative: Easy Access System Europe, Mustamäe tee 50, 10621 Tallinn, Estonia, gpsr.requests@easproject.com

www.ingramcontent.com/pod-product-compliance
Lightning Source LLC
Chambersburg PA
CBHW031241290426
44109CB00012B/390